Diagnostic and Remedial Reading

for Classroom and Clinic

Second edition

Robert M. Wilson

University of Maryland

CHARLES E. MERRILL PUBLISHING COMPANY
A Bell & Howell Company
Columbus, Ohio 43216

The author and publisher gratefully acknowledge the following for permission to reprint:

"Invitational Address to the International Reading Association—1965" by Ruth Strang. In *The Reading Process and Its Ramifications* by Ruth Strang. Reprinted by permission of the International Reading Association.

From *Minimal Brain Dysfunction in Children*, p. 13, by Sam D. Clements. Reprinted by permission of the author.

Photograph from *Word Tracking* by Donald E. P. Smith. Reprinted by permission of the author.

From "The Use of Nonstandard English in Teaching Standard" by Irwin Feigenbaum. In *Teaching Standard English in the Inner City*, edited by R. W. Fasold and R. W. Shuy. Paraphrased by permission of the publisher, the Center for Applied Linguistics.

International Standard Book Number: 0-675-09152-7

Library of Congress Catalog Card Number: 79-181027

1 2 3 4 5 6 7 8 9 10 — 76 75 74 73 72

Printed in the United States of America

Foreword

All who will read this book, and especially the reading teacher and/or consultant will find it most helpful. It reflects the cutting edge of new developments as well as those time-tested techniques and approaches which will greatly assist the teacher as she organizes the optimal reading/learning environment. Since it is *diagnostic-teaching* oriented, this same teacher will find practical suggestions which will enable her to judiciously adjust the reading/learning environment to allow for the different learning rates and learning problems manifested by the learner. Although a few recipes are given, I sense a core philosophy that the reading teacher in all her endeavors should be a creative teacher utilizing to a maximal degree those self-made exercises which represent her own unique background and skill.

Several features of this book are worthy of mention. As with the first edition, the types of diagnosis are: *informal-on-the-spot, classroom, and clinical.* The emphasis carried throughout these aspects is continuous diagnosis in order that a shift in instructional strategies and materials can be effected, thus assuring that each child will progress towards the ultimate goal of maturity in reading skills. Sufficient content has been provided for the teacher to glean understandings, knowledges, and skills to conduct appropriate diagnosis and the subsequent therapy so the child will acquire the cooperatively agreed-upon terminal behaviors.

Again, although this book is not necessarily designed for the clinician, it does contain sufficient substantive content to enable the classroom teacher to properly interpret a formal case study. Furthermore, it goes beyond the above to a greater degree in that the clinician will find information which not only will assist in diagnosis, but will also recommend the appropriate therapy.

It should be noted that Chapters 1, 4, 6, and 7 have been revised to a greater extent than the others. A section titled "Accept and Challenge" in Chapter 1 is worthy of mention. In brief, the author is saying that teachers must accept the child as he is — the product of the experiences

iii

society has provided for him — and that although each child should be challenged, he must also experience a measure of success. The title of Chapter 4 has been changed from "Educational Diagnosis" to "Classroom Diagnosis." It has been expanded and includes only classroom diagnosis leaving clinical diagnosis to be explored in another section of the book. The reorganization of the book results in a new chapter titled "Remedial Activities in Readiness Skills." It includes such needed sections as: *language mismatching, underdeveloped language, auditory difficulties, visual difficulties, orientation,* and *extended remediation in the areas of readiness.*

Another section of the book which is worthy of mention is Chapter 10 "Evaluation in Reading." As is well known, all too frequently the results of therapy and developmental reading have been expressed in the ubiquitous *grade equivalent.* Such a system for expressing growth places too great an emphasis on *skills development,* resulting in an insufficient emphasis on the *affective aspects* of reading. It is gratifying to note that the author has given attention to this important aspect of reading.

Furthermore, the author is cognizant of the fact that, during the formative years, the child spends approximately thirteen (13) percent of his time in the public or private schools, and that he is subject to conditioning by other segments of society for the remaining eighty-seven (87) percent. Chapter II, "Parental Roles in Diagnosis, Remediation, and Prevention," will strike a responsive chord in all teachers. The chapter emphasizes that in addition to providing adequate physical care and a balanced emotional atmosphere, the parents can and should provide an educational climate that would reinforce the therapy given by teacher and/or clinician. The final part of the book, Chapter 12, "Professional Responsibilities and Roles," stresses the important role all must assume in the total education of the child. Although the chapter is short, it is a fitting climax to a series of chapters.

As would be expected, this revision is an improvement over the original text. It is a testimonial to the integrity and scholarship of the author. As might be expected, scholars may disagree with some of the viewpoints, postulates, and hypotheses abstracted from relevant data; nonetheless the book is informative and challenging. After all, no one book can be everything. *And shouldn't a book be challenging?* I invite your thoughtful and reflective reading of this scholarly manuscript — it will be a rewarding experience.

Donald L. Cleland

December, 1971
University of Pittsburgh

Preface

One makes certain assumptions in preparing a manuscript for general dissemination. The reader should be alerted to these assumptions so that the reading of the book can be facilitated.

First, this book is not a beginning text in reading. Rather, it is assumed that the reader will have had some experience with the teaching of reading to children; a basic course in reading; familiarity with the concepts behind such techniques as the directed reading activities, the language experience approach, and word attack skills; and some understanding of current learning theory.

Second, the book may best be seen as a beginning book in diagnostic teaching. It is not designed to answer all of the questions about problem readers nor is it meant to cover all aspects of teaching reading.

Thirdly, it is assumed that the reader has worked with children who are experiencing difficulty in reading while not knowing exactly what he could do about it. Such a situation seems to be essential for effective use of this manuscript.

For the reader's information, the ideas in this revision come from experiences with thousands of children and hundreds of teachers, all of whom would like to see learning as a stimulating and pleasant experience. One tends to become leary of generalizations about problem readers, knowing full well that each case is indeed unique.

At the same time, the general philosophy of this book has been tried and found to be effective with most of the children with whom we have worked.

Our clinic, at Maryland, is an exciting, stimulating environment for children. The staff members have been open to change and are thoughtfully critical of their techniques. This book, to a large extent, reflects the thinking and activities of that staff. Of course, their effectiveness with children who are experiencing extreme difficulty in learning to read goes far beyond technique — it also incorporates a sincere desire to help each child in his own special way to become a happy, successful learner.

And so, while the reader must beware, it is hoped that this book will reflect the practical experience of many persons and the best thinking which those persons can produce. The ultimate measure of the success of such a publication will be determined as you, the reader, initate programs based upon these ideas. The successes which your children have as a result of these ideas will be the final test.

For the reader who may lack the necessary background for most effective understanding of this book, the author would like to suggest several excellent books which may well serve as an overview of the reading process for you.

Cohen, S. Alan. *Teach Them All To Read.* New York: Random House, 1969.

Heilman, Arthur W. *Principles and Practices of Teaching Reading,* 3rd ed. Columbus, Ohio: Charles E. Merrill Publishing Co., 1972

Wilson, Robert M., and Hall, MaryAnne. *Reading and the Elementary School Child: Theory and Practice for Teachers.* New York: Van Nostrand Reinhold, 1972.

Spache, George D., and Spache, Evelyn B. *Teaching Reading in the Elementary School.* Boston: Allyn and Bacon, 1969.

Stauffer, Russell G. *Teaching Reading as a Thinking Process.* New York: Harper and Row, 1969.

Further readings are suggested at the end of each chapter. Those with limited experiences are encouraged to pursue these sources so that contrasting points of view can be considered.

Acknowledgments

The author wishes to acknowledge the many people who have encouraged and guided him toward the completion of this revision.

The inspiration and memory of my father C. B. Wilson has been a constant source of help. The generous encouragement and helpful criticism of my friend and former teacher Donald L. Cleland has always been appreciated.

Many of my colleagues and students have offered valuable suggestions and criticisms; in particular, the efforts of Louise Waynant and Donald McFeely have been deeply appreciated.

Dr. William Powell reviewed the book for the publisher. His diligence and positive attitude greatly affected the final product, and to him I offer sincere appreciation.

In the first edition, the comments from Ward H. Ewalt, optometrist, and William H. Druckmiller, neurologist, were very helpful. These contributions have remained in the revision.

The excellent typing of Mrs. Ruthellen Campbell and the editorial reviews by Mrs. Barbara Wainier are hereby acknowledged.

And to my family — wife, Barbara, and children, Richard, James, and Sharon — who have sacrificed much to permit the completion of this revision, my earnest thanks.

R.M.W.

August, 1971
College Park, Maryland

Contents

1

Working With Problem Readers

Who knows better than the teacher of a child with a reading problem the importance of reading for school success? And who other than the classroom teacher better realizes that the inability to read, coupled with the lack of desire to read, leads directly to school failure? A teacher knows the type of problems presented by the child who cannot or will not read, for he faces this reality daily. He must be armed with the diagnostic and remedial techniques necessary to instruct children as effectively as possible, since the atypical child is not included in the generalizations of most teachers' guides for instructional material.

A study of problem readers, then, must include the reality that the classroom teacher not only is in the best position to help the student, but also is professionally responsible to continue the education of the child as intelligently and efficiently as he can.

CHARACTERISTICS OF PROBLEM READERS

Although there is no single observable characteristic which isolates the problem reader from his classmates, it is likely that he will demonstrate the characteristics of one or more of the three basic types of problem readers.

1

A child is a problem reader because, for one reason or another, he does not read as well as his ability indicates he should. He should not be judged by his reading skills in relation to his grade level in school, but rather in relation to his potential. That a dull child reading below his grade level in school may become a problem does not necessarily imply that he is retarded in the development of his reading skills. On the other hand, the bright child, although reading well above his grade level, may be considered a problem reader when his reading level falls short of his intellectual potential. It becomes important to assess accurately the reading level and ability of each child to arrive at a comparison determining whether or not he is operating below his potential.

TABLE 1

Ability Compared to Reading

	Grade Level	Ability Level	Reading Level
Child 1	4	3	3
Child 2	4	6	3

Child Number 1 is operating in comparison with his ability; child Number 2 is not.

A child may be considered a problem reader when, with the exception of a specific skill deficiency, all other measures of his reading are up to his level of potential. He reads satisfactorily in most situations, but becomes a problem because of a specific deficiency. Although he is difficult to locate because most of his reading skills appear normal, his deficiency, once located, is readily corrected due to the precise nature of the remediation necessary. The classroom teacher, being constantly alert to this deficiency, is now less likely to label the child either lazy or careless.

For example, since many adults read slowly, they have a specific skill deficiency. They can perform on tests and seem to read very well, but their slow speed makes reading a bore and reduces their inclination to read. Children, while appearing to read well, also may have specific skill deficiencies, such as speed, oral reading fluency, word attack, and study skills.

A child also may be considered a problem reader when, in spite of reading skills in good relationship to his potential, he lacks the desire to read. Strang points clearly to this problem when she says:

> If the book is interesting they read it eagerly and with
> enjoyment . . . . Students confronted with dull, drab, uninter-
> esting reading material show the opposite pattern. They
> read reluctantly, they skip and skim so that they can get it
> over with more quickly.[1]

These factors mentioned by Strang discourage a child from using available skills and tend to dampen his desire to read. It is important that a lack of desire to read be considered a reading problem since it often appears that this child has no problem. Clinic reports for such children show that they are frequently subject to ridicule and disciplinary action, since it is often assumed that there is no excuse for their poor reading habits. An understanding of the child's real problem, however, will indicate the need for adjustment in the school situation to develop a better attitude toward reading.

Perhaps the most common characteristic of a problem reader is that in the past he has experienced a year or more of work with a teacher who did not know how to meet his needs. One notices that problem readers seem to cluster in certain classrooms with certain teachers. The child with a skill deficiency or general reading deficiency has trouble with certain teachers. He is criticized, blamed for what he cannot do, and subjected to penalties which range from subtle to direct. In other words, the problem teacher creates problems for children whose learning development is not concomitant with that of other children. A year or more of such treatment causes the child's educational lag to become compounded by a poor self-concept, emotional overlay, and a tendency to give up. From this point of view, any child who is in a learning situation from which he cannot profit can be considered to be having a reading problem.

As problem readers are studied on the following pages, it must be kept in mind that a child can have these characteristics in any combination and with varying degrees of severity.

Specific Traits

In order to look specifically at the traits of the problem reader, one also must look at the traits of problem teachers. The problem teacher is difficult to identify prior to entering his classroom. He is frustrated by his inability to help the children who are not progressing "normally." His frustration stems from inadequate teacher

---

[1]Ruth Strang, *Diagnostic Teaching of Reading* (New York: McGraw Hill Book Co. 1969), p. 106.

education programs, senses of inadequacies, lack of dedication to the task of teaching, or pure inability. He seeks ways out of his frustration through ability grouping, labeling children (careless, dyslexic, or deprived), excessive requests for special services (reading teacher, psychologist, or medicaide), and eventually by simply not working with the child. While adequate teachers also may possess one or more of these traits, they continue to work with the child as a developmental human being whom they believe can and will learn.

How convenient it would be if a problem reader could be described through easily identifiable traits, but such is not the case. He certainly cannot be identified by sight, for his appearance does not reveal him as an outcast of society. The problem reader — usually a boy — can be seen in almost any classroom. A study of this type of child generally reveals an individual who recognizes that the majority of his scholastic activities are unsatisfactory experiences. It is likely that he sees little possibility of school's being anything but a series of frustrations and failures. As a result, this child is likely to react in one of the following ways: he may withdraw and shyly avoid the reading process whenever possible; he may show resentment and become belligerent toward the reading situation; he may cover his deficiency by showing a lack of concern, acting as if his problem does not make any difference; and, finally, he may try to escape the reality of his problem by drifting and by spending abnormally long periods of time with television and comic books or by diverting the teacher's attention with unacceptable behavior. These and other responses to failure in reading provide us with insights into the difficulties of the problem reader.

A closer look at the problem reader reveals that his problem has been recognized for some time, usually since first grade. Early identification often results in program adjustments which allow differing rates of growth, thus, diminishing the problem. In other cases, such identification results in the types of frustrations already discussed.

Occasionally, the child has been successful in the early grades in which required reading skills were fewer and less complicated. His problem becomes more pronounced when he is introduced to the content areas and is expected to learn for himself from a textbook. Here he can no longer rely purely upon memory for word recognition; therefore, he reacts poorly to new reading situations.

As his scores in all verbal areas fall below the norm, his arithmetic computation scores probably will remain relatively high. The teacher finds it difficult to separate the child's reaction to failure from the failure itself. As a result, the child is often misunderstood, coaxed, bribed, threatened, and punished until he no longer has any confidence that school will ever be a successful situation for him. Thus, the problem reader faces many frustrations beyond his failure to read.

RAMIFICATIONS OF THE PROBLEM READER

The problem reader is not only a problem to himself but eventually causes problems among his peers, in school, and at home.

In school: In school, where children often are pressured to achieve a certain grade level of performance, the problem reader is a source of never-ending disappointments. Whether the pressure is subtle or direct, both the child and the teacher sense failure. The teacher may react by giving up on the child or by feeling that he is indifferent, lazy, or troublesome. This reaction may be followed by punishment that usually fosters a hostile attitude between the teacher and a child who is ill-equipped to accept hostility. Frustrated by the rejection and the labels which he has received, the child either cannot or will not work independently. As more and more frustrating material is heaped upon him, he is likely to busy himself with noneducational activities. He finally decides that an education is just not worth the effort. As he falls behind in his classroom work, he is likely to be forced to repeat a grade, with the threat of further repetition constantly being called to his attention. Excessive absenteeism and complete rejection of the school program are inevitable as he proceeds through school being promoted on the basis of age alone. A brief look at the reading level of high school dropouts tells the remainder of the story. Penty says, "More than three times as many poor readers as good readers dropped out of school before graduation."[2]

We realize that not all problem readers end as school dropouts; however, the strained school-pupil relationship increases

---

[2]Ruth C. Penty, "Reading Ability and High School Drop-Outs," *Journal of the National Association of Women Deans and Counselors* (National Education Association, October, 1959), p. 14.

dropout possibilities with this type of child. An additional possibility exists for there is also the child who drops out emotionally although he continues to attend class. Psychological dropouts are in every school; they generally create problems for both the teacher and pupils who are there to work. In either case, the situation is critical.

With his peers: Although his peers often treat him kindly, it is not uncommon for the problem reader to be teased and taunted. He is not with the "in" group and is often found alone at play as well as in the classroom. Other children are not likely to seek his efforts for committee work since his contributions are limited. Rejection encourages him to seek companionship with others in the "out" group. A further complication is the problem reader's repetition of a grade, which places him one year behind his peers; he clearly recognizes that he does not "belong" either in the group with which he is placed or with his peers. If he continues to meet peer group disapproval, he is highly susceptible to undesirable influences, the consequences of which are seen in the reports of police authorities who handle juvenile delinquents. Summarizing a study from the Children's Court in New York, Harris reports, "Among those tested . . . 76 percent were found to be two or more years retarded in reading, and more than half of those were disabled five or more years."[3] Again, we do not conclude that all problem readers turn to delinquent behavior, but merely that continued rejection from his peers makes a child more susceptible to undesirable influences.

With his parents: Parents become anxious when their child is not succeeding in school. Even the most intelligent of these parents are likely to try to solve the problem by urging or forcing the child to make a greater effort. This often means piling on more of the same type of frustrating work which makes the child reject school. When he balks, it is not unusual for him to be compared openly to his brother or sister or to his playmates. Seemingly ashamed of their child's behavior, parents often will look for someone to blame. The child is not blind to this shame and rejection, and he too will look for someone to blame. Even more important, he is likely to look elsewhere for that acceptance which all children need from their parents.

[3]Albert J. Harris, *How To Increase Reading Ability* (New York: David McKay Co., 1970), p. 3.

By observing the problem reader, it can be concluded that the ramifications of his problem are felt not only by himself but also by the school, his peers, and his family. His inability to solve his own problem causes the future to look dark indeed.

Not all problem readers follow the patterns mentioned above. Indeed, some are capable of reasonable adjustment, usually with the help of an understanding, intelligent teacher. The problem facing the teacher, then, is what can be accomplished in a regular classroom of twenty-five to thirty-five children when a child with a reading problem is among them. A classroom without at least one such child is rare. The following pages will provide several possible solutions to this problem.

REACTIONS TO SYMPTOMS — REACTIONS TO CAUSES

When a child with a reading problem is found in the school situation, what diagnostic procedures should be used? Should the *symptoms* of the problem be considered valid enough for a diagnosis, or is it more desirable to conduct a thorough diagnosis designed to establish *causation*? An examination of the following situations will help to place each of these approaches in proper perspective.

Tony is not alone. He is one of many children across the country who, day after day, sit in an elementary school classroom in which he encounters reading situations well above his level. Tony, however, may be ranked among the fortunate, for his teacher realized that Tony could not read well enough to do fifth grade work. He quickly discovered that Tony could read accurately at the third grade level and that he could read only with frustration at the fourth grade level. He noticed that Tony would refuse to attack unknown words, and, on the rare occasions when he would try, his pronunciation was inaccurate.

He also noticed that Tony's reading was characterized by word pronunciation without fluency, that he was uncomfortable in the reading situation, and that he seemed hindered by what the teacher called "word reading." A quick check of the school records indicated that Tony was average in ability but that each year he seemed less responsive to the reading instruction.

Therefore, after carefully considering the information available to him combined with his analysis of Tony's reading performance in the classroom, the teacher set into motion a two-pronged program to supplement Tony's regular reading. First, he encouraged Tony to read more fluently by providing highly interesting reading material at a lower level of difficulty; second, he taught essential phonic skills from the sight words that Tony knew. Realizing that Tony's problem might be more deeply rooted, the teacher asked for an evaluation by a reading specialist. This approach to the situation reflects the presence of an interested, informed classroom teacher analyzing a child's problem and attempting to correct it, while waiting for the services of the reading specialist.

When the reading specialist saw Tony, he knew that to arrive at the cause of Tony's problem a careful diagnosis would be essential. He realized that, among other things, he needed to have complete information concerning Tony's ability, his knowledge of phonics, his auditory skill, and his emotional stability. Therefore, the specialist set into motion a thorough diagnosis in an attempt to establish the cause of the problem; without such diagnosis he doubted that he could properly recommend a program of correction.

This example clearly illustrates two different reactions to Tony's symptoms. The classroom teacher used a pattern of symptoms to set into motion a program of correction. The specialist realized that the problem could best be understood by a more careful study of the child. Both the classroom teacher and the reading specialist reacted properly! The teacher instituted a program of correction as quickly as possible after carefully considering the symptoms; his basic concern being the continuation of Tony's educational program. The specialist initiated a program of diagnosis attempting to determine, as accurately as possible, the cause of Tony's difficulty; his concern being the recommendation of the most appropriate program of remediation.

To further clarify the difference between symptoms and causes of reading disability, symptoms are defined as those observable characteristics of a case that lead to an educated guess about a reader's problems. Teachers must look for reliable patterns of symptoms so that an intelligent program of correction can be initiated with minimal delay to the child's educational progress. Harris states, ". . . many of the simpler difficulties in reading can be corrected by direct teaching of the missing skills, without an intensive search for reasons why the skills were not learned before."[4]

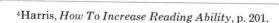

[4]Harris, *How To Increase Reading Ability*, p. 201.

One must consider that the average classroom teacher has neither the time, the training, nor the materials necessary to conduct a thorough diagnosis. He must use a reliable pattern of symptoms. His procedure is to:

1. Examine observable symptoms, combined with available school data
2. Form a hypothesis
3. Begin work

With the possible necessity for referral in mind, he must formulate and conduct the most effective corrective program possible within the limitations of the regular classroom situation. It then becomes obvious that the reliability of a pattern of symptoms has a direct influence on the effectiveness of his instruction with problem readers. Reference may be made to the following chapter for patterns of symptoms applicable to the classroom diagnosis of problem readers.

Causation may be defined as that factor or those factors which, as a result of careful diagnosis, can be accurately identified as being responsible for the reading problem. Robinson[5] presents data to support the multiple nature of causation in reading problems. The reading specialist is acutely aware that since there is rarely one cause for a given problem a careful examination for causation is necessary. Poor home environment, poor physical health, inadequate instruction, lack of instructional materials, personality disorders, and many other factors have been established as interfering to some degree with the development of reading skills. More specific references to causative factors are made in future chapters.

The reading specialist realizes first that it is through the analysis of cause that programs of prevention are made possible; for as Robinson states, ". . . preventive measures can be planned intelligently only if causes of difficulty are understood."[6] The cause, in Tony's case, may have been a lack of auditory discrimination skills needed to learn phonics or, perhaps, an overemphasis on isolated word drill in earlier grades. The reading specialist, after a diagnosis designed to determine causes, sets the groundwork for a program of correction. In Tony's case, this might involve a revision of portions

---

[5]Helen M. Robinson, *Why Pupils Fail in Reading* (Chicago: The University of Chicago Press, 1946), p. 219.
[6]Robinson, *Why Pupils Fail in Reading*, p. 219.

of the reading curriculum from grade one on or, perhaps, the establishment of a more thorough readiness program in the early grades.
Thus, a careful diagnosis is the first step toward the implementation of a preventive program.

The reading specialist may also be interested in causation to
lead more accurately to the most effective program of correction,
especially with the more seriously retarded reader. Strang[7] states,
however, that diagnosis is complex and that causes are difficult to
uncover. If Tony's classroom teacher's program of correction is not
effective, it is obvious that a more thorough diagnosis will be essential. This, then, is the other function of the reading specialist. Based
upon his diagnosis, he will be able to assist the classroom teacher
with recommendations to implement the most effective corrective
program.

That the specialist looks for causation and the classroom
teacher for patterns of symptoms in no way excuses the classroom
teacher from being aware of possible implications and complications
concerning the causes of reading problems. Nor does it excuse him
from gathering as much diagnostic information as possible. Certainly, the more informed he becomes concerning causation, the
more effective he will become in analyzing a pattern of symptoms
intelligently. And, as Harris states, he should be ". . . able to carry
out the simpler parts of a diagnostic study."[8] At the same time, the
teacher's major job is to better instruct all the children in his care,
and, as stated above, this obligation generally precludes thorough
diagnosis in any one case. It is also possible that after a most careful diagnosis the reading specialist will not yet be able to accurately
identify all of the causes of the child's reading problem. Causative
factors may be elusive, but the elusiveness of the problem does not
free the reading specialist from attempting to identify those causes
as accurately as possible.

To better understand these concepts, the following examples
illustrate the effectiveness of both procedures when applied to the
four major areas of reading problems: the physical, intellectual,
emotional, and educational. For a more complete pattern of symptoms and a more thorough discussion of causation, see chapters
three and four.

Physical Problems: "Bill, how many times have I told you not to
hold your book so close to your face?" Despite repeated efforts to

---

[7]Strang, *Diagnostic Teaching of Reading*, p. 26.
[8]Harris, *How To Increase Reading Ability*, p. 201.

have him hold his book at the proper distance, Bill insisted on this type of visual adjustment. Knowing this to be a symptom of a visual disorder, the teacher began to observe Bill more closely. He noticed unusual watering of the eyes and an unusual amount of blinking, especially after longer sessions involving seat work. His response was to adjust the classroom situation to allow Bill the maximum amount of visual comfort (i.e., regulating visual activities to shorter time periods and assuring Bill of the most favorable lighting conditions). Realizing that he might have a serious vision problem, the teacher referred him to a vision specialist.

The teacher's job then was to recognize the symptoms and react: first, to continue to teach Bill by adjusting the physical setting to enable him to perform as comfortably as possible; and, second, to refer him to a specialist for whatever visual correction was necessary.

The reading specialist's reaction to Bill was a little different. He saw the symptoms of the difficulty, and he too realized that referral was a possibility. However, in this case, a visual screening test involving near point vision was first administered in an attempt to determine whether Bill's problem was one of visual disability or one of bad habit.

In all physical problems, referral to the proper specialist is the appropriate action for personnel in education; therefore, both the reading specialist and the classroom teacher considered the referral of Bill for visual analysis. The difference in their approach is important. The classroom teacher observed a pattern of symptoms which told him that there was a good possibility that vision was interfering with his educational progress. Since Bill's education is his first responsibility, the teacher's proper reaction was to adjust the educational climate so that Bill could operate as effectively as possible. The teacher also was obligated to make a referral for the proper visual analysis. The reading specialist, however, was not immediately confronted with Bill's day-to-day instruction; rather, he was obligated to determine as accurately as possible whether vision was the factor interfering with Bill's education. He was justified in his attempt to screen thoroughly before making recommendations for visual referral or for adjustment to educational climate.

Intellectual Problems: Jim scored poorly on the group intelligence test given at the beginning of fifth grade. His teacher noticed that his mental age and his reading achievement age were about the

same; however, the teacher realized that his oral vocabulary
seemed much above average and that he seemed to be much better
in arithmetic than in other content areas. Jim was also more atten-
tive than average. His teacher concluded that Jim might have more
ability than his mental age indicated and that perhaps his intelligence test score was a result of the reading performance necessary
in this type of test. His assumption, then, was that Jim had more
ability than his records indicated. Therefore, the teacher urged him
to perform at a higher academic level. To assure himself of the
most accurate information, he referred Jim for an individual intelligence test. While waiting for the results of this test, he motivated
Jim to achievement beyond his present levels. He was obligated to
rely upon a pattern of symptoms for his analysis of Jim. (That
pattern involved arithmetic ability, oral vocabulary development,
and attentiveness in school.)

The reading specialist's reaction was to administer, or to have
someone else administer, an individual intelligence test to determine, as closely as possible, Jim's actual potential. Without accurate knowledge in this area, it would be difficult to make precise
recommendations for his educational program. Again, we notice
that the reactions of the classroom teacher and of the reading
specialist were proper, for both realized the necessity for the administration of an individual intelligence test due to the limitations of
group tests with children who do not read well. The teacher, however, while waiting for the results of this examination, relied upon
a pattern of symptoms which indicated that Jim might well have
more potential than the school records indicated. He, therefore,
increased the tempo of instruction and encouraged Jim toward a
higher level of academic performance. The specialist again used
diagnostic procedures. His first task was to determine as accurately
as possible the degree of the student's actual potential. In the area
of intellectual problems, we notice that the classroom teacher is
seriously limited by training, time, and the availability of testing
materials. He has no recourse but to rely upon a pattern of symptoms of scholastic aptitude such as group intelligence tests, oral
vocabulary, and arithmetic skills. It should also be noticed that the
reading specialist, who has the training, the time, and the appropriate materials, is in an excellent position to conduct an examination for a more precise measure of scholastic aptitude. It is also
important to notice that in both cases the personnel involved were

aware that they should not rely upon *one* measure of ability and that each searched for the most effective technique available.

Emotional Problems: "Sally, haven't you finished your library book yet?" Sally continually resisted her teacher's efforts to encourage her reading. She lagged behind in all personal reading assignments. Concerned about Sally's attitude, her teacher also noticed that she seemed extremely anxious for praise, but, at the same time, frequently drifted off into a private world of day dreams.

A check of the development of Sally's reading skills through the school records assured the teacher that his primary task was not going to be one of instruction in the basic reading skills. Correspondingly, it became obvious that her reading situation was in need of adjustment to insure more successful, pleasant experiences which would merit her teacher's praise. In an effort to alleviate Sally's rejection of her personal reading, the teacher lowered the level of difficulty in reading assignments. At the same time, he continued to observe any reaction for possible emotional complications. If such occurred, he would make a referral for a thorough psychological evaluation.

When the reading specialist saw Sally, his first reaction was to administer certain personality evaluations and to study her life at home, with her peers, and in the classroom to determine the degree of deviations as they might apply to her reading problem. If such deviations appeared to be significant, the specialist would refer Sally's case to a psychologist, a psychiatrist, or a social worker.

While recognizing the potential of Sally's emotional problems, the classroom teacher realized that though he could not give up on the child, he did not have the training, the time, nor the materials to make a thorough diagnosis. Again we see both the classroom teacher and the reading specialist willing to refer the child elsewhere. The teacher's willingness was based upon the recognition of a pattern of symptoms. Since his primary concern was for immediate educational progress, he attempted to make adjustments in the learning climate to facilitate Sally's progress.

The specialist, being alert to the possible complications in this case, again used diagnostic procedures. Although he realized that he was not a psychiatrist, he knew that a thorough evaluation through tests and case analysis would put him in a better position to, first, refer the child to the proper person and, second, make recommendations for the adjustment of the educational situation. So, again, we see that both reactions were proper although different. The specialist does not feel inclined to start corrective programs with children who, in his opinion, have basic emotional problems. The classroom teacher does not have that choice; so, with an intelligent reaction to a pattern of symptoms, he proceeds with the education of the child, ever alert to problems which may arise!

Educational problems: As you may recall, Tony was weak in his ability to use word attack skills and was considered by his teacher to be a word-by-word reader. The teacher clearly saw that his reading problem was educational in nature (i.e., he had either missed some instruction, his teachers had skipped instruction, or he had received poor instruction). Although he was concerned about the cause of Tony's problem, he could not stop to trace the problem to its source; rather, he attempted to improve his learning situation through individualization of the classroom procedure. Bond and Tinker[9] hold the view that remedial reading instruction is the same as good classroom instruction which is individualized. Quite properly, the teacher arranged for this individualized instruction and proceeded with Tony's education. The reading specialist began a thorough diagnosis. He was aware of Betts' warning. "Poor teaching in a large sense is the chief cause of retardation in reading."[10] He realized further that, at best, the teacher has closed the gap for Tony, but that unless a preventive program were instituted, Tony's problem would appear again and again in other children. The specialist finds support again in Betts who says that ". . . each community will find the need for a careful analysis of its peculiar problems."[11] It is obvious that the reading specialist is more capable of making this "careful analysis" and that it cannot be the responsibility of the classroom teacher. By analysis of groups of students, often in different grades, the reading specialist may well find the flaw in the educational program and prevent future problems from occurring. Herein lies a major responsibility for the reading specialist to alleviate the problem through preventive educational programs. Because of his insights into the problem, the specialist has the additional opportunity of advising the classroom teacher

---

[9]Guy L. Bond and Miles A. Tinker, *Reading Difficulties: Their Diagnosis and Correction* (New York: Appleton-Century-Crofts, Inc., 1967), p. 15.

[10]Emmett A. Betts, *Foundations of Reading Instruction* (New York: American Book Co., 1946), p. 52.

[11]Betts, *Foundations of Reading Instruction*, p. 54.

concerning individual students with the more serious reading problems.

EARLY IDENTIFICATION

Much has been written about the possibilities of early identification of children who are not likely to pass successfully through the school program without serious problems. Most first grade teachers feel they can identify these children early in the school year. Their oral language skills, their auditory discrimination skills, and their visual discrimination skills often are deficient. de Hirsch[12] has produced interesting data concerning the possibilities of early identification. Her index, currently undergoing further analysis, is unfortunately too complicated for large scale classroom use.

Program adjustments for these children can be of several kinds. First, a child may be placed in a modified kindergarten program which will provide developmental experiences as well as an additional year of mental and physical development. Second, a child can be put into an intensified readiness program designed to stimulate his strengths and to provide practice in areas of identified weaknesses. Third, a child can be channeled into a modified reading program which stresses the use of language experiences as opposed to traditional reading programs. In such cases, formalized reading is withheld until a child operates easily with language experience stories. Practice with readiness skills is provided from the material developed in the experience stories.

Of the three approaches, this author strongly recommends the third. It is closely related to the actual reading process; it stresses the child's natural strengths (ability to think and to talk); and it allows for easy and natural transfer to other types of reading programs.

Techniques suggested in the following chapters can be utilized for early identification and for program adjustments which have been recommended.

ACCEPT AND CHALLENGE

Throughout our efforts in working with children who are having

---

[12]Katrina de Hirsch, Jeanette Jansky, and William Langford, *Predicting Reading Failure* (New York: Harper & Row, 1966).

difficulty reading, we have adopted the following motto: Accept and Challenge. This motto is suggested for all who plan to work with children in reading.

One must *accept* the child, for he is but a product of his experiences. If one rejects and criticizes those experiences, he is, in fact, rejecting and criticizing the child. Instead, one must accept those experiences as real and good. He must genuinely accept the total child, his language, his habits, his attitudes, and his skills. By accepting, he gains the child's confidence and encourages him to continue to try. Several examples of specific "accepting" activities might be used as illustrations.

1. Provide instruction in a child's strengths. He needs to show you, his peers, and himself the things he can do well.
2. Keep testing to a minimum. If his problem is serious, most tests reveal little. Teach to his strengths and help him start on a positive note before doing extensive testing.
3. Provide alternatives to every activity. Let the child make choices. Show him you trust and respect his judgments.

All teachers illustrate in numerous ways that they are accepting a child. They should utilize these methods in their early work with every child and should continue to utilize them because accepted children learn, while rejected children do not.

Each child should also be *challenged*. Learning situations should be so planned that they require effort from the child and result in success for the child. Children who are having difficulty learning often find that their efforts result in failure and frustration. Challenge also involves teaching strategies which are highly interesting. Several examples may help.

1. Let slower children work in teams and in pairs with faster children. Slower children can read, study, help make reports, and even lead discussions with the faster children.
2. Utilize pictures from comic strips and magazines to teach the reading-thinking skills. Minimize the amount of reading required, but not the amount of thinking.
3. Teach skills through the use of games. Win or lose, games are a challenge and children will work at them.

All teachers have used many other challenging activities with children. While all children need to be challenged, children who have trouble with learning need acceptance and challenge desperately. As we consider the Accept and Challenge motto, the following selected authorities add insight into its value:

> Waetjen stresses that ". . . if a person is accepted and valued and esteemed, he becomes an inquiring person and he actualizes himself."[13]

> Raths claims, ". . . if our meanings gained from our experiences are frowned upon, are devalued — it constitutes a rejection of our life, and that is intolerable to everyone of us so treated . . ."[14]

> Bowers and Soar say, ". . . the more supportive the climate, the more the student is willing to share, the more learning will take place. . . ."[15]

> Cohen says, ". . . tolerance for failure is best taught through providing a background of success that compensates for experienced failure. . . ."[16]

> Prescott puts it, ". . . the unloved child who fails is in double jeopardy . . . to his insecurity is added the feeling of inadequacy, and he becomes more and more reluctant to try again with each failure."[17]

While planning work for children experiencing reading difficulty, some time should be spent developing techniques which will help children develop a desire to learn. Perhaps the most crucial factor in successful program adjustment lies in the area of teacher attitude toward children.

---

[13]Walter B. Waetjen, "Facts about Learning," *Readings in Curriculum*, edited by Glen Hass and Kimball Wiles (Boston: Allyn and Bacon, Inc., 1965), p. 243.

[14]Louis E. Raths, "How Children Build Meaning," *Childhood Education*, 31 (December 1954), pp. 159-60.

[15]Norman D. Bowers and Robert S. Soar, "Studies in Human Relations in the Teaching-Learning Process," *Evaluation of Laboratory Human Relations Training for Classroom Teachers* (Chapel Hill, N.C., 1961), p. 111.

[16]S. Alan Cohen, *Teach Them All To Read* (New York: Random House, 1969), p. 231.

[17]Daniel A. Prescott, *The Child in the Educative Process* (New York: McGraw Hill, 1957), p. 359.

If the motto Accept and Challenge can be followed, school can be a happy, fun-filled environment for all learners. As you read on, keep the motto in mind and notice the activities, both diagnostic and remedial, which are being suggested which will fit into it. Use them. Try some that you are not too certain of. Discard those that do not allow for accepting the child and those that do not challenge.

THE CULTURALLY DIFFERENT CHILD

Much has been written about children who come from culturally different environments. Some claim these children come to school with a cultural disadvantage and therefore label them "disadvantaged." Others attribute their difficulty in school to their cultural background, implying not only differences but undesirable influence as well. Labels such as "disadvantaged" and "undesirable" hold no value for diagnosis, while they do create many assumptions which hurt children. That numerous children from poor families, particularly from minority groups, have difficulty in school is a fact. Children from restricted urban environments and isolated rural environments are often far below their peers in reading skills.

However, it is not true that the environment alone has caused the reading problem. Indeed, evidence also points to a lack of equal educational opportunity.[18] Yet culturally different children come to school with a fully developed language and with wide backgrounds of experiences. Teachers who work with these children should be alert to their strengths, not to their degree of difference. Teachers must recognize culturally different children as having distinct and good cultures. They are not cultureless. They can be taught if their strengths are evaluated and their programs adjusted so that they feel accepted and challenged. For example, if they can talk, they can be taught through the language experience approach. Therefore, variations in technique are recommended on the basis of diagnosis rather than on the basis of generalizations about culturally different children. Alan Cohen claims, "Learning disability patterns as measured on clinic tests of disadvantaged retarded readers do not differ markedly from the learning disability patterns of middle-class children who are retarded readers."[19]

[18]James S. Coleman, *et al*, *Equality of Educational Opportunity* (Washington, D. C.: U. S. Department of Health, Education and Welfare, 1966).

[19]S. Alan Cohen, "Cause vs. Treatment in Reading Achievement," *Journal of Learning Disabilities* (March 1970), p. 43.

P = the perceptions which develop as a result of many such experiences.

That a child and his perceptions cannot be separated illustrates the cyclic nature of the learning process. Teachers can teach better when they have information about previously developed perceptions. They should attend to responses during and after the learning situation for effective diagnostic teaching. Therefore, diagnosis can take place prior to instruction, at the O level, to assist the teacher in the selection of the learning situation, S. Also, it can take place at the response level, R, where the teacher can evaluate the effectiveness of the learning situation which was developed for the children.

The classroom teacher should enter diagnosis with as much accuracy and confidence as possible. The day is past when the diagnosis of reading problems could afford the aura of mystery which once surrounded it. Since diagnosis is most useful if the person conducting it also interprets the results and institutes the instructional adjustments, teachers must become skilled at diagnostic teaching. The failure of teachers to develop these skills may be attributed to three myths which have developed about diagnosis.

1. Diagnosis requires the use of specially designed tests. On the contrary, the best diagnostic procedures rely upon observing the child in the learning situation. When tests are called for, many of the single purpose tests, either commercial or teacher-constructed, are the most worthwhile.
2. Diagnosis requires a highly specialized, well-trained person. As in all educational areas, there are levels of competency. Some diagnosticians are highly competent and well trained. However, every teacher who is willing to adjust instruction for his students can use diagnostic teaching procedures. These procedures are not reserved for specialists; most teachers use them regularly. They can be improved with but a little effort and knowledge. Therefore, one function of the reading specialist in today's schools should be assisting teachers to become effective diagnostic teachers.
3. Diagnosis calls for a case-study write-up. College and university reading training programs traditionally have included case development in their programs. While case development is an extremely useful educational experience, diagnosis does

In this book, the emphasis will be on doing away with unneeded labels and the inferences which go with them. Instead, diagnose for strengths and adjust programs so that all children can profit from reading instruction. With culturally different children, accept and challenge may be a most useful philosophy.

SUMMARY

It should be remembered that the teacher's first responsibility is to educate all of the children in his classroom as effectively as possible, reading problems notwithstanding. He most effectively fulfills this responsibility by: examining observable symptoms; evaluating the child's difficulty through this pattern of symptoms; adjusting the educational climate; and considering the possibility of referral. In contrast, the reading specialist's first responsibility is to upgrade the effectiveness of the reading instruction of all the children through diagnosis of reading problems within and among the various classrooms. Furthermore, he is responsible for the accurate diagnosis of seriously retarded readers. Herein lies the basic difference between diagnosis using a pattern of symptoms and more thorough diagnosis for causation, both of which are acceptable and proper when dealing with problem readers in the schools.

SUGGESTED READINGS

Bond, Guy L. and Tinker, Miles A. *Reading Difficulties, Their Diagnosis and Correction.* New York: Appleton-Century-Crofts, Inc. 1967. The reader will find Chapter 4, "General Nature of Reading Disability," of particular benefit under this topic; it is quite thorough.

Harris, Albert J. *How To Increase Reading Ability.* New York: David McKay Co., 1970. Chapter 5 (III) provides a broad outlook to supplement students' reading under this topic. The more inexperienced reader will want to examine this reference closely.

Strang, Ruth. *Diagnostic Teaching of Reading.* New York: McGraw Hill Book Co., 1969. Chapter 2, "The Role of the Teacher in Diagnosis," is an excellent discussion of diagnosis in the classroom. The student will find this a handy reference for both this and the following chapter.

Waetjen, Walter R. and Leeper, Robert R., ed. *Learning and Mental Health in the School*. Washington, D.C.: ASCD, 1966. Several chapters by diffierent authors illustrate the necessity for consideration of a theory behind your instructional strategies. Of particular value to the Accept and Challenge motto are the writings of Syngg.

2

Introduction to Diagnosis

Regardless of the educator's professional position (i.e., classroom teacher or reading specialist), diagnosis is essential to good teaching. Diagnosis implies that the educator will actively search for clues to assist in evaluating the present state of the child's skill development and the developmental history of the child's attitudes and habits toward reading and learning.

Strang has developed a model to use in explaining the reading process. This model clarifies the role of diagnosis in instructional situations.

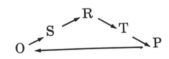

o = the child or children being taught.
s = the learning situations into which these children are placed.
R = the responses of these children to the learning situation.
T = the impressions or traces from the response left upon the nervous system.

---

[1]Ruth Strang, *Invitational Addresses* — 1965 (Newark, Delaware: International Reading Association, 1965).

2

NOT always call for such an approach. Notes from diagnostic observation should be maintained, but they are often of the simplest form. Teachers with a classroom of children waiting to learn can seldom accomplish formal case analysis. Instead, the teacher often will modify instruction without using notes or records. As the teacher reflects upon the lessons, he might jot down several of his observations while continuing his teaching.

As teachers realize that diagnostic teaching is not reserved for those with specialized training and materials, the likelihood of more children benefiting from the advantages of diagnostic teaching will increase greatly. Realistically, the reading specialist will be unable to handle the number of referred students unless the classroom teacher assumes major responsibilities in diagnosis. The type of diagnosis used will be dependent, however, upon the educator's ability to use the diagnostic tools at his disposal and upon his specific educational situation. Thus, the teacher or the reading specialist must evaluate the need for extended diagnosis in terms of the difficulty the child is having, the availability of specialized services, and the needs of the other children in the room. The three types of diagnoses to be discussed in this chapter are: informal on-the-spot, classroom, and clinical.

INFORMAL ON-THE-SPOT DIAGNOSIS

Diagnosis is taking place constantly in the modern classroom where the teacher recognizes symptoms of educational lag through informal procedures. As a result of such diagnosis, the alert teacher makes immediate adjustments in his teaching techniques to provide maximum efficiency in his classroom. Involved in this type of diagnosis are evaluations of the child's reaction to such classroom situations as questions asked by the teacher's informal teacher-made tests, class exercises read, and the use of library facilities. Ever alert to the first signs of pupil frustration, the teacher will prevent serious reading problems from developing by using informal diagnosis, followed by immediate instructional adjustment. Informal on-the-spot diagnosis takes place both during and after instruction (o—s—r). Through evaluation of the responses of children, plans are made for the next learning situation. The good teacher tries to determine through evaluation of a child's performance if that child is ready for the next step in learning. He will assess continuously the child's learning performances, repeating or adapting instruction as necessary. Some of these diagnoses may be conducted with groups of children and some may be individualized, but the process is an ongoing, vital part of the total learning situation in the classroom. How well a teacher can conduct informal on-the-spot diagnosis will relate directly to his understanding of the children whom he is teaching and the skills which they need.

The following examples illustrate the types of situations which can be used to diagnose children's responses to instruction.

1. Oral reading: By having several pairs of children read orally at the same time, a teacher can move from pair to pair, listening to the children's oral reading. The teacher, after noting various students' strengths and weaknesses on index cards, can make instructional adjustments. This technique permits the children to practice oral reading in an environment which does not call for a "performance," for reading before the entire group; it also allows the children to read long portions of material, for as the teacher listens to one pair, the others are practicing.

2. Question asking for comprehension checks: Attending to successes and failures in answering questions is diagnostic. If a teacher uses a modification of Durrell's every-pupil-response technique**, all children can respond to every question. For example, "yes" and "no" cards can be used to check the literal understanding of the story. If, in answer to specific questions, the teacher notices that certain children are in error or are responding sluggishly or not at all, the learning situation should be adjusted immediately. Perhaps, those who respond well can read independently while the teacher alters the learning situation so that the other children can be successful.

3. Book selection: When children are free to choose books for independent reading, a teacher can make observations which

---

**See Appendix B. Double asterisks throughout the text refer the reader to Appendix B; a single asterisk to Appendix A; and a triple asterisk to Appendix C.

may indicate the interests of certain children. Also, he might observe reading habits, which can be utilized in other instructional situations. Alert teachers often can note strengths which, when included in instructional periods, assure children of successes.

4. Spelling: A valuable clue to code-breaking skills is spelling ability. By analysis of successful and unsuccessful spelling attempts, teachers often notice patterns which can lead to instructional needs. For example, if a child always spells the first consonant and vowel in attempted words correctly but misses endings, instruction can stress auditory discrimination lessons. These can start with strengths (initial sounds) which help children listen to other parts of words.

We could cite other examples of on-the-spot diagnosis. However, one has only to watch for opportunities in his own classroom to realize the numerous opportunities available. One should remember that children's inabilities to perform after instruction *must not* be considered failures; they must be noted and combined with their successes to modify the learning situation for better opportunities for success.

CLASSROOM DIAGNOSIS

If a problem persists even after informal adjustments have been made, the teacher initiates a classroom diagnosis which involves a more formal and directed effort without removing the child from his classroom environment. In this type of diagnosis, the teacher utilizes the diagnostic material available to him to formulate a pattern of symptoms which will assist him to understand more clearly a particular child's reading skills. This understanding necessitates the direct observation of the child in the reading act, the use of school records, the direct testing of noted skill deficiencies, the assessment of intellectual potential, and a compilation of relevant data. In this type of diagnosis, the teacher gathers information, evaluates its appropriateness, and relates his findings to the instructional situation. During instruction, he observes the child's responses to the adjusted situation. Classroom diagnosis calls for formal diagnosis at the o level and informal diagnosis at the R level (o—s—R).

Diagnosis Often Precedes Instruction

This, in contrast to on-the-spot diagnosis, involves more analysis and time in a directed study of an individual child. Based on the resulting understanding, the teacher then carefully plans the child's reading program.

Classroom diagnosis might reveal information about a child's reading level. A brief check of the child's vocabulary level is valuable. Using a group test, such as the Botel Word Opposites (Reading), the teacher makes several observations and instructional adjustments. These observations will be tested by the child's ability to handle the new situation. Also, the teacher might ask the child to read from two or three books written at different levels. Instructional situations should be conducted at the level at which the child seems most comfortable. If the child is able to respond to the adjusted instruction, classroom diagnosis was successful.

Classroom diagnosis does not call for long periods of testing nor for reliance upon test results alone. Classroom diagnosis should be more prevalent early in the school year than later on. Once the accuracy of the classroom diagnosis has been affirmed, informal on-the-spot diagnosis will be more efficient.

CLINICAL DIAGNOSIS

As the term implies, this type of diagnosis is reserved for the more complex type of reading difficulty. Conducted by the reading specialist, often with the assistance of noneducational specialists, it usually requires the removal of the child from the classroom so that individual examinations may be administered by a qualified person in surroundings that are conducive to full performance. Characteristic of this type of diagnosis are more precise measures of intellectual potential, word attack skills, visual screening, and the like. These measures will be evaluated to diagnose as accurately as possible the precise nature of the child's reading problem. Clinical diagnosis involves more detailed planning, more careful analysis, and more precise instruments for testing than does classroom diagnosis. We recommend that diagnostic teaching lessons follow clinical diagnosis. If visual discrimination exercises are called for from the diagnostic data, the reading specialist should construct several activities to test his diagnosis. Only then can he place considerable reliance upon his results. If he is in error, he can reanalyze his data and perhaps reexamine the child in certain areas. Clinical diagnosis emphasizes the o with checks on the diagnosis at the R (o—s—R). Clinical diagnosis usually results in formal reporting in the form of a case analysis.

While clinical diagnosis has the advantage of highly individualized study and the use of precise instruments for evaluation by a carefully trained person, it is not without its limitations. One limitation concerns the behavior observed in a one-to-one situation and how that behavior relates to a child's behavior in the classroom when he is working with other children. A second limitation is the manner in which a child reacts to two different people, a teacher and a reading specialist. A third is that while the specialist may check his diagnosis with the diagnostic teaching lessons, he finds that the teacher is unable (for one of many reasons) to make that instructional adjustment. For these reasons, the results of the diagnosis should be discussed with, as well as written out for, the teacher. Also, in order to illustrate the techniques being recommended in the report, the reading specialist should offer to work with the child in the classroom for a lesson or two.

SEQUENCE OF DIAGNOSIS

The following sequence will provide a better understanding of the relationships between the types of diagnosis.

The classroom teacher makes an informal on-the-spot diagnosis and adjusts instruction accordingly. If this fails, the teacher conducts a classroom diagnosis and again individualizes instruction. Should this step be unsuccessful, the teacher refers the student to a reading specialist for a more thorough analysis via clinical diagnosis. Once more instruction is adjusted according to the recommendations of the specialist. If the entire sequence cannot produce the desired results, the necessity for referral outside the school is likely. It is unlikely that a single failure will result in the

CHART 1

Sequence of Diagnosis

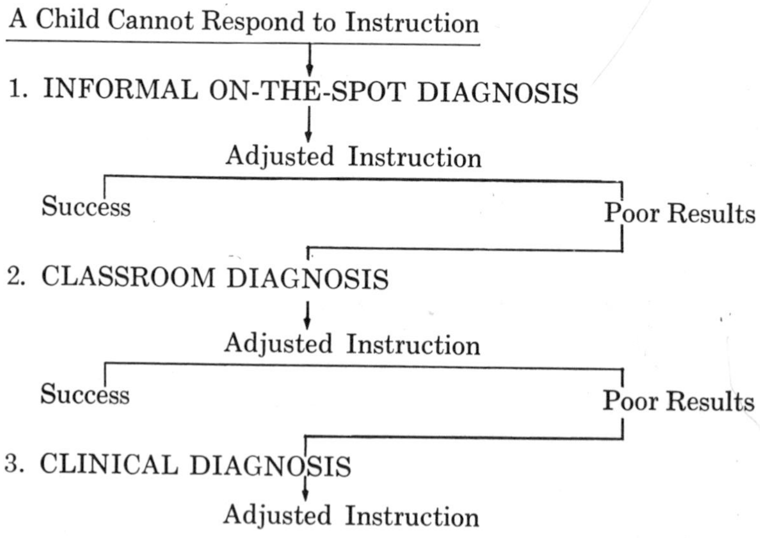

A Child Cannot Respond to Instruction

1. INFORMAL ON-THE-SPOT DIAGNOSIS

Adjusted Instruction

Success   Poor Results

2. CLASSROOM DIAGNOSIS

Adjusted Instruction

Success   Poor Results

3. CLINICAL DIAGNOSIS

Adjusted Instruction

Referral to non-educators might take place at any step.

teacher's moving immediately to the next type of diagnosis; rather, he will utilize each diagnostic step thoroughly and repeatedly, if necessary, before moving to the next. It should be noticed that at each step in this sequence the possibility of referral is present (for an illustration refer to Chart 1.).

Since all effective learning relies upon informal on-the-spot diagnosis and its subsequent follow-up, it is assumed that this type of diagnosis is normal to good teaching situations. It is also obvious that the types of diagnosis are not clearly separated. Neither are specific techniques reserved for the reading specialist; classroom teachers might use clinical diagnostic tools, when appropriate. All types of diagnosis rely upon observation of the child once instruction is adjusted. However, in most instances, the burden of making diagnosis work falls directly upon the classroom teacher. Diagnosis which fails to assist the teacher's daily instruction is of little value.

DIAGNOSTIC PROCEDURES

Diagnostic procedures vary with the purpose and scope of the diagnosis. While similarities exist, there are noticeable differences between informal on-the-spot, classroom, and clinical diagnostic procedures.

Informal On-the-spot Diagnostic Procedures

Informal on-the-spot diagnosis implies that a teacher is concerned about the ability of a child to respond to instruction, that he can observe symptoms of frustration, and that he has alternate strategies for immediate implementation. Therefore, in this type of diagnosis, the child is identified by his inability to respond to instruction. The teacher will note the inability, consider the child's abilities and immediately attempt to adjust the instructional situation so that the child can be successful. The teacher also will record appropriate notes for use in future planning of instruction in that particular area.

Classroom Diagnostic Procedures

Classroom procedures must be designed around the idea that the teacher has obligations and responsibilities to other children as well as to the problem reader. The following procedures may be studied in chart form on Chart 2.

CHART 2

Procedures for Classroom Diagnosis

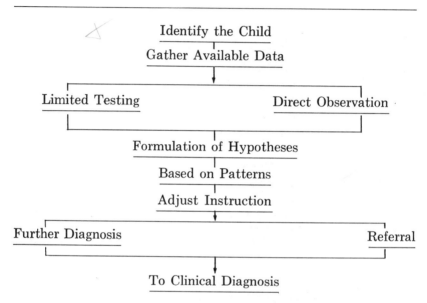

1. Identifying the child: The classroom teacher, unlike the reading specialist, is in the best position to first notice potential problem areas. In this way, the classroom diagnosis is actually underway by the time the child has been identified; informal on-the-spot diagnosis has previously established certain diagnostic information which the teacher will use in classroom diagnosis.

   Hopefully, the tendency for educators to wait until a problem is well developed can be avoided by increased attention to classroom diagnosis at all age levels, including first grade. It is through immediate attention to first symptoms of the reading problems of children that the number of seriously handicapped readers can be reduced.

2. Gathering available data: The classroom teacher then makes an intensive search for available information on the

child and organizes it for further consideration during the diagnosis. Using school records, interviews with past teachers, health reports, and other such sources, considerable data may be available concerning past development, successes, and failures of this child. Obviously, notes made during informal on-the-spot diagnosis will be extremely useful, particularly if the teacher doing the classroom diagnosis did not conduct the previous one.

3. Limited testing: When necessary, the classroom teacher may be prepared to administer and interpret appropriate tests designed to provide information in the area of the difficulty. Testing, of course, is limited in terms of the time that a teacher has for individual testing as well as his skill in using these instruments.

4. Direct observations: Based upon the information available at this stage of classroom diagnosis, the classroom teacher will find it advantageous to observe the child in various reading situations with particular emphasis on the verification of this information. Again, the link to informal on-the-spot diagnosis is clear. When observations and other data complement previous findings, the next step can be taken. When they do not support each other, there is a need for a reevaluation, more observation, possible testing, and new conclusions.

5. Formulation of hypotheses: Based on the patterns observed, the teacher will then form hypotheses about adjustment of instruction, within the group or individually, and about the possibility of referral.

By following the suggestions in this book and by adapting this material to information which the classroom teacher already has available to him, classroom diagnosis should be conducted effectively within one hour. The classroom teacher will need to find periods of time, not necessarily in single blocks, for this type of individual study. As the teacher grows proficient in classroom diagnostic techniques, he will find them more rewarding and less time-consuming.

The classroom teacher's job has obviously just begun, as he will now teach in accordance with his hypotheses, adjust his instruction, evaluate his effectiveness, and, possibly, consider making referral; in addition, he must ever be alert to the possibility that a more thorough diagnosis may be necessary. His situation permits continued diagnosis through the remediation periods. In fact, classroom diagnosis has the strong advantage of often achieving better understandings by working with the child than were possible by preremedial diagnosis itself. In the remedial program the finer points of technique and the real interests of the child can be determined.

Clinical Diagnostic Procedures:

Clinical procedures may be implemented without attention to the needs of other children in the classroom. Clinical procedures are shown on Chart 3.

CHART 3

Procedures for Clinical Diagnosis

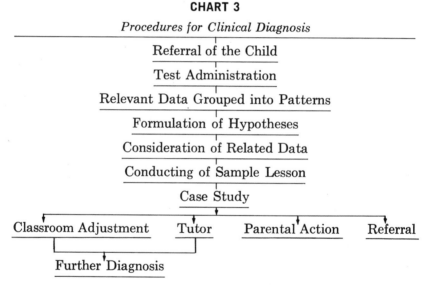

1. Referral of the child: The specialist has the advantage of starting to work with a child previously identified as a possible reading problem. The classroom teacher either has attempted classroom diagnosis or identified the child as one in need of clinical diagnosis. He should be expected to have accumulated all available information about the child and, upon referral to the reading specialist, should submit such information for the specialist's use. It is not uncommon for parents to identify the child as needing clinical diagnosis;

however, it is the specialist's job in these cases to consult with the classroom teacher to make certain that clinical diagnosis has not been conducted previously. He encourages the teacher's support and obtains his opinions and records.

2. Administration of a battery of tests: Based upon a tentative evaluation of the child and his needs, the reading specialist proceeds with the administration and analysis of a battery of tests necessary to gathering objective data concerning the child's reading skills.

3. Observation of patterns: The reading specialist then makes careful observations of behavior patterns during the testing; when combined with test scores and an inner analysis of the child's errors on tests administered, these observations will permit him to group relevant data into more meaningful patterns.

4. Formulation of hypotheses: From the observable patterns, the reading specialist then forms tentative hypotheses concerning the causes of the child's problem. The hypotheses are formulated upon his findings alone. It is important that his original hypothesis be untainted by parental opinion, for often this fresh, unbiased examination of the child leads to the discovery of previously unavailable information.

5. Consideration of related data: Once the hypotheses have been formed, the specialist weighs related data in the form of parent and teacher conferences, school records, previous diagnostic results, and so on. In many instances, the specialist, finding that his hypotheses are true, becomes more confident about his findings. At other times, conflicting information forces him to reconsider his original hypothesis and, in many cases, to test the child further or to reexamine the results of previous tests to gain clearer insights into the child's problem.

6. Conducting of sample lessons: The lesson conducted during a clinical diagnosis is brief and specifically related to diagnostic hypotheses. Parts of that lesson should be directed to the child's strengths and parts to the child's weaknesses. Diagnosis is thus verified through short-term instructional sessions.

7. Formulation of recommendations and referrals: After consideration of all relevant data, the reading specialist develops a case study which includes recommendations for adjust-

ments of school programs, remedial treatment, possible parental action, further testing, and/or necessary referral.

The amount of time needed for effective clinical diagnosis will vary with the age of the child; the effectiveness of classroom diagnosis; and practical matters, such as clinician load. Normally, a clinical diagnosis should be conducted in an hour or so. However, in some cases, much more time will be needed.

But the reading specialist's job does not end here, for he is often involved directly in remediation, in assisting the classroom teacher, or in the initiation of preventive programs, each of which may call for further diagnosis. Morris includes the following thoughts in his discussion of diagnosis: " . . . the challenge is to get to grips more directly with the problem and by working with the individual pupil try to understand what is leading him astray."[1] It is sufficient to say that diagnosis often may reach its ultimate conclusion during instruction.

SOURCES OF DATA

The reading specialist and the classroom teacher have many sources of diagnostic data available to them. Much, but by no means all, of the data available in a reading diagnosis is in the form of tests. Harris views the diagnostic use of tests as follows:

> . . . the heart of diagnosis is not testing; it is, rather, the intelligent interpretation of the facts by a person who has the theoretical knowledge and the practical experience to know what questions to ask; to select procedures, including tests, which can supply the needed facts; to interpret the meaning of the findings correctly; and to comprehend the interrelationships of these facts and meaning.[2]

The reader, therefore, should remember that it is the person conducting the diagnosis and his ability to interpret the data, not the data itself, which leads to effective diagnosis. The reader should also remember that the person who is the object of the diagnosis is more important than the results of test scores.

---

[1]Ronald Morris, *Success and Failure in Learning to Read* (London: Oldbourne, 1963), p. 159.

[2]Albert J. Harris, *How To Increase Reading Ability* (New York: David McKay Co., 1970), p. 201.

Data for classroom diagnosis are less formal than that for clinical diagnosis. School records, observations of the child in his classroom reading, evaluation reports from past teachers, interviews with students and parents, home visits, and available test scores form the major sources of data for a classroom diagnosis.

Data for clinical diagnosis normally take the form of tests of intellectual performance, tests and evaluations of personal adjustment, physical screening tests, tests of reading performance, interviews and questionnaires, observations during model lessons, and professional reports. Data are supplemented by observation of the child during testing and are normally compiled in the form of a case study which illustrates the importance and inter-relationships of the data collected.

Anyone conducting a diagnosis will want to use all of the available diagnostic data which he is competent to interpret. The classroom teacher who has had course work and/or experience in clinical diagnosis will find considerable use for portions of the data listed for the reading specialist. Normally, however, the factors of time, educational background, experience, and access to materials will limit the classroom teacher to less formal types of data.

PRINCIPLES OF DIAGNOSIS

The examiner conducts a diagnosis to understand and then correct a child's difficulty. Implied in principles of diagnosis is the examiner's thorough knowledge of the learning process and of the procedures of teaching reading. Without this knowledge, the educator will find it difficult to apply properly the information gained in a diagnosis, for he will tend to rely solely on the data he has collected instead of interpreting that data in terms of reading skills and learning environment for the child.

Although the classroom teacher is not always able to comply with each of the following principles of diagnosis, it is important for him to be as aware of these principles as is the clinician, for to violate them threatens the reliability of his diagnostic findings.

1. To establish rapport: For a child to perform at his best, a situation must be established where tensions are relaxed and the child is encouraged into a cooperative attitude. The reading specialist confronted with conducting his diagnosis

outside normal classroom situations must be more alert to the necessity for establishing rapport than must the classroom teacher who, through daily contact with the child, is more likely to have rapport established.

2. To provide for individual and group study: Since group testing procedures tend to produce unreliable results for the child with a reading problem, individual study becomes requisite. This principle demands that the individual be studied apart from, as well as within, the group to assure as accurate as possible analysis of his reactions to learning. Through individual and group study, it is possible to analyze accurately the child's skill development, alleviating the aspects of competition which often cause this type of child to perform below his capacity. An error made by many diagnosticians is their failure to observe the child in group situations. Yet much of the child's learning is likely to be in group situations. Obviously, both group and individual study are imperative.

3. To test, not to teach: During testing procedures, special effort must be made to resist the temptation to prompt the child to give the proper answer through "teacher-type" comments, such as "Sound out the first letter," or "That's almost right, try again." The teacher's comments can make the child justifiably encouraged or discouraged. In either case, this action invalidates the diagnostic findings. This principle applies only to the diagnostic period in which the child is expected to perform in a variety of ways without the encouragement or discouragement of success and/or failure. As has been previously stated, both the classroom teacher and reading specialist will find numerous diagnostic opportunities while instruction is taking place.

4. To assure thoroughness: Normally continuing in remedial sessions, diagnosis seldom terminates with the initial diagnostic period. In most cases, informal diagnosis and shorter periods of formal diagnosis will be interspersed during remedial sessions where precise diagnostic findings are formulated and put to use. In such cases informal on-the-spot diagnostic techniques will prove invaluable.

5. To maintain efficiency: In terms of efficiency, a diagnosis includes only those tests which are likely to help the

examiner arrive at pertinent results. There is a tendency
to rely upon a systematic diagnostic procedure regardless
of the needs of the child, creating pointless testing situations which, at best, are often frustrating experiences. An
efficient diagnosis, then, is one which includes those measures needed by the educator to properly arrive at a
solution to the problem; it eliminates those which have
questionable value in relation to the final objective of the
diagnosis. Most testing conducted with children does not
result in adjustment in instructional situations. Therefore,
it is important to stress that diagnostic results which do
not assist in instructional adjustment are of questionable
value. It is also important to note that observations during
instruction often are more valid diagnostically than are test
scores. No doubt many problem learners are the victims of
excessive testing.

6. To evaluate diagnostic data in terms of patterns: The
examiner must look for patterns in data and hesitate to
rely upon a single measure as being meaningful or significant. This principle, then, requires a diagnosis to, in effect,
include several interrelated measures of the child's reading
abilities. For example, it would be best to compare one's
results on a word recognition test with the results on both
oral reading and word meaning tests. When similar errors
occur on all three tests, a pattern of error is established;
when they occur on only one or two tests, a different pattern appears. If reversals occur in one situation but not in
another, the diagnostic conclusions should indicate the situation in which reversals occur.

DIAGNOSIS FOR STRENGTHS

While a child's weaknesses naturally might be the concern of the
teacher, diagnosis for strengths is equally important. Since instructional adjustment should start with areas of strengths, deliberate
diagnosis to determine those strengths is necessary. However, as
we observe diagnostic reports of children with reading problems,
we seldom find mention of their strengths. *All children have
strengths.* Each child should be made aware of them, and the

teacher should note them with as much accuracy as he notes weaknesses. In fact, given a choice, this author would favor diagnosis for strengths. What a child knows is important. What he does not know can be assumed from what he does know. Unfortunately, many case reports seem to indicate that the child has only weaknesses. We all can be placed in reading test situations in which we will fail. For example, I can test most teachers in the area of word attack until they fail. But what is most important, of course, is what they know, not what they do not know. The stress on diagnosing for strengths is a reflection of the motto, Accept and Challenge.

DIAGNOSIS FOR CAUSATION

As diagnosis has been presented thus far, the role of the reading specialist in clinical diagnosis has been contrasted to the role of the classroom teacher in informal on-the-spot and classroom diagnosis. Each has been encouraged to use the best diagnostic procedures and data available. The classroom teacher will utilize his time and efforts most effectively in diagnosing patterns of symptoms in order to adjust his classroom approach to the child with a reading problem. The reading specialist, in clinical diagnosis, will be more thorough in attempting to arrive at a cause. Although diagnosis directed toward the detection of causation is primarily the responsibility of the reading specialist, and although it is through clinical diagnosis that causes are most accurately evaluated, a classroom teacher's awareness of the causes of reading difficulties will aid him in obtaining a better diagnostic understanding of the child. Likewise, the reading specialist must always be concerned about diagnosis which will assist in helping the teacher to adjust classroom instruction in order to help the child become a successful learner.

We have previously established that reading disabilities are caused by a variety of factors. The areas indicated by Bond and Tinker[3] (intellectual, physical, emotional, and educational) are inclusive enough to provide consideration for this variety of causes. Noneducational causes (intellectual, physical and emotional) will

---

[3]Guy L. Bond and Miles A. Tinker, *Reading Difficulties: Their Diagnosis and Correction* (New York: Appleton-Century-Crofts, Inc., 1967), Chapters 5 and 6.

be discussed in Chapter 3. Chapter 4 will contain a discussion of educational causes. It is important for the reader to remember that it is the specific responsibility of educators to diagnose and correct reading problems in this fourth area, educational.

SUMMARY

Through an understanding of the similarities and differences in the diagnostic procedures, data, and principles as they apply to the classroom and clinical situations, the educator is most likely to be effective and satisfied with his efforts. The nature of classroom and clinical settings establishes clear limitations. There are advantages and limitations to both types of diagnosis, and, therefore, each can be viewed objectively and used most effectively. Consideration of the importance of the individual child, his strengths and weaknesses, his feelings, and his self-concept must be of utmost importance to the diagnostic teacher. Without diagnosis, instruction can be effective only by chance.

SUGGESTED READINGS

Bond, Guy L., and Tinker, Miles A. *Reading Difficulties, Their Diagnosis and Correction*. New York: Appleton-Century-Crofts, Inc., 1967. Chapter 7 contains a careful introduction to the broad principles of diagnosis. The reader who desires more specific information on this general topic will find this chapter rewarding.

Harris, Albert. *How to Increase Reading Ability*. New York: David McKay Co., Inc., Chapter 1. Harris' discussion of reading and reading disabilities will provide another view of the role of diagnosis.

Strang, Ruth. *Diagnostic Teaching of Reading*. New York: McGraw Hill Book Co., 1969. As an introduction to this book on diagnosis, Chapter 1 provides an up-to-date, carefully organized discussion of the principles, approaches, and other concepts related to the diagnosing of reading disabilities.

Strang, Ruth. *Invitational Addresses — 1965*. Newark, Delaware: International Reading Association. The address sets the background for the reading model presented in this chapter. The reader may want to refer to the original source for more detail.

3

Noneducational Diagnosis

Diagnosis which is noneducational in nature refers to situations in which the final diagnosis rests with a specialist outside of the field of education. The responsibility of the educator in noneducational diagnosis is to screen the child either with the tools which he has available or through observations of symptoms of difficulty. Once a problem is identified, the child is referred to the appropriate specialist who will conduct a thorough examination and either correct the deficiency or make recommendations to the educator for remedial approaches. This chapter will assist the educator in identifying potential problems, referring effectively, and recognizing the difficulties involved with diagnosis in each of the areas, intellectual, physical, and emotional.

INTELLECTUAL DIAGNOSIS

Estimates of intellectual potential are useful in diagnosing reading problems. An estimate of the child's potential can assist the teacher in setting realistic instructional goals. Such goals should be flexible, for the best measures of intelligence are subject to error. Therefore, recognition of the advantages and limitations of measures of intelligence is essential for interpretation of such data in a reading diagnosis.

As a cause of reading disabilities, intelligence is suspect. In fact, intelligence is related to *causes* of reading problems only in relation to the ability of the school to adjust the educational program to the abilities of various types of children. It is important to realize that it is not intelligence — or lack of it — that prohibits a child from reading up to his potential; rather, it is the fact that school programs which are often geared to the majority of average children do not give ample consideration to children at the extremes (the bright and dull children). The inability or the impossibility of a given situation to provide these necessary adjustments often *causes* bright or dull children to become reading problems. Although accurate measures of intellectual performance are essential to the diagnosis of children's reading, the intelligence of a given child per se is not the cause of his problem.

Complications of Intellectual Testing

Complicating the use of intelligence tests is the educator's tendency to misuse test scores by grasping at high or low scores as the most easily observable division between the problem and the normal reader. How many children have thus been labeled can only be guessed at, but that many have been mislabeled is fact.

A brief review of the limitations of measures of potential will indicate the difficulties encountered when such data is used in diagnosis.

Reliability: Has the test measured accurately? Has the test measured by chance? If the child were to retake the test, would he obtain the same score? All tests are subject to error; therefore, most test constructors provide information about the test error in the teacher's guide. Error information is of two types, reliability coefficient and standard error of measurement. Reliability coefficients are usually reported in decimals (.90). Made into a percentage (90 percent), the test may be said to measure the true score ninety percent of the time and error ten percent of the time. Reliability coefficients below the .90 level cause concern about the reliability of the test. The standard error of measurement usually is reported in terms of the raw score or mental age score on the test (4 months). The standard error, in theory, is explained as follows: If the student were to take the test repeatedly, his scores would fall within a range of plus or minus four months of the score he obtained with the current administration. Therefore, if a child obtained a mental age score of 9.5 months and the test had a standard error of 4 months, his score would be interpreted as falling somewhere between 9.1 and 9.9 months about two-thirds of the time. For children who score in the extremes, very high or very low, errors of measurement are greater than for those scoring in the middle or average ranges of the test. The necessity for awareness of reliability and standard error scores becomes clear. Without them, one cannot interpret a given score. Such information shows the folly of labeling a child with a given score.

Validity: Does a test measure what it purports to measure? Validity involves the problem of what intelligence is. Most tests include items which encompass the ability to perform in school. Of the many dimensions which intelligence must surely have, most tests measure only a few; some measure only one. Presumably, the most prominent aspects of intelligence have been included in the best constructed tests. While a test which measures listening comprehension is measuring a significant aspect of intelligence, the resulting score — called a mental age — implies more than can be covered by such a narrow measure. Another complication is encountered when a given test also requires specifically learned skills, such as reading. The test's validity is then in interference with the reading achievement of the person taking the test.

Most test constructors attempt to prove the validity of their measure by comparing the results of their test with another test, usually one of established reputation. These figures usually appear as decimals (.70). For interpretation purposes, the decimal must be squared (.49) to find the percent (49 percent) of the variance measured, in common, by each test. Other test constructors are content to logically defend the test's content as an obvious factor or factors of intelligence.

When two tests of intelligence are administered, a child probably will obtain two different scores which, at times, are quite different. Then the problem is to determine which score is most valid. However, an obvious concern arises. Would the child have scored even better on another measure?

To complicate validity further, many tests contain problems which are dependent upon cultural experiences. Children from cultures other than those on which the test was normed score significantly poorer than will children from cultures similar to the ones on which the test is based. In such cases, is the test a fair measure of the child's intelligence? Obviously not.

Test administration, scoring, and interpretation: Despite the efforts of the American Psychological Association, persons other than qualified psychologists administer intelligence tests. Many of these people do so without training under directed supervision; they often make serious errors in test administration, scoring, and interpretation. Tests administered by unknown personnel must be held suspect and normally should not be considered useful information in a reading diagnosis.

Group intelligence tests: For several reasons, group tests of intelligence are inappropriate for children suspected of having a reading difficulty. First, many of the group tests require that a child read in order to take the test. Obviously, if the child cannot read well, his score will reflect his poor reading as well as his intelligence, and the two will be hopelessly confused. Second, rapport is difficult to establish in group testing. For a child who has been subjected to considerable failure, any group test may threaten him further and result in a poor performance. Third, the reliability of many of the group tests is very poor, making score interpretation nearly impossible. MacDonald comments on the difficulty with group intelligence tests.

> Because both group type intelligence tests and reading achievement tests involve reading, the common element present in both kinds of tests represents two measures of the same categories of skill. Poor readers are doubly penalized with significant underestimation of probable mental ability.[1]

Awareness of the limitations inherent in measures of intellectual performance will lessen the possibility of intelligence test scores being used or interpreted improperly. For the best assessment of intellectual performance, at least one of the measures of

---

[1]Arthur S. MacDonald, "Research for the Classroom," *The Journal of Reading,* VIII (November 1964), pp. 115-18.

intelligence must be individual and nonreading in nature. Major discrepancies between test scores are justifiable reasons for referral for psychological examination. An accurate I.Q. is *not* found by averaging conflicting scores.

Acknowledging these limitations, one should establish as accurately as possible the level of intellectual performance (an index of potential reading ability) to measure the degree to which the child is retarded in reading. A fifth grade child with the estimated intelligence of the average fourth grader, reading one year below his grade level, normally is not considered retarded in reading; he reads as well as he is able. He is, however, a problem to his teacher, for he is not likely to profit from instruction with the materials available to his fifth grade class. This child is a problem, not as a retarded reader, but as a product of our schools' failure to provide materials at varying levels of difficulty (or of a teacher to use effectively available materials and techniques). This child does not need a reading diagnosis; rather, he needs the normal developmental program available in fourth grade. Harris claims, " . . . if the dull child's reading ability is up to his mental age, relatively little return may be gained from remedial instruction."[2] On the other hand, a fifth grade child, reading at a sixth grade level with the estimated intellectual performance of the average eighth grader, may not cause instructional problems, but he *is* retarded in reading. So, quite often, the retarded reader is of normal or above average intelligence, but reading below his potential. It remains important, therefore, for the person conducting a diagnosis of reading problems to evaluate carefully the intellectual performance of each child or to obtain that evaluation from a reliable source.

Considering the limitations of intelligence testing and particularly of group testing, it seems inconceivable that school reading personnel would use such scores to control admission to a program to aid those having reading difficulty. However, many schools limit admission to reading programs to those with group intelligence test scores above 80, 90, or 100. Such a practice seems indefensible and should be changed. Imagine that a child with a group-tested I. Q. of 79 might be denied help, although he easily might score 110 on an individual measure. Discriminations of this type are not based on a knowledge of the instruments being used.

---

[2]Albert J. Harris, *How To Increase Reading Ability* (New York: David McKay Co., 1970), p. 217.

Instead of relying on such scores, other options are available. What is the nature of a student's problem in reading? How long has the problem existed? How does his teacher feel about it? How did last year's teacher feel about it? Are there any evidences of school success outside the language areas? Eventually the school will have to deal with such a case, for every child has the right to the best programs possible.

Measures of Potential Reading Ability Suitable for Clinical Diagnosis*

*Revised Stanford Binet Intelligence Scale:** Considered by many to be the most accurate single test for measuring intelligence, the Binet test may be administered and scored only by personnel with formal course work and laboratory experience. The test ranges from preschool to adulthood, yielding a mental age and an intelligence quotient. The test measures several aspects of intelligence, is heavily verbal, takes about one hour to administer, is individual in nature, and requires precise administration and interpretation for reliable results.

Wechsler Intelligence Scale for Children (WISC):* Another popular, accurate test of intellectual performance, the WISC requires individual administration and formal course work and laboratory experience for reliable results. Measuring several aspects of intelligence, the WISC yields a performance and a verbal score, with the verbal score normally considered the most valid predictor of performance in reading. With problem readers, however, the performance score probably provides the best measure of reading potential. The child's verbal score may be limited by the same factors that limit his performance in reading. When WISC scores show a higher performance than verbal rating, there is just cause to encourage a child with his development in reading. Deal[3] summarized fourteen studies of WISC subscores and found that the researchers were far from unanimous in their findings concerning interpretation of subscores. Farr,[4] summarizing sixteen studies, found several fairly consistent subscore patterns on the WISC for retarded readers. No cause-and-effect relationship was determined,

---

[3] Margaret Deal, "A Summary of Research Concerning Patterns of WISC Subtest Scores of Retarded Readers," *The Journal of the Reading Specialist*, IV (May 1965), pp. 101-11.

[4] Roger Farr, *Reading; What Can Be Measured?* (Newark, Delaware: International Reading Association, 1969), pp. 93-4.

however. The teacher is cautioned about the use and interpretation of such subscores for reading diagnosis and subsequent adjustment of instruction. Since WISC scores are best interpreted by psychological personnel, most reading personnel should await their analysis. The *Wechsler Adult Intelligence Scale* (WAIS), also available, may be used with older children and adults. Both the WISC and the WAIS take approximately one hour to administer.

The Peabody Picture Vocabulary Test (PPVT):* Designed to test the child's ability to associate one of four pictures with the word pronounced by the examiner, the PPVT is a test of listening vocabulary taking approximately fifteen minutes for individual administration and requiring little special preparation by the teacher. Although limited to one aspect of intelligence (i.e., *auding*), Neville[5] found no significant difference between the performance scores of fifty-four children on the PPVT and on the WISC. Strang contends, "Ability to comprehend by listening (sometimes called *auding*) is another indication of potential reading ability."[6] We have found it valuable to refer to the M.A. score on the PPVT as the child's "auding age" and to the I.Q. as the "auding quotient." By changing these names, we find that teachers who work with these tests are more likely to use the resulting scores properly. For a quick indication of intellectual performance, the PPVT is considered to be practical and useful when Binet and WISC scores are not available. The Slossen Intelligence Test* and the Ammons Full Range Picture Vocabulary Test* are also useful instruments for quick indications of intellectual performance.

*Durrell Listening-Reading Series:** As another measure of auding ability, these tests require children to associate words and paragraphs which have been read to them with pictures. The auding scores then are compared to reading vocabulary and reading paragraph scores. Testing time requires approximately eighty minutes and requires little formal preparation for either administration or scoring.

*The Knox Cube Test:** This subtest from the *Grace Arthur Point Scale* is useful in reading diagnosis since it provides a measure of the

---

[5]Donald Neville, "The Relationship Between Reading Skills and Intelligence Test Scores," *The Reading Teacher*, XVIII (January 1965), pp. 257-61.
[6]Ruth Strang, *Diagnostic Teaching of Reading* (New York: McGraw Hill Book Co., 1969), p. 15.

child's performance in memorization of nonverbal sequences. Most children with reading problems will score two to three years below their chronological age. Scores which fall below this margin may be considered as one symptom of more complicated organizational disabilities.

Arithmetic computation: For children who have attended school for two or more years, a test of arithmetic computation, not involving verbal problems, is useful in estimating academic potential. Included as a factor on several intelligence scales, arithmetic computation scores show how well the child succeeds in school in nonverbal tasks, thus indicating his level of potential. Arithmetic computation scores verify suspicions of potential that have gone undetected when they vary noticeably from reading achievement. In some types of more seriously handicapped children, arithmetic computation scores do not indicate potential. This is especially true when the child reacts against the total learning environment with emotional rejection. Arithmetic computation, however, remains a valuable tool as one of the first indicators of intellectual potential.

The tests mentioned above, which are the most likely ones to be available, provide fairly accurate measures of reading potential. Other measures of intellectual performance also are available for clinical diagnosis; however, most of them require special preparation and laboratory experience, as do the Binet and the WISC.

Measures of Potential Reading Ability
Suitable to Classroom Diagnosis

The Binet and the WISC:* These are not normally administered by the classroom teacher, but their scores are often found in the school records of the problem reader. The other tests mentioned under clinical diagnosis can be administered by a classroom teacher as a part of normal school procedures or as a part of classroom diagnosis.

Group intelligence tests: Although group intelligence tests are inherently unsatisfactory in reading diagnosis, several of them do separate reading and nonreading factors. The *California Test of Mental Maturity,** for example, provides a mental age and I.Q. for both language and nonlanguage performance. The teacher who uses this type of test and finds a major discrepancy between the two scores (nonlanguage I.Q.—140; language I.Q.—100), should be encouraged to look for other signs of intellectual performance, for the child may be capable, but hindered in the language section by his lack of reading ability. Other measures of reading potential, such as those mentioned under clinical diagnosis, should then be checked, or the child should be referred for an individual intelligence examination. However, unless group intelligence tests have nonlanguage features, they are not useful in estimating the reading potential of children with reading problems. Even then, their usefulness is highly questionable.

Teacher observation: The experienced teacher often is able to note characteristics of reading potential through direct observation of the child's response to various school activities. Roswell states that a teacher "... can form some idea of the child's intellectual ability from his general responsiveness in class."[7] Specifically, noticeable characteristics are:

1. Ability to participate effectively in class discussions, both listening and speaking.
2. Ability to achieve more successfully in arithmetic than in subjects requiring reading.
3. Ability to participate effectively in peer group activities.
4. Ability to demonstrate alert attitudes to the world around him.
5. Ability to perform satisfactorily on spelling tests.

Admittedly, such observations are neither highly valid nor reliable indications of reading potential. Teacher observation is limited by the possibilities of teacher bias; he may well see just what he is looking for. For example, his observation may be controlled somewhat by previous test performances and prior impressions of the child. Ability in these areas is, however, often the first symptom to be noticed. By such observations, children who have been intellectually misjudged may be referred for a more accurate evaluation.

Remember that a child's score on a given test is only a reflection of his total ability. He is always greater as a person than any test score can show. Therefore, teachers are encouraged to look for the best in all children, and such an approach to observation should be communicated positively to the child.

---

[7] Florence Roswell and Gladys Natchez, *Reading Disability* (New York: Basic Books, Inc., 1964), p. 27.

Reading Potential and Degree of Retardation

Measures of intellectual performance greatly aid in determining the degree of reading retardation. A comparison of the best estimates of reading potential with the best estimates of reading achievement will result in an arithmetical difference. When potential exceeds achievement, one is concerned that the child is not working up to his capacity. The larger the difference, the more serious the degree of retardation.

Perhaps the most common technique for estimating the seriousness of retardation is a simple comparison of the child's mental age [I.Q. divided by 100, multiplied by chronological age (C.A.)] to his reading achievement.[8] This technique is particularly limiting with very young children of high ability, for it assumes a considerable development of reading skills prior to school attendance. A six year old child with an I.Q. of 140 entering first grade may be considered to have a mental age of 8.4 ($\frac{140}{100}$ x 6.0 = 1.4 × 6.0 = 8.4), but should not normally be expected to be reading at the third grade level because he lacks social, emotional, and educational experiences for that degree of achievement. Even with older, bright children, this technique tends to place reading potential scores unrealistically high. Acknowledging these limitations, an estimate of the seriousness of retardation can be determined by this technique.

Harris recommends a formula which places priority on mental age (Reading Expectancy $= \frac{2\ \text{MA} + \text{CA}}{3}$) as another alternative.[9]

Bond and Tinker circumvent the limitations mentioned above by using the formula ($\frac{\text{I.Q.}}{100}$ multiplied by years in school + 1.0)[10] as compared to reading achievement. The child discussed above would have a reading potential of 1.0 upon entrance to first grade.

$$(\frac{140}{100} \times 0) + 1.0 = 1.0$$

As a child advances through school, this approach expects him to make accelerated progress so that upon entrance to third grade this same child is expected to be reading at the 3.8 grade level:

---

[8]Harris, *How To Increase Reading Ability*, p. 211.

[9]Harris, *How To Increase Reading Ability*, p. 212.

[10]Guy L. Bond and Miles A. Tinker, *Reading Difficulties: Their Diagnosis and Correction* (New York: Appleton-Century-Crofts, Inc., 1967), p. 92.

reading specialist and the classroom teacher can refer children either on the basis of reliable patterns of symptoms or as a result of certain screening devices available to educators. Conceivably, the educator, who is in daily contact with the child in a variety of situations, often sees symptoms of possible physical limitations which nonspecialized medical personnel in a given, brief medical examination cannot detect. This is not to say that the classroom teacher's observation is a substitute for a specialist's evaluation; rather, it is to emphasize strongly the place of the teacher in the initial identification of a physical problem through the observation of symptoms in his daily contact with the child.

Specifically, the areas of physical diagnosis of reading problems are general physical, visual, auditory, and neurological. Limitations which are serious enough in these areas to interfere with the child's performance in reading are also likely to interfere with the child's general educational performance. However, a general educational deficiency does not necessarily indicate physical disabilities.

As we consider various types of physical limitations to educational performance, we should keep in mind that physical *comfort* is all-important. For example, serious tooth decay can cause enough discomfort to limit a child's ability to concentrate in school. While there is no evidence to correlate tooth decay with reading problems, an understanding teacher should be alert to symptoms of discomfort which might interfere with instruction.

General Health

Large numbers of children are not healthy enough to profit efficiently from the instruction provided, even under the best of conditions. Although difficult to estimate, the exact size of a given school population affected by general physical limitations varies greatly from one community to the next. It behooves the educator to know those aspects of general health which interfere with school progress and which should be evaluated in the diagnosis of reading problems.

Malnutrition causes the child to lose weight or to lag behind in physical and mental vitality. Malnutrition does not necessarily show itself in loss of weight, however. Many children suffering from diet imbalance are quite chubby (e.g., those suffering from imbalance of starches). The sluggish behavior which results interferes with school performance.

Glandular defects have also been diagnosed as causing educational problems. When the glands which maintain important balances in the body fail, more than physical discomfort may result.

Mental or physical fatigue, caused by lack of sleep, poor sleeping habits, lack of exercise, or overexertion, can cause children to be inattentive and easily distracted in a learning situation.

Poor general physical condition, often characterized by frequent illness, causes a lack of stamina with resulting gaps in the educational instruction. Factors such as overweight, underweight, poor teeth, hay fever, etc. can result in difficulty with school tasks.

Alertness to signs of poor health is essential in a reading diagnosis. Many such cases are first identified by individual attention to a child's performance during diagnosis.

The classroom teacher combines information from school records, reports from the school nurse and the family doctor, information from the parents, and observable symptoms which are characteristic of children with general physical deficiencies. Sluggishness, inattentiveness, failure to complete assignments, apparent lack of interest, sleeping in school, and general lack of vitality often are symptoms which cause a child to be labeled lazy or indifferent. A classroom teacher, finding a pattern of these symptoms, properly contacts the home to report his evaluation of the problem and makes a medical referral when it is appropriate. At the same time, he adjusts the instruction to make the learning environment as comfortable as possible for the child. This adjustment may take the form of relaxing the tension caused by the child's apparent indifference, allowing the fatigued child a program of varied activities and necessary rest periods, and, if possible, following the recommendations of medical personnel. It does not take a medical report to make us aware that all children, not just those with reading problems, need good health for optimum school performance. Necessities, such as adequate rest, a balanced diet (particularly a good breakfast), annual physical checkups, and large doses of play activity after school, are vital requirements for good school performance.

Referral, then, is the responsibility of the teacher any time that a child in academic difficulty shows symptoms of general physical limitations. It is the responsibility of school personnel to consult the home and make medical referrals when there is evidence that a child needs medical attention.

The reading specialist's job in diagnosing is to evaluate reports received from medical personnel in terms of the total case picture of the child involved and to recommend the appropriate classroom adjustment and/or remedial program. Prior to referral, the reading specialist is likely to obtain much of his diagnostic information from the same symptoms mentioned under the classroom teacher's diagnosis or from the classroom teacher himself. His duty, then, is to apply this information to his overall diagnosis. The reading specialist must note particularly the onset of the physical deficiency. Was this limitation prevalent at birth or did it arise later in the child's life? By considering the time element, the reading specialist most accurately assesses the degree to which a limitation may have actually interfered with the child's learning processes.

Visual Diagnosis

The classroom teacher is aware that deficiencies in visual ability and ocular comfort may well impede a child's growth in reading. Reports relate that from fifteen to forty percent of our school children need professional visual attention. The relationship of vision to reading problems is complicated since many children with visual problems are not problem readers. The more careful research reports[13] show a relationship between certain types of visual deficiencies and failure in reading and have found that certain visual disabilities and ocular discomfort greatly interfere with a child's reaching his reading potential. In general, functional problems, such as awkward eye movements and poor fusion, more often cause reading difficulty than do organic difficulties, such as nearsightedness, farsightedness, or astigmatism. A review of some of the aspects of vision and ocular comfort pinpoints the relationship.

Acuity: Acuity, the clearness of vision, is normally measured at far point targets (a Snellen Chart[14] 20 feet away from the child). Such screening tests of acuity provide us with information concerning the child's acuity at the far point (e.g., his ability to see the chalkboard). The results of this type of visual screening are expressed in terms of what the average person can see at twenty feet. The term 20/20 means that a child can see at 20 feet the same target

---

[13]Charles A. Kelley, *Visual Screening and Child Development* (Raleigh, North Carolina: North Carolina State College, 1957), Chapter II, p. 11.

[14]"The Snellen Chart" (Southbridge, Mass.: American Optical Co.).

that a person with normal vision can see at 20 feet. This test, when used alone, however, cannot detect all visual deficiencies. In the first place, we do not normally read targets which are 20 feet from the eyes; neither do we read with one eye at a time. The eyes must efficiently move from one target to another rather than merely fixing on and identifying a target. Kelley claims, "The misconception that the Snellen Chart will do an efficient job of screening out children who need visual care is a major block in the road of those trying to establish good school visual screening programs."[15]

Screening devices to measure near point acuity are essential in the diagnosis of a problem reader, although they generally take more time and training to administer properly. Today, a child who passes the Snellen Chart may still have a visual deficiency which is causing problems in his reading performance. The farsighted child, seeing far point targets better than near point targets, may pass the Snellen Chart yet not see well enough or efficiently enough to read with comfort at the near point. The nearsighted child, who sees near point targets better than far point targets, is likely to fail the Snellen Chart, but, while obviously limited by a visual defect, may read effectively in most cases. Therefore, proper visual screening must measure both far and near point acuity. This need has been partially met by the development of a type of chart for use at a distance of fourteen inches. Additional techniques, described below, are generally more desirable for accurate near point screening.

Fusion: Fusion involves the ability of the brain to blend or fuse the image from each eye into an adequate image. A child who looks with one eye and psychologically blinds the other gets a clear image but does not have good fusion. A child with sluggish fusion seldom sees a clear target adequately; thus, he experiences ocular discomfort and inefficiency that should be identified in a near and far point visual screening. It is not the educator's job to determine the degree of fusion; rather, he must identify the problem area for referral purposes.

Color recognition: It is important for the young child to recognize colors accurately. Simple far point color blindness tests generally are adequate for screening, with the precise measurement of color limitation left to the vision specialist. The reading teacher, with a knowledge of the child's color confusion problems, does not expect the child to perform in tasks requiring color discrimination.

---

[15]Kelley, *Visual Screening and Child Development*, p. 11.

Ocular motility: The efficient operation of the eye in motion is a requisite for effective reading. In particular, we are referring to good left-to-right motion (pursuit), saccadic movement, fixations, and focusing power. Screening devices are available for evaluation in these three areas and should be considered in a diagnosis of reading problems.

1. Left-to-right motion: In the reading act, the eyes must fix on a target, move to the right, fix on another target, move to the right, fix on another target, then sweep back and take hold of the next line in a manner which is not natural at birth, but learned. A child who is grossly inefficient at this task of left-to-right eye movements or accurate fixations will likely experience difficulty in the reading act.

2. Pursuit eye movement: Eyes should be able to follow a moving target smoothly, not stopping and starting, but following with an effortless fluid movement. The ability to do so allows a child the efficient eye motion between fixations without which he is likely to have trouble following a line of print.

3. Saccadic eye movement: Accurate change of fixations from one word to another or from the end of a line of print to the beginning of the next line is an important ocular-motor skill related to reading. When deficient in this skill, the child loses his place, skips words, and reads more slowly than is necessary.

4. Focusing power: Prolonged reading further demands the power to maintain focus on a target for a long time. The child with deficient focusing power is likely to become fatigued much sooner than others.

5. Binocular vision: During the reading act some children tend to suppress the vision of one eye and do all the reading with the other. The continuation of this type of reading can lead to serious visual complications which can only be evaluated by the visual specialist.

The areas of ocular motility are seldom investigated in usual school screening; however, when diagnosing a reading problem, every effort should be made to evaluate them.

The reading specialist should refrain from diagnosing visual deficiencies. Instead, he should consider the possibility that visual discomfort might be interfering with the ability or the desire to read. Justifiably, a child can be referred for visual examination when he has a serious reading problem and has not had a visual examination within the last year. Should a reading specialist desire to screen a child's visual abilities, several procedures are available. Regardless of the results, however, the reading specialist must remember that he is only *screening* the child. Diagnosis of visual deficiencies belongs to the visual specialists. The following techniques are useful for visual screening:

1. A *Telebinocular** test provides near and far point screening of acuity, stereopsis, and fusion, as well as a test of color visual. The proper administration and analysis of this test requires supervised experience to assure reliable results. It should be noted that the telebinocular screens the visual skills related to the ability of the eyes to fix only on a given target.

2. The reading specialist must also be concerned about the eyes as they operate in reading situations. The *Binocular Reading Test** by Spache provides an analysis of binocular vision during the reading act. In this test, the child looks at a card that has been placed in the telebinocular and reads a story containing some words that only the right eye can see and some that only the left eye can see. By marking the child's responses, the examiner can determine the degree to which each eye operates in the reading act. Referral is based on certain characteristics which are identified in the accompanying manual.

3. Another test of the operation of eyes in the reading act is the *Reading Eye Camera.** Similar to an eye motion camera that is formally called the opthalmograph, the film produced in this examination supplies information concerning the number of fixations, regressions, span of fixation, and duration of fixation of a child's reading. As the Spaches have explained, "The use of the camera reveals that many pupils of primary and intermediate levels manifest reading errors that reflect faulty or inadequate training in the visual components of the reading act."[16] When carefully interpreted,

---

[16]George D. Spache and Evelyn B. Spache, *Reading in the Elementary School* (Boston: Allyn and Bacon, Inc., 1969), p. 12.

an analysis of eye motion in the reading act can supply important information. Although the equipment for this test is costly and the administration is time-consuming, it enables a reading specialist to obtain a picture of the eye in motion.

4. For screening pursuit, saccadic eye movements, and focusing power, a pocket flashlight is used in the following way: holding the light upright, approximately eighteen inches from the eyes, the examiner asks the child to look at the light. The examiner then moves the light in a plane eighteen inches from the eye in straight, vertical, horizontal, and diagonal lines twelve-eighteen inches in length, and, then, in a circle with a radius of about twelve inches clockwise and counterclockwise. The child should be considered for referral if: he cannot follow the light without moving his head, even after being told to hold still; the reflection of the light cannot be seen in both pupils at all times; or the eye movements are saccadic (i.e., they follow the light jerkily instead of smoothly). To test converging power, the light is again held eighteen inches from the eye, moved slowly to a position one inch directly between the eyes and held for one second. Since some children do not understand this test the first time, there is justification for referral only if the child cannot hold this fixation after three attempts.

Not having any of this screening equipment available to him, the classroom teacher must rely upon a pattern of symptoms observable in the reading act or in other school situations. The check list prepared by the American Optometric Association[17] (Table 3) includes a list of these symptoms. Copies of this check list may be secured from the American Optometric Association, 4030 Chouteau Avenue, St. Louis, Missouri. Note that this check list recommends that *all* students who are not performing well in terms of their capacity should be referred for visual examinations.

Children with these symptoms normally will be referred to the school nurse; however, if her screening equipment is limited to the Snellen Chart, the classroom teacher is obligated to present his information to the parents, with the suggestion of a complete visual

---

[17]"Teacher's Guide To Vision Problems " (St. Louis: American Optometric Association, 1953).

TABLE 3

*Teacher's Guide to Vision Problems
with Check List*

To aid teachers in detecting the children who should be referred for complete visual analysis, the American Optometric Association Committee on Visual Problems in Schools has compiled a list of symptoms — a guide to vision problems. The committee recommends:

1. That all children in the lower third of the class, particularly those with ability to achieve above their percentile rating, be referred for complete visual analysis.
2. That every child in the class who, even though achieving, is not working within reasonable limits of his own capacity be referred for a complete visual analysis.

Following are other symptoms which may indicate a visual problem, regardless of results in any screening test:

Observed in Reading:

Dislike for reading and reading subjects.

Skipping or re-reading lines.

††Losing place while reading.

Slow reading or word calling.

Poor perceptual ability, such as confusing o and a; n and m; etc.

Other Manifestations:

Restlessness, nervousness, irritability or other unaccountable behavior.

Desire to use finger or marker as pointer while reading.

††Avoiding close work.

††Poor sitting posture and position while reading.

Vocalizing during silent reading, noticed by watching lips or throat.

Reversals persisting in grade 2 or beyond.

Inability to remember what has been read.

Complaint of letters and lines "running together" or of words "jumping."

††Holding reading closer than normal.

††Frowning, excessive blinking, scowling, squinting, or other facial distortions while reading.

††Excessive head movements while reading.

Writing with face too close to work.

††Found to be particularly significant in a recent study.

Table 3 — Teacher's Guide Continued

Fatigue or listlessness after close work.

Inattentiveness, temper tantrums or frequent crying.

Complaint of blur when looking up from close work.

Seeing objects double.

Headaches, dizziness or nausea associated with the use of eyes.

††Body rigidity while looking at distant objects.

Undue sensitivity to light.

Crossed eyes — turning in or out.

Red-rimmed, crusted or swollen lids.

Frequent sties.

Watering or bloodshot eyes.

Burning or itching of eyes or eyelids.

††Tilting head to one side.

††Tending to rub eyes.

Closing or covering one eye.

Frequent tripping or stumbling.

Poor hand and eye co-ordination as manifested in poor baseball playing, catching and batting or similar activities.

††Thrusting head forward.

††Tension during close work.

Only a complete case study will determine whether inadequate vision is a significant factor in nonachievement.

††Found to be particularly significant in a recent study.

---

case study by a specialist. Until the child receives treatment, the teacher should make every effort to provide him with the most comfortable and efficient visual environment. This may be accomplished by placing the child in a position of maximum lighting, by eliminating glare, by adjusting seating to ease board work, or by reducing the reading load.

Visual referral problems. Referral in vision is complicated by the reluctance of educators to overrefer (i.e., referring a child who may not be in need of help). Kelley views the problem as follows:

The cardinal purpose of school visual screening procedures is to refer children who may need visual care. It generally is considered more serious for a screening program to *fail to refer* a child in real need of care than for it to *refer* a child not actually in need of care.[18]

Shaw says:

My opinion is that a child's first ophthalmological examination should be given at about age three . . . The persistance of abnormal symptoms would suggest the need for eye examination regardless of the results of a screening test.[19]

Underreferral is the only alternative since it is unlikely that a visual screening test will result in completely accurate referral. Ewalt sees the problem of overreferral as follows:

You have heard screening programs seriously criticized because they refer too many youngsters for visual examination. Nonsense! Most of the agencies of this country, dealing with vision, whether they represent the ophthalmologists as the National Association for the Prevention of Blindness, or the optometrists as the American Optometric Association agree that every school child should have an annual examination. If all school children need an annual examination, we need not be too concerned with an occasional over referral.[20]

The schools, through their notorious reluctance to refer, have caused many children to operate daily with eye strain which leads to more complicated, permanent problems. The author is of the opinion that all children should have periodic visual examinations by a specialist. Until the schools assume this responsibility, it remains a parental obligation. The teacher then, should not hesitate to refer any child who demonstrates the symptoms indicated in Table 3. This in no way implies that an indiscriminate attitude toward referral should be adopted; however, this procedure is the best way by which many children can receive necessary visual attention.

The necessity for visual referral is complicated further by changes in the eyes following visual adjustment. The nature of school, requiring hours of close work, may make it necessary for lenses to be changed periodically. Therefore, the teacher should

---

[18]Charles A. Kelley, *Visual Screening*, Chapter 2, p. 11.

[19]Jules H. Shaw, "Vision and Seeing Skills of Preschool Children," *The Reading Teacher*, XVIII (October 1964), p. 36.

[20]Ward H. Ewalt, Jr., "Visual Problems of Children and Their Relationship to Reading Achievement," *The Optometric Weekly* (October 22, 1959).

not hesitate to refer a child who has symptoms of visual discomfort, even if the child is wearing glasses.

A third complication of referral is the strongly motivated student who, regardless of visual strain and discomfort, persists in his school work and shows no signs of academic deficiency. Again this child, showing symptoms listed in Table 3, should be referred without hesitation before the possibility of consequential harm.

Finally, one must choose to whom the referral should be made. We have used the term vision specialist to avoid complication. By vision specialist we mean either an optometrist, an ophthalmologist, or an oculist. A competent specialist in any of these fields should be considered satisfactory for referral. Ophthalmologists and oculists are medical doctors who have specialized in vision. The optometrist has a doctor's degree in optometry. Each is qualified to prescribe lenses and visual training. In the case of eye disease, an optometrist will refer the patient to the ophthalmologist or oculist. Regardless of the degree held by the vision specialist, educators should make an effort to seek out those who have a special interest in the visual development of children and in the problems of functional vision that relate to reading achievement.

To aid in the referral, a form, such as the following, will aid the vision specialist to understand the reasons for referral and will provide him with basic educational information.

Visual Referral Form

_____(name)_____ was screened visually and did not perform satisfactorily in the following areas(s):

_____

_____

His present reading level is _____, but his reading potential is about _____.

Will you please inform us if, after your examination, a visual deficiency may have been causing this student some problems in reading.

_____

Signed

The educator's tone when making a referral is especially important. If his tone is authoritative, he may come into conflict with visual specialists and parents when he overrefers. We have found it best to state the referral in terms similar to these; "Since Tom appears to be having serious difficulties in reading and since he has not had his eyes checked recently, we would like you to take him to a specialist for an examination. As we start to work with Tom, it will be best to correct any visual disorder first. If he has none, then we will not need to be concerned about visual discomfort."

In summary, both the reading specialist and the classroom teacher should consider every child with a reading problem to have a potential visual problem. Therefore, they should use screening devices and observe symptoms to refer possible problem cases. Under no circumstances should the teacher or the reading specialist consider a battery of screening devices, no matter how highly refined, as a substitution for a thorough eye examination and visual analysis. Screening tests, at best, are limited to their designed function: the identification of children in need of visual attention.

Auditory Problems

Obviously, a child who cannot hear adequately faces problems in school. Many children with auditory limitations are placed in special schools or special classes for the deaf and hard of hearing so that they can receive specialized educational opportunities. Many other children with hearing losses, however, remain in the normal school situations. For the most part, school nurses have been able to identify these children early and to refer them to specialists. Nevertheless, for one reason or another, auditory problems continue to plague children.

It has been our experience that very few children need auditory referral; only those who do show marked difficulties in reading. In the first place, a child with a significant hearing loss is likely to find phonic instruction beyond his grasp because of a distortion of sounds or the inability to hear sounds at all. Most auditory deficiencies concern high frequency sounds; therefore, due to the high frequency of many of the consonant sounds, the most common limitation that a hearing deficiency places upon a child is in the area of consonant recognition and usage. A child with a hearing difficulty is hindered as well by his inability to follow directions since he may not hear them clearly. He is, therefore, likely to lose his place in oral reading class when listening to others, fail to complete home assignments, and appear inattentive and careless.

It is important to recognize the difference between the child who is unable to hear a word and the child who is unable to discriminate between sounds. In the first case, the child has a hearing loss which is a physical problem; and, in the latter, he has an auditory discrimination problem which has educational implications. Auditory discrimination will be discussed under educational diagnosis in Chapter 4.

Ideally, auditory screening should include a test of pitch (frequency) ranging from low to high and one to measure varying loudness (decibels). This screening can be adequately conducted using an *audiometer*,* an instrument adaptable for either group or individual auditory testing. Although opinions vary concerning a satisfactory audiometer score, it is safe to conclude[21] that a screening score which reports a loss of 25 decibels at 500, 1,000, 2,000 and 6,000 frequencies and 30 decibels at 4,000 indicates possible interference with reading instruction and that such a child should be referred.

The classroom teacher: Again, it is unlikely that the classroom teacher has the time, experience, or equipment to conduct the type of screening mentioned above. Classroom teachers have been advised that a watchtick test or a whisper test is possible in the classroom. However, we feel that classroom teachers do not use these tests because they have not had enough supervised experience with them, and the possibilities of overreferral are too great. Therefore, the classroom teacher should be encouraged to rely upon a pattern of symptoms which, when occurring in a child who has failed in reading, is justified cause for referral. These symptoms are:

Physical Symptoms:

1. Speech difficulties (particularly with consonant sounds)
2. Tilting of the head when being spoken to
3. Cupping of the ear with the hand in order to follow instructions
3. Strained posture

---

[21]Darrell E. Rose, *et al*, *Audiological Assessment* (Englewood Cliffs, New Jersey: Prentice-Hall, 1971), p. 150.

   5. Persistent earaches
   6. Inflammation or drainage of the ear
   7. Reports of persistent buzzing or ringing in the head

Behavioral Symptoms:

   1. Inability to profit from phonic instruction
   2. Inability to follow directions
   3. General inattentiveness
   4. Excessive volume needed for comfortable radio and phonograph listening.

Normally the pupil is referred to the school nurse for audiometric screening. In an effort to encourage as much success as possible in the classroom for a child with a suspected hearing loss, the classroom teacher should not hesitate to move the child's seat so that it is: in the center of a discussion area; close to the teacher; and away from outside distractions, such as radiators, fans, cars, and traffic noises. A teacher must also be willing to repeat assignments for this child to insure that they have been properly understood. Referral outside the school normally would be made to a general practitioner or to an otologist, a medical doctor who specializes in hearing problems. Again, the medical referral is to be made in terms of the observed symptoms of auditory difficulty, with a request for results of the audiometric examination.

The reading specialist: Required information may be obtained from a recent report of a medical examination or from a screening conducted through the use of an audiometer. Although the reading specialist may not plan to conduct an audiometric examination with every child, such an examination is called for when the child shows signs of problems in speech and/or phonics instruction. The reading specialist must also attempt to establish the period of time during which the hearing loss first noticeably interfered with school work and then relate this information to the entire case study. For example, the child affected by a hearing loss after the primary years, in which oral instruction and basic phonic sounds are presented, *had* the opportunity to learn his basic skills while he had normal hearing. Although this child may be handicapped, remedial techniques will vary in terms of the type of instruction the child received prior to the hearing loss.

Neurological Disorders

Neurological disorders include direct damage to the brain and defective neurological systems resulting in either malfunction or disorganization. There is little evidence that neurological disorders are a major cause of reading problems. Bond and Tinker state, "Evidence indicates that brain damage is a relatively rare cause of reading disability."[22] Nevertheless, there continues to be a large number of investigations annually based upon the observation that many problem readers show symptoms of abnormal neurological patterns. Robinson[23] named neurological disorders as one of the causal factors in eighteen percent of the cases in her classic study. It is our experience that approximately eight percent of the children tested in the university clinic have enough symptoms of neurological disorders to be referred for neurological examination. It should be noted that our population in the clinic is drawn from children having serious difficulties in school and is by no means a normal population. Initially, the problem for the educator in this complex area is to identify the child who may be neurologically handicapped; however, precise identification ultimately is the job of medical specialists who themselves have some concerns about the accuracy of diagnosis in this area. Let us say simply that most problem readers are adequate enough neurologically to preclude this area as a cause of reading disability; at the same time, let us admit that there remains a small percentage of problem readers who, in fact, do have these symptoms and need medical referral.

The classroom teacher and the reading specialist are likely to find themselves relying heavily upon a pattern of symptoms for initial identification. Because individual symptoms used for neurological referral are, when viewed in isolation, not peculiar to the neurologically disturbed child, it becomes necessary to seek a highly reliable pattern. Without this pattern, the educator is subject to the error of interpreting educational indifference to neurological causes. If the identification is made in the initial diagnosis, it is necessary to have a pattern of several symptoms (three to four) to properly refer a child for neurological examination. However, if a child fails to respond after the best diagnosis and remedial instruc-

---

[22]Bond and Tinker, *Reading Difficulties*, p. 118.
[23]Helen M. Robinson, *Why Pupils Fail in Reading* (Chicago: University of Chicago Press, 1946), p. 218.

tion, one or more of these symptoms or any history of the following causes of neurological disorders should be considered when deliberating a neurological referral. These causes include:

1. Difficulties at birth — birth complicated by prematurity, use of instruments, or by anoxia or hypoxia.
2. Head injuries — blows or accidents in which the head is severely bruised.
3. Diseases — those resulting in inflammation and/or pressure in the area of the brain (i.e., rheumatic fever, encephalitis, continuously high temperature, and the like).

Symptoms for neurological problems fall into two categories — physical and educational. Physical symptoms include:

1. Physical incoordination — grossly awkward walking, running, writing, etc., in relation to overall physical development.
2. Overactivity — inability to concentrate which causes the child to complete his assignments rarely, to annoy others, and to appear disinterested.
3. Headaches — history of persistent headaches.
4. Speech impediments — persistent blockage of speech or articulation difficulties which are peculiar for his age level.
5. Visual incoordination — saccadic eye movements, inability of the eyes to focus or to visually hold a line of print.

Educational symptoms of neurological problems include:

1. Average or better than average intelligence — general educational development deficient in terms of valid measures of intelligence.
2. Phonic blending deficiency — knowledge of sounds but inability to blend them into words.
3. Poor contextual reader — knowledge of the sight vocabulary but inability to use known words in sentences.
4. Slow reading speed — poor reading rate, even with easy, familiar material.
5. Poor auditory discrimination — inability to discriminate between sounds of letters, without evidence of a hearing acuity deficiency.

6. Distractability — inattentive to designated tasks.
7. Abnormal behavior—over-reaction to stimuli (i.e., he laughs long after others have ceased).
8. Poor ability to remember sequences — although apparently normally intelligent, difficulty in remembering sequences, verbal and nonverbal. [The *Knox Cube Test* is good for this evaluation. Scores here must fall well below the chronological age (4-8 years) to be significant. Smith and Carrigan[24] cite the Knox Cube as one of the first tests to give in cases for screening of neurological disorders. References for further study of children with these symptoms are often found under the terms dyslexia and specific language disability.]

Obviously, these symptoms in isolation do not necessarily indicate neurological disorder. It is imperative to gather a pattern of symptoms which includes four or more of the above. Children with this number of symptoms, whether identified in classroom or in clinical diagnosis, should be considered legitimate referrals for neurological examinations. It does not follow that a strong pattern of symptoms leads the educator to a neurological diagnosis, just to a referral.

Clements[25] summarizes the ten most frequently cited characteristics of minimal brain dysfunction from over 100 publications. They are:

1. Hyperactivity
2. Perceptual-motor impairments
3. Emotional lability
4. General coordination defects
5. Disorders of attentions
6. Impulsivity
7. Disorders of memory and thinking
8. Specific learning disabilities in
   reading, arithmetic, writing, spelling
9. Disorders of speech and hearing

---

[24]Donald E. P. Smith and Patricia M. Carrigan, *The Nature of Reading Disability* (New York: Harcourt, Brace and World, 1959), p. 47.

[25]Sam D. Clements, *Minimal Brain Dysfunction in Children*, (Washington, D. C.: U. S. Department of Health, Education, and Welfare, 1966), p. 13.

10. Equivocal neurological signs and electroencephalographic irregularities

Many educators seem reluctant to make neurological referrals, however, for they are overly concerned about either the psychological effects of such a referral or the great possibility of over-referral. An understanding of the procedure generally followed in a neurological examination may reduce the educator's hesitancy to refer. Neurological referral normally will include an office appointment during which the child will receive a detailed neurological examination and the medical specialist will obtain case history information. If, at that time, the medical specialist finds symptoms of abnormal tendencies, another appointment will be made for a more involved neurological examination, often requiring hospitalization. For those interested, Clements[26] discusses diagnostic evaluation in more detail.

Professionally justified in the use of patterns of symptoms, educators should not be reluctant to refer. If, in fact, they should overrefer, they are relieved to find that the child's problem is *not* neurological in nature and can proceed with an educational diagnosis.

The reading specialist, upon receipt of the neurological report, relates the findings to other information which he has gathered for the case study. Again the relationship of neurological problems to the entire case history must be considered in the recommendations for educational adjustment.

The classroom teacher, while waiting for the neurological report, should relieve the child from unnecessary frustration by relaxing tension and providing reading experiences in the area of the child's strengths. If the report indicates that the child does not have a neurological problem, the teacher will continue with a classroom diagnosis in an effort to find the area where correction should start. However, if the report does reveal a neurological problem, the classroom teacher should refer the child to a reading specialist who will conduct a careful case evaluation of the child, noting all educational aspects and precise recommendations concerning remedial techniques.

Medical personnel should be encouraged to write reports so that educators can understand them. A neurological report stating the findings in technical terms is difficult to interpret and of little

---

[26]Clements, *Minimal Brain Dysfunction*, p. 14-15.

value to most educators. Reports written for educators, however, are of value. For example, a recent report stated in relatively simple terms that the child had a receptive problem in the tactile areas, although auditory and visual receptive areas were normal. Such a report leads to effective educational adjustment, which, in this case would not include the tracing or VAKT technique.

The final analysis of all physical difficulties is the responsibility of medical personnel; however, since physical problems frequently interfere with reading efficiency, the educator often finds himself identifying a physical problem first. Having based his judgment upon reliable patterns of symptoms, the educator is obligated to refer to the medical specialist and, while awaiting his diagnosis, to make practical classroom adjustments. The educator considers medical recommendations carefully in terms of the child's total diagnosis.

EMOTIONAL DIAGNOSIS

Emotional difficulties, when considered as causes of reading problems, create cause-and-effect confusion. Sometimes emotional disturbances cause reading problems; however, many emotional problems are not the cause, but the result of a failure in reading. Unfortunately, there is often no clear line of distinction. When emotional disturbances cause reading problems, performance in all learning areas suffer. Often, it is in the diagnosis of a problem reader that this area of difficulty is first uncovered; however, assessing the severity of that difficulty is properly the task of psychological personnel. Conversely, although emotional reactions may complicate a reading problem, they are often not the cause, but rather an effect of the reading failure itself. It is our experience that most children referred to as problem readers exhibit some symptoms of emotional conflict and that these symptoms often diminish or disappear with effective instruction after the diagnosis. In summarizing the research, Bond and Tinker conclude, "Examination of all the evidence, however, does make it pretty clear that the emotional maladjustment is much more frequently the effect than the cause of reading disability."[27] An effective diagnosis may result in relieving the child of some home and school pressures by exposing the fact that the child's difficulty is not due to a poor attitude or a

---

[27]Bond and Tinker, *Reading Difficulties*, p. 129.

low level of intellectual potential, but rather to a skill deficiency which, when corrected, will permit the child to perform as expected. When these diagnostic conclusions are explained satisfactorily to cooperative parents, a more favorable learning atmosphere can be established.

The classroom teacher and the reading specialist must be aware that most children with reading problems react emotionally to their failure through such behavior patterns as refusing to read, not enjoying school, disliking their teacher, or causing problems at home. Emotional reactions to specific situations, however, may be opposite within a given child at a given moment, and they may be opposite between two disturbed children. For example, when frustrated, an emotionally disturbed child may withdraw and be quiet or slash out in defiance. In comparing emotional diagnosis to intellectual diagnosis, Carroll states: "Personality traits are more complex and less consistent than intelligence and so more difficult to measure objectively."[28] The more thorough an understanding the teacher has of the child's intrafamilial, peer, and school relationships, the more likelihood of an effective diagnosis. The examiner must anticipate certain types of emotional reactions, note them, include them in his diagnosis, and consider them in his recommendations; however, it is with caution that these reactions be labeled as causative, for their presence does not necessarily make the child a candidate for referral.

Realistically recognizing their limitations as detectors of emotional difficulties and at the same time recognizing the emotional entanglement of these types of children, the reading specialist and the classroom teacher follow similar diagnostic procedures. Through the cooperation of all the educators in contact with the child, information may be gleaned concerning the child, his home, his school situation, and his reactions in peer group situations.

INFORMATION CONCERNING THE CHILD

Due to his daily contact with the child, the classroom teacher is in a unique position to obtain valuable information about the child's reactions to many situations. The reading specialist is obligated to rely upon the information supplied by the teacher and parents

---

[28]Herbert A. Carroll, *Mental Hygiene* (New York: Prentice-Hall, Inc., 1947), p. 246.

or to obtain it from a personal interview with the child. Desirable information should include:

1. The child's attitude toward his family, school, teacher, and friends.
2. The child's awareness of his problem and his suggestions for its solution.
3. The child's attitude and reaction to reading.
4. The child's development of worthwhile personal goals.

Gathered informally by the classroom teacher or formally by the reading specialist, all information in questionable areas must be checked for reliability. One can do this easily by comparing sources of available data; if they concur, one can view the sources as both reliable and respectable. A child may have said that he makes B's and C's in school. One will rely more readily on his other statements about school if, when checking the school records, one finds that he does indeed make B's and C's.

Personality testing of a formal nature is available. *The California Test of Personality,** one of the more popular instruments for classroom use, provides standardized evaluations of the child's reactions to questions concerning personal and social adjustment. This test may be administered individually or in classroom-sized groups. Since adequate performance requires the child to possess reading skills close to the grade level of the test, the seriously retarded reader will be unable to read the questions. In evaluating the *California Test of Personality,* one is cautioned against the tendency to place undue emphasis on any low set of scores; however, such scores may be considered indicative of areas of potential personality problems. Scores indicating the necessity for referral are described in the test manual. Final verification will not come from this type of testing, but rather from teacher observation and referral to psychological personnel.

Personality testing through the use of incomplete sentences is an informal way of obtaining valuable information. The child is expected to respond to twenty to thirty incomplete sentences, some examples of which might be: "I like books, but. . . " "My home is . . ." "I like my brother and. . . " Strang[29] provides an example of responses in informal inventories including some advice on the techniques of interpretation. The most reliable use of this type of in-

---

[29]Strang, *Diagnostic Teaching of Reading,* pp. 262-63.

formation is to note patterns of responses and to verify them by direct observation of the child in situations where these responses may be reflected in the child's behavior. Again, the examiner is cautioned against excessive analysis of any slightly deviate responses, leaving for psychological personnel final assessment of the child's emotional stability.

Personality tests of the paper-and-pencil variety are considered inherently weak since the child often anticipates what he considers to be the acceptable response. They tend to record "of-the-moment" responses. A child who has had a bad day may score poorly on such tests; however, twenty-four hours later, he could score many points higher. When this occurs, it is obvious that the scores obtained, besides not validly indicating personality traits, have severely limited use in diagnosing emotional problems in children.

A technique for noting personality characteristics in a more natural situation is to observe the child at play. An investigation of play behavior may be based on the following type of questions: Does he play with others his own age? Does he prefer to play with children of his own sex? Does it appear that he is accepted by his peers? Does he play fairly? Does he play enthusiastically? Answers to such questions provide further analysis of the child's total behavior pattern without the limitations of paper-and-pencil tests. Shafer and Shoben feel that the analysis of free play has definite advantages in emotional diagnosis. "Many diagnostic suggestions may be drawn from watching a child in free play. . . . The communications of very young children tend to be symbolized only in the activities of play. . . ."[30] Forest also feels that such observation of play is desirable. "Emotional release through play activities due to a sense of competency and mastery may be observed in normal groups of children."[31] Note that both of these authorities suggest that play analysis has particular value with younger children.

A STUDY OF THE HOME

Although the home usually is not visited as a result of a reading diagnosis, under certain circumstances, such a visit is profitable. When it appears that situations at home are impeding the child's

---

[30]Laurance F. Shafer and Edward J. Shoben, Jr., *The Psychology of Adjustment*, 2nd ed (Boston: Houghton Mifflin Co., 1956), p. 508.

[31]Isle Forest, *Child Development* (New York: McGraw Hill Book Co., 1954), p. 64.

language and/or emotional development, the educator who hopes to improve these conditions must make a home visit. In cases where a home visit would be of little value, one may gather information concerning home conditions through parental interviews or questionnaires. These are constructed to obtain the following types of information: socioeconomic status of the home; availability of books; intrafamilial relations; parental efforts to assist the child; general family activities; and overall acceptance of the child in the home.

Abnormal home conditions should be brought to the attention of appropriate personnel (school officials, home-school visitors, social workers, and psychologists). Neither the classroom teacher nor the reading specialist is justified in offering unsolicited advice to parents about home conditions unrelated to the child's educational progress. There are times when parents will turn to an educator and ask for consultation in noneducational areas. Although it depends upon the individual situation, it is the author's opinion that an educator is normally acting out his proper professional role in offering advice in such cases. However, caution is urged. Offering advice concerning domestic affairs implies that one has training or information about "best" solutions.

The educator will want to contact the social worker when home problems appear to be a basic source of difficulty for the child. These professional persons are skilled in working with parents and investigating home situations. Many schools have found it worthwhile to have social workers on their professional staff.

A STUDY OF THE SCHOOL

The classroom teacher gathers relevant data for a classroom diagnosis and submits it to the reading specialist for his case analysis. From the school it is necessary to obtain information relating to the child's attendance, his behavior, his ability to work and play with others, and his reactions to various types of success and failure. School records do not always contain this type of information, although teachers are often encouraged to write comments concerning outstanding characteristics of the child. When such notations are available, they should be included in the diagnosis; when not accessible, the information should be gathered through interviews or questionnaire responses from the teacher.

While children are reading, teachers should note peculiar reactions which reflect anxiety, frustration, and emotional disturbance.

Roebuck[32] found that emotionally disturbed children tend to read orally with tense voices, to react more definitely to the material being read, and to read compulsively. In compulsive reading, the child never stops or hesitates; rather, he reads on whether he knows the words or not, skipping and/or mispronouncing unknown words. Other noticeable symptoms are refusal to read aloud, profuse sweating of the hands during oral reading, and peculiar book selections for free reading.

If the educator is to be effective in obtaining such information, students and parents must be assured that it will be handled confidentially and will not find its way into the hands of irresponsible people. A cooperative attitude on the part of both parents and educators is necessary for reliable data collection.

One justifiable reason for an educator to consider emotional difficulties, other than for possible referral, is to discourage improper labeling of children. It is easy to decide that a problem reader is lazy, troublesome, or delinquent before considering his emotional difficulties. These symptoms are displayed quite often by children with emotional problems; the unwarranted label complicates the difficulty of accurate diagnosis and remediation.

After psychological referral has been made, the classroom teacher adjusts his instruction to avoid further complicating potential emotional difficulties while awaiting referral recommendations. Adjustments include avoiding placement of the child in failing situations which cause unnecessary embarrassment, avoiding implications that the child is lazy or stupid, and providing a sensible program of discipline by which the child can gain a degree of composure and self-reliance. Carroll points out some of the difficulties involved with discipline for children with these symptoms:

> The causes of misconduct insofar as classroom conditions are concerned are not hard to identify. Every child needs to succeed. If the academic tasks set for him are too difficult, he feels frustrated. Frustration is uncomfortable, and he feels driven to do something about it. . . . Denied the opportunity to satisfy his need for scholastic achievement, he strikes out against environment.[33]

---

[32]Mildred Roebuck, "The Oral Reading Characteristics of Emotionally Disturbed Children," *International Reading Association Proceedings*, VII (1962), pp. 133-38.

[33]Carroll, *Mental Hygiene*, p. 210.

He also says that this child must have his success recognized by the group and by the teacher, whether the success is large or small. Furthermore, he states, "She (the teacher) will be more lavish with praise than criticism. She will help every child to maintain his self-respect."[34] In discussing the control of the group when this child is disruptive, Carroll points out that the teacher will have to take disciplinary measures but adds, "She should never use fear as a technique of control."[35]

The classroom teacher must consider this child to be one who needs and deserves special considerations; negative reactions from him can only drive the child to further reject the learning processes and the environment. At the same time, the teacher has an obligation to the other children in the room and is obliged to provide an environment conducive to learning.

When the child with symptoms of emotional problems disrupts this environment to the detriment of the entire group, the teacher must meet the needs of the group.

Prevention of complex emotional disorders is also in the hands of the classroom teacher. His reaction, for example, to the initial signs of frustration and failure within a given child may cause the child's acceptance of his temporary situation or a reaction against it. Although children must be challenged in school, not all children will meet these challenges with the same degree of success. The teacher may relax tensions and feelings of failure by his attitude toward the efforts of the less successful. Conversely, all children must succeed in school. The successes of all children, but particularly the less successful, should be highlighted. Beware, however, of false praise — children resent it. Instead of false praise, one should structure situations in which — with a little effort — a child can legitimately succeed and be praised. More of these types of techniques are discussed under remediation and in Chapter 10.

All information and notations concerning the child's emotional behavior should be included and evaluated in the case analysis. The reading specialist should apply the recommendations for the necessary educational adjustment. If the classroom teacher, after the institution of these recommendations, finds further complications, he should refer the student to the reading specialist.

---

[34]Carroll, *Mental Hygiene*, p. 210.
[35]Carroll, *Mental Hygiene*, p. 211.

A note of caution concerning emotional referral may be helpful. We find that teachers are prone to interpret obscure symptoms as signs of emotional problems within a child. A child is suspect, for example, if his parents are divorced, if he is an only child, if he does not talk much, or if a parent is under psychiatric care. While such observations should be noted, they do not constitute a legitimate referral; the child's behavior must call for it. Nor should emotional diagnosis be made on the basis of test performance alone. Abnormal scores *do not* call for psychological evaluation unless observed performance confirms the test score. Referring on too little evidence clogs the referral system with children who are not in need. Many times this causes parents needless anguish and expense.

SUMMARY

Educators are involved in noneducational diagnosis. They are likely to be the first to identify a child's potentially noneducational problem. Knowing that he cannot finally judge the severity of noneducational problems, the educator collects his data carefully, refers the child to an appropriate specialist, follows the advice of the specialist, and makes classroom adjustments. The reading specialist will be expected to give more careful consideration than would the classroom teacher to these noneducational areas in his diagnosis. Both educators, however, have important roles, and it is imperative that the roles be understood by each. By refraining from involved noneducational diagnosis, the educator frees himself for the task of educational diagnosis and adjusted instruction.

SUGGESTED READINGS

Cleland, Donald L. "Clinical Materials for Appraising Disabilities In Reading." *The Reading Teacher*, XVII, March 1964, p. 428. This interesting, easy-to-read article presents summaries of the various appraisal materials available for clinical diagnosis. Of particular interest is the discussion of reading capacity and appropriate techniques for determining it.

Clements, Sam D. *Minimal Brain Dysfunction in Children*. Washington, D. C.: U. S. Department of Health, Education, and Welfare, 1966. In fifteen pages, Clements summarizes terminology to clarify several issues and to offer a blue print for action on minimal brain dysfunction. The information contained in this monograph will be useful to those who have not read widely in this area.

Harris, Albert J. *How To Increase Reading Ability*. New York: David McKay, 1970, pp. 216-21. Harris discusses several techniques for the use of mental age in determining reading expectancy scores. For a review of alternate methods, the reader is encouraged to refer to these pages.

Kelley, Charles R. *Visual Screening and Child Development*. The North Carolina Study. Raleigh, North Carolina: North Carolina State College, 1957. This book reports a little-known, but carefully organized study concerning the scope and sequence of vision and scholastic effectiveness. The reader who is interested in a more detailed study will find it worthwhile.

Money, John. *The Disabled Reader*. Baltimore, Maryland: The Johns Hopkins Press, 1966. A book of readings collected by Money under the topic of dyslexia. Attention provided to medical and psychological opinion as well as to educational opinion. Essential reading for those working with the seriously handicapped.

Reeds, James C.; Rabe, Edward F.; and Maniken, Margaret. "Teaching Reading to Brain-Injured Children." *Reading Research Quarterly* (Summer 1970), p. 379. An excellent review for those interested in brain-injured children. Claiming a lack of evidence for specific program adjustments for brain-damaged children, the authors review several of the most highly respected sources.

Robinson, Helen M. *Why Pupils Fail in Reading*. Chicago: University of Chicago Press, 1946. Robinson presents a discussion of the multiple causation theory in terms of the most prominent authorities and also in terms of her research in this area. Of particular importance are the conclusions which she reaches through her technique to determine causation.

Strauss, Alfred A., and Lehtinen, Laura E. *Psychopathology and Education of the Brain-Injured Child*. New York: Grune & Stratton, 1947. This book provides the rationale for the syndromes of distractability and perseveration. It is a basic book for those who are interested in more thoroughly understanding the aspects of minimal brain injury. Explanations are given in terms designed for educators.

Stuart, Marion. *Neurophysiological Insights Into Teaching*. New York: Pacific Books, 1963. This book provides relatively elementary explanations of diagnosis and treatment of readers with neurological limitations.

Woolf, Maurice D. and Woolf, Jeanne A. *Remedial Reading*. New York: McGraw Hill Book Co., Inc., 1957. This selection is a detailed discussion of the emotional involvement of problem readers. Theory backed by case study illustrations makes meaningful reading in this difficult area.

4

Classroom Diagnosis

An analysis of the child's reading skills and attitudes is the major function of educational diagnosis. Unlike noneducational diagnosis in which final evaluation is the concern of a specialist outside the field of reading, educational diagnosis rests solely with the classroom teacher and the reading specialist. It is here that their professional competencies best suit them to complete the task which has been delegated to them by the public (i.e., the education of children).

A classroom teacher, who has a relatively long acquaintance with a child, relies heavily upon observation and informal testing procedures for educational diagnosis. A reading specialist, who is permitted only short-term pupil acquaintance, finds a more formal testing and evaluation program effective. Before careful examination of the two approaches to educational diagnosis, one should consider briefly the causes of problems in this area. Educational difficulties can be said to cause a reading problem when the problem can be corrected or prevented from recurring by the adjustment of the learning climate. That educational causes of learning difficulties can be complicated by one or more noneducational causes was discussed earlier. However, one should remember that educational adjustment alone might not correct a problem which has been ignored for a long period of time and to which there is a severe emotional reaction.

EDUCATIONAL CAUSES

Educational causes can be grouped into the following six categories: lockstepping, instructional techniques, reading methods, absence, classroom size, and materials for instruction.

Lockstepping: Perhaps the most serious educational problem is the system of lockstepping children through school. We are referring to such practices as having all children in a group read the same book at the same time, all children in a group learn the same skills at the same time, children who do not learn in the specified time labeled as failures, children who have not finished book one by the end of first grade or book two by the end of second grade labeled failures, and second grade teachers starting the year with book two and so on within each following grade regardless of where each child ended the preceding year.

Fortunately, lockstepping as we have defined it is decreasing. Many school systems and thousands of teachers now recognize that children need to be involved in decisions involving the pacing of the amount of time needed for learning to take place. Emphasis on mastery of material is replacing 'covering' the reader in a year. However, the problem continues to exist, and children are falling farther and farther behind within a group which is moving on.

Instructional techniques: In the primary grades, a child normally has one teacher each year. If that teacher is incompetent, indifferent, poorly educated, or insensitive towards children, one year of exposure to him can seriously harm some children. While most children survive a year of poor teaching without permanently harmful results, others fall far enough behind in their reading skills to be considered problem readers. The solution to the reading problems caused by this type of teacher is twofold: first, the handicapped children must receive the appropriate instruction at a later date; second, incompetent teachers must be helped to improve their instructional techniques. The former solution relates to a child's next teacher; the latter becomes the problem of the reading specialist in cooperation with the school administration. Many consider poor instruction the major cause of reading problems in children. With this assessment, we must agree but hasten to add that commonly other interferences complicate the problem.

Reading methods: In addition to instructional techniques as a cause of reading problems is the closely related area of method. While instruction focuses on what the teacher does regardless of the method, method focuses upon the basic approaches and materials used to teach reading. School systems which impose innovative teaching methods on teachers not skilled in their use and not committed to their philosophy can become responsible for their students' learning problems. A given innovation may or may not be right for a given group of children or a given group of teachers. Some innovations so control what a teacher does that he actually relinquishes responsibility for the instruction which takes place.

Again, we find this situation improving as teachers become more professional. They are insisting on being a part of decision making which affects their instruction. They best know the children. By their involvement in innovation, commitment replaces imposition and instruction is improved.

Absence: When a child experiences long periods of continuous absence, the sequential development of his skills may suffer. Yet he may be pushed along to more advanced skills without the background upon which to develop them successfully. It is often difficult for a teacher to provide the instruction ncessary to counterbalance excessive absence. Therefore, reading disability can occur if the child is not taught the skills he has missed. Unless his program is modified, the child may fail in future assignments. Teachers are finding many useful techniques for overcoming the problem of excessive absence which include: using peer instruction, teacher aides, volunteer parents, telephone instruction, and programmed instruction. As teachers consider the many means available to assist children whose absences are excessive, the problem will lessen.

Classroom size: In overcrowded classrooms a teacher may have difficulty following the sequential development of each child's reading skills. Here a child may falter undetected until he falls too far behind to catch up without special instruction. Although particularly damaging in the primary grades where the development of reading skills follows a closer sequence than in the later elementary years, the failure to provide basic skill development may cause difficulty during any period in the remainder of the child's schooling. Therefore, as a child starts slipping behind, procedures must be available to assist him before he is lost.

To alleviate overcrowded classrooms, some schools have hired teacher assistants. By assuming many of the less important routine tasks, the assistant frees the teacher to provide the needed instruction. As in the case of excessive absence, the use of peer instruction, volunteer parents, and special programs can assist children in overcrowded classrooms. Individualization of instruction through diagnostic teaching and the use of learning centers permits the teacher to work with small groups or individual students even in large classrooms. We have found pairing of children useful (i.e., a strong student works cooperatively with a weaker one on a given assignment). Such pairing can be changed frequently and eliminated whenever desirable, but through its use learning becomes more effective and problems can be identified more quickly. Teachers in overcrowded classrooms will find it necessary to alternate between group instruction and individualized instruction, between large and small group work. Flexible grouping to avoid the pitfalls of lockstepping is essential.

Materials for instruction: Economy-minded school administrators frequently fail to provide adequate materials to enable the classroom teacher to adjust instruction. Therefore, unless a teacher can devise materials and techniques to instruct children with minor skill deficiencies, the possibility of these children becoming problem readers increases. With adequate materials and knowledge of their use, most teachers can prevent serious skill deficiencies. Considering the wealth of materials available to educators today, one must seek the most helpful aids for his particular situation.

Many larger school districts have established curriculum libraries in which a wide variety of materials is available for individual teachers and teacher committees to examine and consider. In this manner, it is possible to maintain reasonable economy and at the same time, to permit careful analysis and wise selection of materials. Other schools have designated small groups of teachers as "materials selection committees" for the various areas. They are the persons to contact concerning the value of particular materials. Teachers also are sharing the instructional techniques they use with new materials. For example, if a given material has been selected for use, three teachers might try it. Each of the three would observe the other, refine their procedures, and then present their collective ideas to the staff. No one knows how much money is spent annually on new materials which never find their way into effective use in the classroom, but one might guess that the amount is quite large.

TYPES OF CLASSROOM DIAGNOSIS

Classroom diagnosis can take place either before or after instruction as discussed in Chapter 2 ($\acute{o}\longrightarrow s\longrightarrow\acute{R}$). While both are appropriate times for classroom diagnosis, each uses different techniques and each has advantages and limitations.

Diagnosis before Instruction

Many teachers attempt to determine the strengths and weaknesses of their students by testing them prior to instruction. These teachers use the test scores to plan future instruction and to group the children. Whether or not testing is useful depends upon the type of instrument used. Three basic types of testing instruments are available for classroom diagnosis: standardized tests, prepared informal inventories, and teacher-made informal inventories.

Standardized tests: Most schools test regularly with one of the major standardized tests (Iowa Test of Basic Skills, California Reading Test, Stanford Reading Test, Metropolitan Reading Test, or the Gates MacGinitie Reading Test). Each of these tests is in common use, and many teachers *have the scores available* to them. The tests usually yield total reading, vocabulary, and comprehension scores. Children take these tests in class-size groups and their performance is to be completed within reasonable time limits; most of these tests can be administered within a half-hour to an hour. Some of the tests have subscores relating to various types of reading vocabulary and comprehension skills.

Standardized test scores are nearly useless for classroom diagnosis.[1] The tests' limitations have been discussed by many authorities in reading. First, that they are administered to groups necessitates multiple choice answers and encourages guessing. Second, the tests' standardizing procedures are subject to error, a fact which causes considerable concern about their reliability. Third, their ability to match the child with a given reading level is constantly under question. Finally, the use of subtests has been discouraged due to the extreme lack of reliability of these measures.

However, since schools administer tests to determine how well the children are doing generally, two diagnostic uses of standardized test scores are recommended.

1. While the earned scores do not reflect accurate reading grade levels, extremely low scores usually indicate reading diffi-

---

[1]Roger Farr, *Reading: What Can Be Measured?* (Newark, Delaware: IRA, 1969), pp. 97; 212-18.

culty. Therefore, prior to instruction, a teacher can gain an idea of which children might experience difficulties; he might identify those children most in need of informal diagnosis.

TABLE 4

Example:	Child	Word Meaning	Paragraph Meaning
	1	1.3	2.1
	2	2.4	2.4
	3	3.4	3.5
	4	2.7	3.7
	5	3.5	3.8
	6	3.6	3.7
	7	3.7	3.9
	8	4.1	4.0
	9	4.2	3.9
	10	4.1	4.1

If the above scores were obtained at the beginning of fourth grade, children numbers one and two logically would be selected as those most in need of informal diagnosis due to their extremely low performance.

2. While sub-test scores do not meet reliability standards, extreme differences in subtest scores can serve as indicators of "possible" skill difficulties. For example, in the above table, children numbers one and four exhibit extreme differences between word meaning and paragraph meaning scores. The teacher should not accept these scores at face value. Instead, they should suggest that something *might* be wrong. The teacher should look into the matter, usually through the use of informal techniques.

These two uses of standardized test scores are suggested only if scores are available. Tests should not be administered solely for the purpose of obtaining such scores, however, since they are more reliably obtained from other sources.

Prepared informal inventories: Several publishing companies have prepared informal testing instruments which are useful for classroom diagnosis. One of the most commonly used instruments is the Botel Reading Inventory. Three sections of this inventory are useful for reading diagnosis: word recognition — the child reads graded lists of twenty words aloud to the teacher; word opposites (reading) — the child identifies antonyms from graded lists of ten words; and phonics—the child identifies graphemes as the teacher reads words to him. Both the word opposites and the phonics sections are group tests. The two group measures can be administered in about thirty minutes. Other informal inventories usually include an oral reading section of selected paragraphs at various grade levels. (One such test in common use is the *Diagnostic Reading Scales.**) An advantage of such instruments is that they use graded lists of words and graded paragraphs which are either taken from or are similar to the materials students will be expected to read in school. Using prepared informal inventories can result in a teacher obtaining results which assist him to identify children's strengths and weaknesses and which also yield fairly reliable estimates of reading levels.

For example:

TABLE 5

Child	Word Recognition	Word Opposites	Phonics* Consonants	Phonics* Blends	Vowels
1	2-1	2-2	ok	ok	ok
2	2-1	2-2	no	no	no
3	2-1	2-2	ok	no	no
4	2-2	2-2	ok	no	ok
5	3-1	2-2	ok	ok	no
6	3-1	3-1	ok	ok	ok
7	3-1	3-1	ok	ok	ok
8	3-2	4-1	ok	no	ok
9	3-2	4-1	no	no	no
10	4-1	4-1	ok	ok	ok

*Note — the Botel phonics section has many more categories.

Results, such as those above, can be extremely useful in matching children to books and in making decisions about skills which children have or need. The word recognition column indicates how well children can decode certain levels of words. The word opposites column reveals how well the students can get at word meanings. The phonics columns show how well they have mastered the various phonics relationships. Now, although in columns one and two, children numbers one and two appear to be operating on the same levels, their phonic skills development is entirely different. And, while child number nine appears to be reading better than most of the others, his phonic skills development is deficient.

When attempting to teach to strengths, data such as that above becomes very important. What are the children's strengths?

If a teacher had a choice between the type of data in the above table and that in the preceding one, his choice should be the data from the informal testing. It is much more useful, valid, and reliable.

A procedure for working with the Botel tests has been developed as follows. Early in the school year, as soon as the children are relaxed and comfortable (second week), the teacher administers the Botel Word Opposites (reading) to the group. After about ten minutes, the teacher has a fairly reliable indication of reading level.[2] Using another ten to twenty minutes, the phonics test can be administered. The word recognition test can be reserved for such children as numbers one, two, and nine on Table 5, scoring lowest on these two tests. As the word recognition test is given, words which are mispronounced or substituted are written down. Error analysis reveals the types of errors being made. For those who appear to have the most severe problems (number two, for example), the teacher can select passages from the reading material he expects the child to read. At the teacher's desk, the child reads several of these passages silently, then aloud. The teacher can ask several questions to determine the level of understanding and can add this data to that which already has been collected. Even if, for a classroom of thirty children, the suggested approach took an hour a day for one week, the time would be well spent. The teacher would then have information upon which to make instructional decisions. What do the other children do while the teacher is working with those who need special diagnosis? They read books of their choosing. This helps children "warm up" to reading after a summer of basically nonreading activities.

---

[2]Morton Botel; John Bradley; and Michael Kashuba, "The Validity of Informal Testing," *Reading Difficulties: Diagnosis, Correction, and Remediation* (Newark, Delaware: IRA, 1970), pp. 85-103.

Teacher-made informal inventories: Obviously, teachers can develop informal tests having the same features as those prepared commercially. Using the material from which they intend to teach the children, the teacher can assess a child's ability to recognize words, to read orally, and to read silently for comprehension. Many school systems develop an informal inventory for use by their teachers. The construction of this instrument can be time-consuming and requires considerable knowledge of both the reading process and test construction. Interpretation can be even more difficult. Powell[3] raises serious questions concerning traditional norms used on informal inventories. Others[4] also have found the subject of norms for informal inventories rather perplexing. The test results can be used in much the same manner as that suggested for commercially prepared informal inventories. A major advantage of teacher-made inventories centers around the convenience of having to make the test cover a wider range of reading materials than do many commercially prepared tests. The larger sampling tends to produce more reliable results. Two serious problems occur with their construction: can the teacher select materials and ask questions which are accurate measures of the child's development; and is the material accurately graded?

In answer to the first question, the answer is yes; with some training, teachers can select materials and ask questions which are accurate measures of the child's development. Also, they are more capable of interpreting the results when they have developed the instrument. However, without training and without a thorough knowledge of the skills of reading, many sloppy, inaccurate, relatively useless instruments have been developed.

In answer to the second question, probably not. Publishers tend to pay little attention to the readability level of materials even if they place grade level numbers on the books.[5] Even then the readability level is generally an average of the readability levels of the individual pages. Through readability checks on several basals, teachers become aware that any "fifth grade" basal can range in

---

[3]William R. Powell, "The Validity of the Instructional Reading Level," *Diagnostic Viewpoints in Reading* (Newark, Delaware: IRA, 1971), pp. 121-33.

[4]William K. Durr, ed., *Reading Difficulties* (Newark, Delaware: IRA, 1970), pp. 67-132.

[5]Robert E. Mills and Jean R. Richardson, "What Do Publishers Mean By Grade Level?" *Reading Teacher* (March 1963), pp. 359-62.

readability from third to seventh grade level. If the teacher uses these materials for an informal inventory and happens to select pages that are at the extremes of the ranges (third and seventh grade levels in the above example), his assessment of a child's reading ability will be inaccurate.

In a student study at Maryland, the *Autobiography of Malcolm X* was rated as having a readability level of fifth grade, eighth grade, and tenth grade. In this study, the students used three different readability formulas.[6] The question raised is — what factors are considered when one discusses "readability level?"

The problem of matching a child's performance prior to instruction with any given material is chancey. In fact, mismatching probably occurs all too frequently. That a child's reading ability tends to change with the material's content contributes to the mismatching. Books tend to be inaccurately marked — particularly in the content areas.

Another general problem occurs during diagnosis prior to the instruction; reading levels in one area of content or interest do not necessarily carry over into other content and interest areas. If the student reads at the college level, he will not necessarily read a physics book with the same ease with which he approaches a novel, even if both are rated at the same level of difficulty. Labeling children's reading levels as independent, instructional, or frustrated through the use of tests comprised of one type of material embodies considerable risk. This becomes even more true when one realizes that no definition of reading level has been agreed upon by authorities.

One approach, closure testing, may help circumvent the problem of mismatching and labeling. Closure tests constructed from the types of materials a child is expected to use can provide relatively useful information concerning the child's ability to work with various types of printed materials. The procedures for closure testing are as follows:

1. Select several passages of at least 100 words from the various books to be used.
2. Retype the selection, deleting every fifth word.
   Mary had a little_____. Its fleece was white_____

---

[6]Mae C. Johnson, *Comparison of Readability Formulas* (Unpublished doctoral student research project, University of Maryland Reading Center, 1971).

snow. Everywhere that Mary _____ the lamb was sure to _____.

3. Have the child read the selection, supplying the printed word. Older children can write the words in, younger children can read the passage to you.
4. Determine a score by counting as correct responses the number of words actually used by the author.

A score of 40 percent or better[7] indicates that the book should be one that the child can handle. A score below that level indicates that the book is probably too difficult for the child; either he will need more help reading it or he should be permitted to use easier material. The use of closure eliminates the necessity of matching a grade-level score with a book, for the test derives from the various types of material which the child will be expected to read. Closure tests are easily constructed, scored, and interpreted. While they are not without flaw, they may be the most useful type of testing instrument for use prior to instruction that is available to the classroom teacher. A word of caution. Considerable research is being conducted with closure testing materials. Adjusted norms will be reported indicating possible differences from the 40 percent criterion mentioned above. As one works with children of different ages and materials from different content areas, adjusted norms can be expected. The reader should remain alert for reports of such changes for the most useful application of closure in reading diagnosis.

Diagnosis after Instruction

The advantages and disadvantages of diagnosis before instruction make an obvious case for diagnosis after instruction. In classroom diagnosis, observation of the child's ability to respond to instruction is of prime importance. Through the direct observation of the child's responses, the teacher can avoid some of the time-consuming, costly, and sometimes questionable testing commonly linked to diagnosis. Through such observation teachers can become skilled in observing reading performances in other basic skill areas.

Readiness skills involve the ability to approach the page with effective mechanical skills (orientation), to operate effectively with

---

[7]John R. Bormuth, "Comparable Cloze and Multiple Choice Comprehension Test Scores," *Journal of Reading* (December 1969), p. 191.

the language, and to display effective auditory and visual discrimination skills.

Sight vocabulary involves the recognition and meaning of a word instantly and constantly.

Word attack involves an efficient ability to decode words not recognized by sight.

Comprehension involves the ability to bring meaning and understanding to words and groups of words and their interrelationships.

The reader should note that each of these skill areas affects the total reading process; that is, each influences the manner in which a child decodes the printed message and associates his decoded message with past experiences. These terms, then, appropriately include the skills necessary for effective decoding and association (i.e., reading). In each of these skill areas, the classroom teacher must obtain the answers to the following three questions:

1. What is the instructional level of the child in this area? It must be determined at which level this child can respond most effectively to instruction; normally, it is a point at which the child makes errors but does not fail completely. The teacher will have numerous opportunities to observe the child reading different types of materials. He will realize that children do not have one instructional level but several. In social studies materials, a given child might read at levels considerably above those at which he reads in other areas. As a child enters materials which are obviously too hard for him, instructional adjustments are necessary in either increased assistance through word introduction and concept development prior to reading or reduction of the difficulty of the material by selecting different books.
2. Specifically, what types of skills does the child possess? (What are his reading strengths?) Diagnostically, the teacher looks for those skills which the child has apparently mastered. He looks for patterns of performance which will assure him of mastery. For example, if the child always attacks the initial portion of the word accurately, initial consonants may be listed as mastered. The teacher also notes observed patterns of errors. Thus, both strengths and weaknesses are credited.

3. What classroom adjustment can be used to teach to the child's strengths? What adjustments can be made to assist the child in his areas of weaknesses? By starting with instructional situations, the teacher clearly can see the necessity for instructional modifications which will enable the child to operate successfully. While all diagnosis has instructional adjustment as its aim, classroom diagnosis which stems from instruction cannot escape this necessity.

To answer each of the above questions, a teacher directly observes a child in three reading situations: word recognition exercises, oral reading, and silent reading. Reading situations differ from skill areas in that each situation requires the use of one or more of the skills for acceptable performance. Improvement in the skill areas results in improvement in reading situations when the diagnosis has been effective in establishing the instructional needs of the child. The teacher adds these observations to any testing information which he might have and formulates diagnostic hypotheses which he will attempt to interpret into instructional adjustments.

In word recognition: During word recognition activities, the teacher should note specific symptoms which lead to diagnosis of both strengths and weaknesses. Word recognition exercises are those activities in which children work with words in isolation (out of context) (e.g., sight word drills, word bank activities, teacher-made games, and so on). Patterns of performances need to be observed to permit the formation of diagnostic hypotheses; one symptom observed now and then is not considered sufficient.

Each of the symptoms is followed by a statement of diagnosis via looking at both strengths and weaknesses. Strengths generally indicate areas in which a child is making a positive effort; therefore attitudes as well as skills are reflected. The teacher using these suggestions must see them as possible listings of strengths and weaknesses. Error analysis and other factors must be taken into full consideration. Inflexible interpretation of these suggestions and the chart is not not intended.

1. The student pronounces words instantly and accurately.

       strengths: sight vocabulary (memory of word form)
                      visual discrimination
      weaknesses: none

2. The student refuses to pronounce words even after a delay of up to five seconds.

    strengths: none
    weaknesses: sight vocabulary;
                  no apparent use of word attack skills

3. The student hesitates to pronounce a word but finally pronounces it after a delay of between two to five seconds.

    strengths: possible use of word attack skills or delayed recall of word form at sight
    weaknesses: sight vocabulary

4. The student partially pronounces the word but fails to pronounce entire word accurately (e.g., *ta . . .* for *table*)

    strengths: use of word attack skills for portion of word pronounced, in this case, initial consonant and vowel sound
    weaknesses: sight vocabulary;
                  possible orientation difficulty;
                  difficulty in word attack with unpronounced portion of word, in this case, word ending

5. The student makes an attempt to pronounce the entire word, but mispronounces it (e.g., *tinble* for *table*)

    strengths: word attack skills for portion of word accurately pronounced; in this case, initial consonant and ending
    weaknesses: sight vocabulary;
                  difficulty in word attack skills on portion mispronounced; in this case, vowel and medial consonant;
                  possible visual discrimination difficulty

6. The student substitutes one word for another while maintaining the basic word meaning (e.g., *kitten* for *cat*)

    strengths: clue to word meaning through association
    weaknesses: disregard of word form;
                  possibly internalized the word form but did not remember it

7. The student substitutes one word for another and distorts word meaning (e.g., *stop* or *stomp* for *step*)

    strengths: word attack skills for portion of word pronounced accurately;
                    observation of general word form

    weaknesses: sight vocabulary;
                    word attack skills of minimal configuration differences;
                    visual discrimination

8. The student confuses letter order — reversals (e.g., *was* for *saw*, *expect* for *except*)

    strengths: observation of word elements (letters);
                    general use of configuration

    weaknesses: directional confusion (orientation);
                    sight vocabulary

9. The student knows word meaning (e.g., he can use the word in a sentence, can define it, or can supply a synonym, and so on).

    strengths: decoding, personal concept for the word
    weaknesses: none

10. The student can pronounce a word accurately, but does not know its meaning.

    strengths: decoding skills
    weaknesses: concept development;
                    may have worked so hard to pronounce the word that he simply failed to think of its meaning

From symptoms observed in word recognition, diagnostic evaluations start to take form. Observations noted should be verified by observation in oral and silent reading activities. Oral reading adds the dimension of context aids to the process of word recognition. Of those symptoms noted during word recognition activities, the following might be signs of the use of context aids in oral reading:

Pronunciation of word
Hesitations
Substitutions which maintain meaning
Knowledge of word meaning

The following might be signs of weakness in the use of context:

Refusal to pronounce word
Partial mispronunciation
Complete mispronunciation
Substitutions which change meaning
Lack of word meaning, but can pronounce word

Other behaviors which are unique to oral reading can be observed. The first three to be mentioned are considered minor errors, and, in many instances, they are signs of thoughtful oral reading.

1. The student repeats words or phrases during oral reading.

> strengths: effort to correct expression;
>   effort to correct error;
>   delaying tactic to attack up-coming word
> weaknesses: directional confusion;
>   sight vocabulary

2. The student omits words.

> strengths: contextual reader if words omitted are of minimal contextual value (e.g., *I see two boys* for *I see the two boys*)
> weaknesses: eye-voice span;
>   directional confusion; word memory

3. The student inserts words.

> strengths: contextual reader if insertion embellishes the author's meaning (e.g., *I see two happy boys* for *I see two boys*)
> weaknesses: eye-voice span;
>   overreliance on contextual clues

The remaining observations from oral reading take on more important diagnostic implications.

4. The student reads word-by-word (all words pronounced accurately, but slowly with pauses between them and with much expression).

strengths: decoding skills
weaknesses: context clue usage;
              sight vocabulary;
              comprehension skills

5. The student loses his place during oral reading.

    strengths: none
    weaknesses: directional confusion;
                  possible visual problem;
                  possible overconcentration on decoding

6. The student observes all punctuation via pauses and inflection.

    strengths: comprehension skills;
                  knows cues implied by punctuation
    weaknesses: none

7. The student fails to observe punctuation.

    strengths: none
    weaknesses: decoding may be so difficult that punctuation is ignored;
                  may be unaware of the function of punctuation comprehension skills

8. The student exhibits difficulty when asked questions although he decoded all words concerning the literal understanding of the story. In oral reading, comprehension checks are usually limited to literal understanding. Higher level comprehension skills are diagnosed following silent reading.

    strengths: decoding
    weaknesses: decoding may be so all-consuming that comprehension does not occur;
                  conceptual development;
                  verbal memory

Symptoms observed during oral reading should be based upon materials which the child can handle fairly well. All symptoms observed during attempts to read frustrating material are invalid due to the difficulty of the material. In those cases, the weaknesses are within the materials, not within the child.

During silent reading, the teacher can observe several behaviors which may aid in the total diagnosis.

1. The student moves his lips and makes subvocalized sounds during silent reading.

    strengths: appears to be working on decoding skills
    weaknesses: may be overworking decoding;
                      may be trying to remember what he is reading;
                      may be a habit carried over from excessive oral reading

2. The student points to words with fingers.

    strengths: may be using touch to keep place or to emphasize words
    weaknesses: orientation skills need touch support;
                      may be having decoding difficulties

3. The student shows physical signs of reading discomfort (e.g., rubbing of eyes, extreme restlessness, constant adjustment of book).

    strengths: perseverance with task
    weaknesses: possible difficulty of material;
                      possible physical defect — vision, nutrition, and the like;
                      possible emotional reaction to frustration

The child's responses to questions following silent reading can indicate strengths and weaknesses in the comprehension-thinking skills. Diagnosis in this area is complicated by such factors as the concept density and difficulty of the material, the quantity of print to which the child is expected to react, the amount of time lapsing between reading and questioning, and the difficulty in pinpointing types of comprehension skills. For the purpose of diagnosis, comprehension skills are classified into three levels: literal understanding (obtaining facts and details, general tone, sequences, and the like); interpretation (grasping main idea, paraphrasing, drawing inferences, and so on); and problem solving (critical and creative thinking, reactions to the ideas of the author; and evaluative thinking about the value of the material read, and the like). Ability to follow directions and to apply reading to study areas are additional comprehension skills which are not included in the above mentioned levels.

The following observations should be made during the questioning and reaction periods that follow silent reading. During each observation the stress is on comprehension skills.

4. The student can decode the material but cannot respond literally to the ideas of the author.

   strengths:　　decoding
   weaknesses:　visual memory
   　　　　　　　concept development relative to material read
   　　　　　　　possible over-concentration on decoding

5. The student can respond to literal understanding questions but cannot interpret those ideas into his own words.

   strengths:　　decoding;
   　　　　　　　literal understanding
   weaknesses:　possible overconcentration on decoding;
   　　　　　　　concept load difficulty;
   　　　　　　　possible failure to reflect on the author's ideas

6. The student can respond literally and can interpret the author's ideas, but cannot apply ideas to problem-solving situations.

   strengths:　　decoding;
   　　　　　　　literal understanding;
   　　　　　　　interpretation
   weaknesses:　problem-solving skills;
   　　　　　　　possible misunderstanding of the problem;
   　　　　　　　verbal limitations

7. The student can recall the author's message but cannot follow the author's or teacher's directions.

   strengths:　　literal understanding;
   　　　　　　　interpretation
   weaknesses:　possible conceptual difficulty — even with a few terms in a passage;
   　　　　　　　work with sequences

TABLE 6

Classroom Diagnosis Check List

Symptom Observed	Diagnostic Hypotheses						
	Pre-reading				Sight Vocab.	Word Attack	Comprehension
	Lang.	Orient.	Aud.*	Vis.			
In Both Word Recognition and Oral Reading							
pronounces word				+	+		+ context
refusal					0	0	0 context
hesitation					0	+	+ context
partial pronunciation		0			0	+/0(e.a.	0 context
complete mispronunciation				0	0	+/0(e.a.	0 context
substitution (meaning)				0			+ context
substitution (no meaning)				+/0(e.a.		+/0(e.a.	0 context
reversals		0		0 e.a.	0		
knows word meaning					+		+ context
no word meaning	0						0
In Oral Reading							
repetitions		0			0	+	+ correction
omissions		0			0	0	+ context
insertions		0					+ context

102

word-by-word meaning		0	+	0 context
loses place	0	0	0	
observes punctuation				+
ignores punctuation				0
fails literal understanding	0	+	+	0
In Silent Reading				
moves lips	0		+	
points to words	0			
physical strain	0	0		
fails to respond				
a. literal	0	0	0	0
b. interpretive (but handles literal)	0	+	+	+ literal 0 interp.
c. problem solving (but handles literal and interpretive)	0	+	+	+ literal and interp. 0 problem solving
fails to follow directions	0	+	+	+ literal 0 sequences
fails to apply to study	0	+	+	+ 0 independent

KEY: e.a. = requires error analysis; + = possible strengths; 0 = possible weaknesses

*To be checked with all weaknesses in word attack.

8. The student can read with understanding while under direction but fails to apply skills in study situations.

strengths: comprehension abilities intact under direction

weaknesses: overdependence on the teacher;
inability to set own goals;
disinterest in the material being studied

As in oral reading, silent reading diagnosis must be conducted with materials suitable to the child. If materials are at his frustration level, the diagnosis will show results which are not the child's weaknesses, but those of the materials selected for his use.

Once observations have been completed, diagnostic hypotheses are established. Further diagnosis can be conducted by designing instructional materials to complement the strengths and weaknesses of the child, through the use of diagnostic hypotheses. For example, if word attack skills seem to be a problem, the teacher can design activities which show how the child operates in auditory or visual discrimination activities. Such verifications of diagnostic hypotheses makes them more reliable; hypotheses also may be confirmed through selected testing.

The use of Table 6 will assist the teacher in linking the appropriate diagnosis of strengths and weaknesses with observed symptoms. The more extensive the observed pattern of symptoms, the more certain the teacher can be of the diagnosis. Use the table for a quick check. Accurate diagnosis requires study of preceding pages.

The use of this table and the diagnostic technique involved is not without limitations. An awareness of these limitations will place the results obtained by this technique in proper perspective. First, most classroom teachers experience some difficulty in their initial efforts to observe accurately errors in word recognition, oral reading, and silent reading. Spache[8] cautions the inexperienced teacher to practice such identification. We have found that with directed practice teachers can record accurately the errors made by children. Exercises with children's readings recorded on tapes and played for students to practice with has been especially effective. Despite the degree of difficulty encountered in his initial attempts to make

---

[8]George D. Spache and Evelyn B. Spache, *Reading in the Elementary Schools* (Boston: Allyn and Bacon, Inc., 1969), pp. 332-333.

such direct observations, the teacher will find that his skills will improve with practice. Second, the technique used in this type of diagnosis lacks the precision and scope found in clinical diagnostic techniques. As has been stated, the classroom teacher normally is not in a position to obtain all the types of information available to a reading specialist. The use of the proposed technique, however, will assist the classroom teacher in detecting many reading deficiencies. With full realization of what the classroom diagnosis is attempting to do, the teacher will find the technique extremely practical and useful. He will note that the symptoms of one type of skill deficiency overlap those of other skills. Obviously, vocabulary development and language development are closely linked. When overlapping symptoms are noted, the teacher should consider educational adjustment in both areas. It is during such adjusted instruction that the diagnosis takes its final form.

Interpretation of Skill Deficiencies

Special consideration will be needed for each identified skill area in order to best interpret skill deficiencies noted through classroom diagnostic techniques.

If *pre-reading–readiness* skills are deficient, answers to the following questions should assist the teacher in pinpointing the difficulty.

1. Is the child's language characterized by differences in dialect that are common to children from low socioeconomic families? Does the child appear to have difficulty following oral instructions? Three problems may be causing these difficulties. One is that the child may be at a disadvantage because his language does not match that of the books and the teacher. Another is that the child may lack sufficient or appropriate language experiences to link words and phrases with ideas. Then, there is also a possibility of limited intellectual development. In any case, instructional adjustments are called for (see Chapter 7).
2. When mispronunciations are common, does the child's speech reflect the same type of mispronunciations? Delayed speech development will indicate further the need for work in auditory discrimination (for instructional adjustments, see Chapter 7).

3. Does the child demonstrate visual discomfort (i.e., squinting, redness around the eyes, and so on)? If so, visual referral may be appropriate.
4. Visual discrimination symptoms may be analyzed further by asking whether the child confuses words of minimal configuration differences (*big* and *dig*), or whether he confuses most words regardless of configuration? Minimal configuration confusions generally indicate difficulties with overreliance on general configuration or with certain portions of words. In either case, instructional adjustment is needed (see Chapter 7).
5. Does the child exhibit visual difficulty in following the line of print from left to right?
6. Were the orientation errors basically ones of habitual letter, word, and/or phrase reversals?
   big-dig = letter reversal
   was-saw = word reversal
   stop-spot = partial reversal
   many were-were many = phrase reversals
7. Were the words habitually omitted without destroying context?
8. Was the symptom one in which the child habitually lost his place? Observation should determine further whether the child lost his place while going from line to line or within a line of print.

If the answer to any one of questions five, six, seven, or eight is "yes," the teacher is advised to seek educational adjustment in an effort to correct the skill deficiency (see Chapter 7).

If *sight vocabulary skills* appear to be deficient, the answer to the following questions will assist in pinpointing the difficulty. To obtain accurate answers, each error must be examined.

1. Does the child miss small, similar words — *sat, cat, mat* — or does he falter on words which are obviously different — *city, water, phone*? It is important to establish that the child has actually looked at the word. It is not uncommon to list a child's errors only to find that, upon instruction, the child knows the word and the word patterns but had not looked carefully at them during testing.

2. Does the word missed represent a concrete or an abstract concept — *boy* and *dog* or *with* and *where?*
3. Does he know the word in isolation but not in context?
4. Does he pronounce the word properly but fail to associate it with the correct meaning?
5. Is the error one in which the child eventually prounounces the word but not without undue hesitation? In this instance, the child is apparently using a word attack skill but does not know the word as a sight word.

A "yes" answer to any of the above five questions calls for educational adjustment (see Chapter 8).

If *word attack skills* appear to be deficient, the answer to the following questions will pinpoint the phonic, structural, or contextual nature of the error. To arrive at these answers, each mispronounced word must be examined.

In examining phonic errors:

1. When the child mispronounces or substitutes words, is there a pattern of consonant or vowel errors? If so, in what part of the word are these errors made — initial, medial, or final?
  dig for *dog* = vowel, medial position
  sat for *mat* = consonant, initial position
2. Does the child need instruction in the usage of known sounds (blending and syllabication)?

In examining structural errors:

3. Do the words which are substituted or mispronounced contain prefixes or suffixes, or are they compound words? Problem readers commonly have trouble with suffixed words. It must further be determined if the child knows the base word without the suffix (e.g., a child can pronounce "want" but not "wanting").

In examining contextual errors:

4. When the child made his contextual errors, were there contextual clues available which, if observed, could have prevented the error?
5. Did the error result from failure to observe punctuation clues?

6. Do the child's errors seriously distort the author's intended meaning? If the child reads the following sentence, "Tom has a big cat," as "Tom has a large cat," the child has *not* made an error which seriously distorts the author's meaning. However, if he were to read, "Tom has a big dog," this would be a serious contextual error and is basically one of sight vocabulary.

A "yes" answer to one of the above six questions calls for educational adjustment (see Chapter 8).

If *comprehension skills* appear to be deficient, an analysis of the errors will assist the teacher in pinpointing the difficulty:

1. Do the child's comprehension difficulties appear to increase as he encounters larger units of material? (Words, to phrases, to sentences, to paragraphs, to combinations of paragraphs.)
2. Were the basic errors due to the type of comprehension expected (i.e., were they in the area of factual recall), or were they involved with the more subtle areas of comprehension such as obtaining main ideas, inferences, sequences, or problem solving?
3. Was the child able to paraphrase the author's ideas, or was he able to relate them only in the words of the author? Quite often, we find children able to parrot the words of the author, although unable to obtain deeper meaning.
4. Can the child recall the author's ideas but remain unable to perform in content area reading situations? Does he have difficulty in following directions and organizing the author's ideas?
5. Is there a total failure to respond to comprehension situations?

A "yes" answer to any of the above five questions calls for educational adjustment (see Chapter 9).

HABITS AND ATTITUDES

An evaluation of a child's reading habits also must be considered in a classroom diagnosis. The classroom teacher is in the most effective position to evaluate accurately the child's reading habits for he sees him in reading situations, such as book selection and independent reading. An effort should be made to note effective and ineffective habits which seem to vary considerably from those of the average children. The classroom teacher is likely to be asked by the reading specialist for information concerning habits and attitudes; therefore, observations should be noted carefully. Specifically, the classroom teacher should obtain answers to the following questions:

1. What use does the child make of free reading opportunity? Does he appear eager to use free time for reading, or is reading only the result of constant prodding?
2. Does the child appear anxious or reluctant to read orally? Silently? Does there appear to be a difference in his attitude between oral and silent situations. His area of least reluctance should be noted specifically, for this gives us direction when remediation starts.
3. Are signs of reluctance noticeable in reading situations only or in all learning situations? A child who hesitates in all learning situations must be motivated, whereas one reluctant in reading alone needs success and reward in reading.
4. In what reading situations is the child most or least effective? Can he summarize or answer direct questions better? Does he do better when he tells you answers or when he writes them? Again, this will direct us to desirable remedial situations.
5. Does the child have to be prodded to finish his reading assignments? If the child cannot work without supervision even when specific assignments have been made, unsupervised reading situations should be avoided in initial remedial instruction.
6. What type of book selections does the child make in the library? Considerable information can be obtained about a child's interests by noticing the type of book he chooses from the library. Remedial efforts should start with the type of material in which he has indicated an interest.

Answers to the above questions will become important guides to the initial remedial sessions. The teacher will find it useful to record his findings so that he will have a record of accurate data and he will be able to inform the reading specialist. Although these questions will be answered for the most part by informal observation, we have found it most satisfactory if the teacher gives them special attention and becomes an active agent in collecting information.

At times, it is not possible to obtain precise "yes" or "no" answers to the questions needed for classroom diagnosis. In these cases, the classroom teacher may continue to observe the child until he can substantiate a more accurate pattern of errors. Specifically, the teacher may provide the child with individualized exercises to do at his seat, go over his responses, and even have a short conference about why he marked the exercises as he did. As a part of informal on-the-spot diagnosis, this technique can be useful in verifying classroom diagnosis. Suppose, for example, that one has diagnosed irregular patterns of difficulty with final consonant sounds. Several carefully prepared exercises with final consonant sounds can be developed, administered, and analyzed for the purpose of verification. Further verification can come from information available in school records, from parental interviews, from past observations, from classroom diagnostic tests, and from subsequent instruction. All information, however obtained, should be used to effect an accurate classroom diagnosis.

FOUR FINAL QUESTIONS

The teacher must reflect upon the answers to the following four questions to complete an effective classroom diagnosis and to assist him in establishing more clearly the validity of his findings.

1. Did the child make the same error in both easy and difficult material or did the observed errors indicate frustration with the material? We are most interested in the errors made at the instruction level, the level at which we hope to make improvement. All children make errors when reading at their frustration level; these errors, however, normally do not lead to diagnostic conclusions, for these are not the errors upon which remediation is based.

2. Were the errors first interpreted as slowness actually an effort on the part of the child to be especially careful and precise? Beware of diagnostic conclusions drawn from the child's responses to questions on material which he did not read due

to slowness, especially when timed standardized tests are used or when testing situations make the child aware of being evaluated.

3. Can the child be helped as a result of this classroom diagnosis or must he be tested further, either in the classroom or in a clinical diagnosis? If the teacher has reached a point at which he can adjust effectively classroom learning situations, he should do so; otherwise, he must consider the need for further diagnosis. Further testing with any of the instruments mentioned under clinical diagnosis may be in order and is entirely proper when the teacher has the time and knowledge of their proper usage and interpretation. At this point, however, the services of a reading specialist may be required.

4. Did the child appear to concentrate while being directly observed, or did he seem easily distracted? The child who appears to be distracted during observation may have produced unreliable symptoms.

Summary Sheet

With a technique for summarizing his diagnostic findings, the classroom teacher may find much of this valuable information more readily applicable to the adjustment of classroom instruction. It is our feeling that much diagnostic information is lost through the lack of recording techniques. Of course, the classroom teacher may form, as does the reading specialist, a case study on the problem reader. However, we have found recording essential information on one page, as in Chart 4, more valuable and less burdensome for the classroom teacher. By consolidating it on one page, the classroom teacher will find the information more accessible for reference; various findings can be related to one another quite accurately.

The summary sheet provides basic information at a glance. In short, it illustrates how far the child is reading below grade level and how far he is reading below his potential. The teacher then indicates the remedial skill areas in which the child possesses strengths and those in which he has identified specifically needed classroom adjustment. And, finally, he notes symptoms requiring referral along with the date the referral was made. The teacher maintains information on the child in a folder with this form stapled on the inside cover.

CHART 4

Summary Sheet — Reading Diagnosis

Grade	CA	AA	KC	Gilmore Acc	Comp	Botel WR	Botel WO	Other
9								
8								
7								
6								
5								
4								
3								
2								
1								

Estimate of Reading Expectancy: _____
Estimate of Decoding Level: _____
Estimate of Comprehension Level: _____
Major Strengths:

Major Weaknesses:

Questions to be answered:

His diagnostic task has been to observe the individual child through analysis of symptoms, to associate the symptoms to appropriate skill areas, to determine the significance of the error, and to organize his information in terms of practical classroom adjustments. On only a few occasions will diagnosis be concluded at this point. An ongoing process, diagnosis will normally continue during the remedial sessions, always attempting to obtain more precise information concerning the child's deficiency. Morris feels that this is the important advantage for the classroom teacher. He states, "To the teacher . . . the challenge is to get to grips more directly with the problem and by working with the individual pupil try to understand what is leading him astray."[9] To this, we add, "and to determine more precisely his skill, *strengths*, and deficiencies."

SUMMARY

Classroom diagnosis, involving both diagnostic teaching and formal assessment of the strengths and weaknesses of the children, is essential to effective teaching. Awareness of the diagnostic areas and resulting identification of skill needs of children guide reading instruction.

Diagnostic teaching is not easy and is time-consuming. As does most effective teaching, it calls for attention to individual needs of children and requires careful study. Those who use diagnostic teaching find it highly rewarding and extremely effective. '

SUGGESTED READINGS

DeBoer, Dorothy L., ed. *Reading Diagnosis and Evaluation.* Newark, Delaware: International Reading Association, 1970. Emphasis is on the diagnostic aspects of reading. This IRA collection features early identification, use of testing, and informal approaches.

Durr, William K. ed. *Reading Difficulties.* Newark, Delaware: International Reading Association, 1970. The second section, The Informal Inventories, includes six articles by different authors on the various aspects of informal inventories. Readers who are unfamiliar with informal techniques will want to study this section.

Farr, Roger. *Reading: What Can Be Measured?* Newark, Delaware: International Reading Association, 1969. An excellent paperback which looks at the value and limitations of the various measuring instruments used in reading. Farr has prepared a valuable resource for teachers in-

---

[9]Ronald Morris, *Success and Failure in Learning to Read* (London: Oldbourne, 1963), p. 159.

terested in classroom diagnosis in terms of both the accuracy of the measure and its reliability.

Farr, Roger, and Anastasiow, Nicholas. *Tests of Reading Readiness and Achievement*. Newark, Delaware: International Reading Association, 1969. These authors review five readiness tests and five reading achievement tests in detail. This is an excellent source for those interested in the selection of such instruments.

5

Clinical Diagnosis

While relying mostly on a formalized testing program, the reading specialist evaluates the same four skill areas that are evaluated in classroom diagnosis. He attempts to obtain the same type of information as did the classroom teacher. What is the child's reading potential? What is the child's estimated reading level? What are his skill strengths and weaknesses? The reading specialist is also looking for possible causes of the difficulty. He is looking for ways to help the child as well as ways to help the child's teachers. He may be looking for clues underlying the difficulty which can be corrected, thus establishing programs of preventon as well as programs of correction. He follows the case from the testing situation to the instructional situation, continuously assessing the child's ability to respond to adjusted instructional programs.

No one diagnostic procedure can be labeled clinical diagnosis, for each clinic uses its own battery of tests to collect data. However, there appear to be three levels of clinical diagnosis; these might be identified as initial screening, selective study, and full case study. Most reading specialists use an initial screening procedure to assist them in identifying those children with whom they will continue to work. Selective studies are conducted when specific diagnostic information is needed. Full case studies are conducted when the child is encountering problems which are difficult to diagnose. Each of these levels of clinical diagnosis will be discussed in detail later in this chapter.

With relatively short time periods for the collection of data on a given child, the reading specialist is likely to resort to test data regardless of the level of diagnosis being performed. He adds his data to the report from the teacher concerning the child's observed behavior from a classroom diagnosis, then he prepares a clinical diagnosis.

THE USE OF TEST DATA

In Word Recognition

The first reading test to be administered in a clinical diagnosis is one of word recognition. This test must be designed to screen the ability of the child to pronounce words normally found at various grade levels accurately. From a screening of word recognition, the reading specialist is able to make the same analysis as that made from direct observation in classroom diagnosis (Chapter 4). It also assists him to make the following two basic judgments concerning the next steps in clinical diagnosis:

1. From the word recognition test (the instructional level varies with the instrument used), the reading specialist is able to select tests at an appropriate level for use in the remainder of his diagnosis. Without this information, it is possible to find oneself administering tests upon which the child cannot score at all or upon which he can obtain a nearly perfect score because they are too easy. In neither case will this type of testing produce usable diagnostic information, for tests must be administered upon which students can start with success and upon which they ultimately will encounter difficulty.

2. From the word recognition test, the reading specialist initially determines the *type* of testing which should follow. He may find, for example, that further testing of *sight vocabulary*, as such, is unnecessary, but that a complete *phonic analysis* is in order. Or he may find that a child has adequate *sight vocabulary* and *word attack skills* but needs a test with words in context to determine his *understanding*

of the meaning of words in relation to each other as well as their pronunciation.

Two of the widely used tests of word recognition are the *Botel Reading Inventory** and the *Dolch Basic Sight Vocabulary Cards.** The Word Recognition section of the Botel Inventory samples groups of twenty words found in the various basal readers in grades one through four. A child pronounces the word while the examiner records his pronunciation errors.

A sample of one-half of the first page of the Botel Word Recognition Test is shown. Notice that the child's responses must be recorded accurately. This child made most of his errors in final consonant sounds and then in vowel sounds. Accurate inner test analysis requires examination and marking of each type of error as shown; v stands for vowel, fc for final consonant, ic for initial consonant, mc for medial consonant, and √ for correct response.

The *Dolch Basic Sight Vocabulary Cards* represent a sample of 220 common words found in most first and second grade basal readers.

Many reading specialists prefer to use informal tests of word recognition. These consist of words randomly selected from basal series which the children might encounter. A minimum of twenty words per reader level should be used. The more words selected, the more reliable are the test results.

The specialist who is inexperienced with informal test construction will find this task quite difficult; he may find it more profitable to use ready-made tests. Informal word lists are available[2] and may be used when desired.

Inner test analysis in word recognition includes the following:

1. Strengths and weaknesses in phonics
2. Strengths and weaknesses in structural analysis
3. Strengths and weaknesses with words which have similar configurations
4. Strengths and weaknesses with service words and words which carry abstract meanings

---

[2]Mary C. Austin; Clifford L. Bush; and Mildred H. Huebner, *Reading Evaluation* (New York: The Ronald Press, 1961), p. 13; and Emmett A. Betts, *Handbook on Corrective Reading for the American Adventure Series* (Chicago: Wheeler Publishing Co., 1956), pp. 37-39.

BOTEL READING INVENTORY A[1]
WORD RECOGNITION SCORING SHEET

Pupil _____

Date _____

Instructional Levels _____

Teacher _____

A (Pre-Primer)		B (Primer)		C (First)	
Word	*Response*	Word	*Response*	Word	*Response*
1. a	√	all	√	about	√
2. ball	√	at	√	as	√
3. blue	blow	boat	boak	be	√
4. come	√	but	bud	by	√
5. farther	fatter	do	√	could	cold
6. get	√	duck	√	fast	first
7. have	half	find	fine	friend	friet
8. house	horse	girl	√	guess	guest
9. in	√	he	√	hen	√
10. it	√	kitten	kitton	how	hot

[1]Morton Botel, *Botel Reading Inventory* (Chicago: Follett Publishing Co., 1962).

In Oral Reading

Next, the reading specialist will find a test of oral reading skills to be valuable. From oral reading tests, the reading specialist again can gather diagnostic information in the same manner as did the classroom teacher when he observed oral reading in the classroom (see Chapter 4). It also enables him to do the following:

1. He will be able to verify the findings obtained on the word recognition test. Does the child consistently display strengths and weaknesses on the same kinds of words or in the same parts of words as those noted in tests of word recognition?

2. Further diagnostic information is obtained while determining whether words unknown in word recognition are known when they are seen in their relationship with other words. The ability of the child to use contextual word attack skills is determined by comparing the word recognition instructional level with the oral reading instructional level. A large difference in favor of oral reading indicates effective use of context. A score difference in favor of word recognition may be an indication of contextual confusion. If the difference is in favor of oral reading, the reading specialist becomes less concerned about the types of errors observed in word recognition. After all, nearly all of the reading a child does is in contextual situations. Better performance in word recognition than in oral reading would only be important if one were concerned about the overuse of context clues; the clue to which is many substitutions which make sense in the context but which do not convey the meaning intended by the author.

3. Oral reading tests also provide the examiner with an understanding of the child's reading characteristics in school situations. Although this particular diagnostic information may not have a direct relationship to specific remedial procedures, it will provide the reading specialist with an understanding of the child's reaction to oral reading, and of the problems which he may be causing in his classroom. It helps him realize the difficulty which might be encountered teaching the child in a group situation.

There are several tests already available with prepared oral reading selections and norms for grade equivalents. Some of these are: *Gilmore Oral Reading Test,* * *Gray Oral Reading Test,* * *Diagnostic Reading Scales,* * *Durrell Analysis of Reading Difficulties,* * and the *Gates-McKillop Reading Test.* * Although the directions for administration of these tests vary, they have the following basic ingredients: the child reads aloud from graded reading selections, ranging from simple to difficult; the examiner records the reading errors as outlined by the manual; then he asks several comprehension questions which normally provide a measure of the child's ability to recall specifically stated facts from the story (the Gates-McKillop test does not have this feature). The reading specialist will want to examine each of these tests and make his selection in accordance with his philosophy of oral reading and the characteristics of the specific tests, especially the standardization data.

As with word recognition, many reading specialists prefer to construct informal tests of oral reading. Using the graded materials which the child might be expected to read, paragraphs are selected from each reader, and questions are designed to measure comprehension skills. Accuracy in oral reading is recorded as it is on standardized tests of oral reading. Using informal tests of oral reading in a diagnosis offers the advantages of larger selections and a variety of content. A major disadvantage is inherent in the assumption that the graded materials used for the test are, in fact, accurately graded. For example, if a given selection taken from a fifth grade book is actually at the sixth grade level, diagnostic conclusions which come from it are faulty. However, by avoiding the problem of mismatching a test score with reading materials, accurate assessments are possible through the use of informal testing procedures.

Oral reading tests as diagnostic tools are plagued by several limitations. In the first place, there is considerable disagreement about what an oral reading error is. Certainly, we would recognize mispronounced words, hesitancy on unknown words, or disregard of punctuation marks as obvious limitations to effective oral reading, at least as far as the listening audience is concerned, but is it an error when a child repeats words to correct oral reading mistakes? Is it an error when a child stops to use word attack skills on words not known at sight? Or are these the types of behaviors which we want children to display? Are all these errors of equal importance, or do some more seriously than others cripple reading efficiency? If weights could be developed for various types of errors, would the same weights hold at various grade levels? For example, would a vowel error made by a first grader be as serious an error as a vowel substitution made by a fifth grader?

Fully aware of these limitations, test constructors, in an effort to standardize oral reading tests, have had to establish some easily recognizable arbitrary standards of accurate and inaccurate oral reading. Although these arbitrary systems vary, most of them include markings similar to those listed in the Gilmore Oral Reading Test Manual.[3] Substitutions and mispronunciations are written above the word for which the substitution was made; omissions are

---

[3]*Manual of Directions*, Gilmore Oral Reading Test (New York: Harcourt, Brace and World, 1952), pp. 8-9.

circled; repetitions are underlined; words inserted are put in the appropriate place; punctuation which is disregarded is marked by an x; hesitations of two seconds or more are marked by a check mark above the word; at five seconds, these words are pronounced for the reader and two check marks are indicated. Diagnosis, of course, depends upon the accurate marking of errors and a valid interpretation of them.

The following paragraph has been marked according to the system discussed.

     √   √ √   surfit x
A spaceman has just stepped on to the surface of the moon.
                                 telephone
<u>He is very</u> careful as he steps from his capsule. Live television
brings the moment to the (entire) population of the Earth. It is
a very
an∧exciting moment.

With such marking, the child's reading is accurately recorded. He hesitated on the word *has* and failed to pronounce the word *stepped* in five seconds. He mispronounced *surface* and disregarded the period after *moon*. He repeated *He is very*. He substituted *telephone* for *television* and *a* for *an*. He omitted *entire* and added *very*. The above paragraph illustrates not only the marking system but also the fact that all errors are not of equal importance. For example: hesitation on the word *has* is not as serious an error as is the failure to pronounce *stepped*.

Another limitation of oral reading tests concerns the ability of the examiner to hear and record accurately the errors which the child is making. It has been our finding that supervised practice is necessary to obtain proficiency in oral reading test administration. It is obvious that if the examiner is not able to hear or record the child's errors accurately, the results of his testing will be of questionable value. Through practice, competency can be developed to assure satisfactory administration and interpretation of oral reading. However, unsupervised testing without adequate practice can lead to extremely unreliable results.

With these limitations in mind, the reading specialist will continue to find tests of oral reading extremely valuable in a reading diagnosis. He will find value in the information obtained from the answers to the analysis suggested above.

In Silent Reading

The third phase of a clinical diagnosis is the evaluation of a child's silent reading skills through specially constructed tests. Through an evaluation of these tests, the reading specialist gathers information as did the classroom teacher when he observed silent reading.

In clinical diagnosis, silent reading tests have several additional advantages. First, information relating to the child's instructional level can be obtained. The instructional level in silent reading is the level at which a child reads without undue frustration, but at which he is obviously in need of instruction for improved performance. The grade score earned on a silent reading test, however, does not necessarily represent the instructional level, as this score usually includes measures of the child's performance at the frustration level. To obtain the instructional level accurately, the reading specialist must examine carefully silent reading comprehension errors to determine where the child falls short of errorless reading. If the test is not constructed using graded paragraphs, such an analysis will be difficult, if not impossible. Second, it is through inner test analysis that the reading specialist is first able to determine the types of comprehension with which the child has successes and with which he has difficulties. Most well-constructed test manuals guide the examiner in this type of analysis. While such analysis is important, the reading specialist must accept such data as evidence rather than as fact. Once evidence is accumulated, hypotheses about possible strengths and weaknesses can be proposed. Third, through a comparison of the child's scores in word and paragraph meaning, the examiner learns whether the child is able to obtain meaning through the use of context; word meaning tests usually contain a minimal use of context while paragraphs contain considerable contextual aids.

From such data, the reading specialist begins developing insights into the manner in which the child is comprehending. In some instances he may have obtained sufficient information that no further testing will be needed, but in others he may discover that other types of additional tests are needed.

Several of the better known tests of silent reading ability are: *The California Reading Tests,** *The Diagnostic Reading Tests,** *Durrell Sullivan Reading Achievement Test,** *The Gates MacGinitie Reading Survey,** *The Iowa Test of Basic Skills,** *The Metropolitan*

Achievement Tests,* and *The Stanford Achievement Test.** Being silent tests, they may be administered in group situations in which the child normally is expected to complete the process in a generously allotted time period. It is important that the reading specialist remember to consult his word recognition test scores to determine the proper level for the selection of silent reading tests, so that he will start the child at a level at which he can have success. Although each of these tests provides a measure of a child's performance in word and paragraph meaning, the differences in the items involved to obtain these scores are great. For example, some tests stress the recall of directly stated facts, while others sample the ability to handle main ideas, inferences, map reading, and the like. Both types of tests are likely to provide scores designed to indicate the child's ability to comprehend. The reading specialist necessarily will need to examine the nature of each test prior to its interpretation.

Silent reading tests are also plagued with limitations. First, if a child's instructional level is not measured by a silent test, the score which he obtains will be meaningless. For example, if a child takes a test designed for intermediate grade children but cannot read beyond the first grade level, his test score is likely to be invalid since the test did not measure his instructional level. He probably will not score on any item except by guessing. This type of test indicates only that he is a poor reader, a fact known before the test was administered, but it gives little useful information beyond that.

Second, the author's definition of comprehension may make a difference in the resulting score. For example, the *California Reading Test* measures comprehension at the elementary level by combining the ability to follow directions, the ability to read maps, charts, and graphs, and the ability to get meaning from paragraphs. Obviously, that score is not comparable to the score on an achievement test measuring only factual recall paragraph meaning. The reading specialist, therefore, will want to administer a test which agrees most directly with his definition of comprehension.

Another limitation is that standardized populations vary considerably, resulting in grade equivalent scores which are not always accurate for the child upon whom the diagnosis is being conducted. Efforts must be made to determine the nature of the standardization population; otherwise, the resulting score cannot be evaluated accurately for a given child.

Finally, the reading specialist should be cautioned about the limitations in using certain silent reading tests to make reliable inner tests analysis and diagnosis. On the *California Reading Test*, for example, the child taking the elementary form of the test answers three questions to indicate whether he can determine the main idea. Conclusions based upon a child's responses to only three questions must be held suspect. If the reading specialist is to interpret this score as an area in which further investigation seems warranted, the test has a useful function. More reliable diagnosis is possible, however, on this same test if one compares the major sections, such as Following Directions, Reference Skills, and Interpretation of Materials. The *Diagnostic Reading Tests* and the *Gates MacGinitie Reading Tests* have entire sections which are devoted to an analysis of a child's competency in specific types of silent reading comprehension. Gates, for example, has separate tests for Speed and Accuracy, Level of Comprehension, and Vocabulary.

INFORMAL DIAGNOSIS IN COMPREHENSION

Using informal inventories for comprehension diagnosis is well justified when one considers the weaknesses inherent in the use of standardized tests. Informal tests can be constructed to include the types and numbers of compehension questions which are valid in terms of the skills to be measured. They can include samples of materials identical to or similar to those used in instruction. They can provide larger samplings of comprehension behavior at what appears to be the instructional level. They can be designed to measure the comprehension skills needed for content subjects, such as science and social studies, as well as for general reading.

Informal measures can take the characteristics of paragraph readings followed by teacher-made questions, or they can take the form of closure tests (see Chapter 4). The measure usually includes several samples from a given book. Informal test questions can measure directly stated facts, or they can measure higher level comprehension skills. The types of questions developed, their purposes, and the interpretation of the resulting scores need to be given careful consideration.

Informal Inventories

Occasionally, scores in the diagnosis conflict to the point that they are confusing. Austin, et al.[4] have prepared an inventory for use with the Allyn Bacon Series Readers. Betts[5] has prepared one for use with the American Adventure Series. Smith, et. al.[6] have developed one for the primary grades. Reading specialists who are unfamiliar with the construction of these inventories will want to refer to these sources or to the book on informal inventories by Johnson and Kress.[7] Spache has carefully prepared standardized paragraphs in the Diagnostic Reading Scales which provide teachers with a rather large sampling of oral and silent reading test materials. However, he has standardized this test, making interpretation easier. Upon examination the reader will note that each authority has established separate norms. Caution is urged in making interpretations — especially from one to the other.

HYPOTHESIS FORMATION

After measuring the strengths and weaknesses of the child in sight vocabulary, oral reading, and silent reading, tentative hypotheses are made. From these hypotheses the reading specialist obtains clues to the child's strengths and weaknesses in the skill areas and plans further diagnosis in terms of his findings. His procedure here is identical to that used by the teacher classroom in classroom diagnosis. Although the questions asked in relation to each skill area are those asked in classroom diagnosis, the resulting conclusions may culminate in further diagnosis since the reading specialist has more diagnostic tools available and is more qualified to interpret the results. Based upon these tentative hypotheses, the reading specialist now will extend the diagnosis to those skill areas which have been identified as needing further analysis. These two aspects of clinical

---

[4]Austin, Bush and Huebner, *Reading Evaluation,* Appendix.

[5]Emmett A. Betts, *Handbook on Corrective Reading for the American Adventure Series* (New York: American Book Co.), Chapter III.

[6]Nila B. Smith et al., *Graded Selections for Informal Reading Diagnosis* (New York: New York Universal Press, 1959).

[7]Marjorie S. Johnson and Roy A. Kress, *Informal Reading Inventories,* Reading Aid Series (Newark, Delaware: International Reading Association, 1965).

diagnosis — preciseness of the tools and the extension of diagnosis based upon the hypotheses—plus the evaluation of information from noneducational diagnosis often make the detection of causation possible.

Extension of Diagnosis

One of the basic considerations for clinical diagnosis concerns the possibility that a child might have a certain mode of learning which suits him. If so, the reading specialist will have valuable information for both himself and the classroom teacher. For example, a child who may learn effectively when tactile experiences are combined with visual stimuli, may not learn through visual stimuli alone. These strengths and weaknesses should serve as guides for instruction.

To identify learning modalities, the reading specialist has such tests as the *Mills Rate of Learning Test*,* the *Monroe Sherman Group Diagnostic Achievement and Aptitude Test*,* and the *Gates Associative Learning Test*.* These tests attempt to identify strengths in visual or auditory sensory systems; the Mills test adds tactile and combination techniques. For the severely handicapped child, identification of strong learning modalities seems to be especially helpful.

If the tentative hypothesis identified other readiness or pre-reading skills as areas for further diagnosis, the examiner has several alternatives. If the student's language appears to be deficient, tests, such as the *WISC** or the *ITPA*,* may identify specific linguistic functions which can be listed as strengths and/or weaknesses. The *Peabody Picture Vocabulary Test* and the *Ammons Full Range Picture Vocabulary Test* measure listening vocabulary and an aspect of modality.

If visual discrimination skills appear to be deficient, the *Monroe Sherman Group Diagnostic Achievement and Aptitude Tests*, the *Frostig Test of Visual Perception*, or informal measures can be used for further diagnosis. The clinician should be certain that his diagnosis will aid in the development of an educational prescription. Generally, we find informal measures of most value. Informal testing, using a simple passage or a child's experience story, can be conducted by asking the child to circle all words which begin with a specific letter after showing him the letter, by asking him to underline all words which have a certain ending, or by finding specific letters in the paragraph. The advantage of such informal testing is that the actual reading passage is the testing media.

If auditory discrimination appears to be the problem, further testing through measures, such as the *Wepman Auditory Discrimination Test*, appear to be of value. Here, auditory discrimination abilities are identified further as initial sounds, medial sounds, or final sounds. Again, informal measures are equally useful and easily constructed. The clinician can read lists of words in pairs (cat — fat) and ask the child to indicate whether they are the same or different. Correct responses and errors can be totaled to determine strengths and weaknesses.

If the tentative hypothesis identifies the orientation area as a problem in reading, diagnosis often is extended through an evaluation of eye motion during the reading act, normally through careful observation of the child during both oral and silent reading. Do the eyes appear to move with a reasonable number of fixations across the line of print? Do the child's eyes move backwards, making many regressions? Everyone makes regressions in reading; without experience in observing children in the reading act, it is difficult to diagnose this area accurately. The reading specialist should observe groups of good, fair, and poor readers so that he can learn what is expected in the observation of eye movements. The Reading Eye Camera* is designed to photograph the precise movements of each eye while a child is reading. With this camera, the reading specialist can evaluate several aspects of the mechanics of reading and compare a child's performance with established norms. Note that the evaluation of eye motion films also requires considerable practice because the eye movements of poor readers do not follow the normal analysis patterns set forth in the manual. Eye motion photography also is made difficult by the restricted reading situation required for testing.

Another extension of orientation of diagnosis often moves into the area of dominance preference. After screening hundreds of cases of severe reading retardation by means of in depth dominance study, we have found no relationship of dominance to orientation problems, nor have we found any remedial solutions based upon such diagnosis. While many children have symptoms of confused dominance, we do not find such cases to be restricted to reading problems. Our conclusion to diagnosis in this controversial area is that there is no justification for continued efforts to link reading difficulties to dominance problems — in fact, such diagnosis often leads educators away from the symptoms which will best offer solutions to the child's educational difficulties. As a result, both eye motion and dominance diagnosis are areas of extended diagnosis which are complicated and often nonproductive.

If the tentative hypothesis identifies sight vocabulary as the problem area, a more careful analysis of tests previously administered may determine consistent patterns of sight vocabulary errors (see Chapter 4).

Aside from measuring word meaning and word recognition, tests may also indicate the speed at which the child responds to recognized words. A word cannot properly be called a sight word unless a child recognizes it instantly. Standardized word meaning tests which are timed provide one measure of speed, especially if the child responds accurately but scores poorly on tests which are designed to test his reading speed alone (*Gates MacGinitie Reading Test,* Speed and Accuracy Section). Durrell[8] suggests that the word not known at sight should be used to see if the child can analyze the word using word attack when time is not a factor. In such cases, the word recognition answer sheet will have two columns, one for instant pronunciation and one for delayed pronunciation. Obviously, if the child does not know the word at sight but does know it when permitted to examine it, we may conclude that he has skills to attack the word properly, but has not overlearned it to the extent that it can be called a sight word.

If the tentative hypothesis finds the area of word attack in need of further diagnosis, the specialist should analyze the errors made in word recognition and oral reading as was done in the classroom diagnosis (see Chapter 4). There are also tests available for clinical diagnosis which measure specific word attack skill performance. *The Botel Phonics Test,* *The Silent Reading Diagnostic Tests* by Bond, Clymer, and Hoyt, *The Roswell-Chall Diagnostic Test of Word Analysis Skills,* and the *Doren Diagnostic Reading Tests of Word Recognition Skills* are four well-known, quite different evaluations of a child's word attack skills. Each of these tests may be administered to groups of students who respond to oral presentations by the teacher. The Botel test is quite short, the Bond, Clymer, and Hoyt test takes about 45 minutes, and the Doren test takes three hours. The needs of a given child determine which is most appropriate in his diagnosis. The various diagnostic

---

[8]Donald D. Durrell, *Manual of Directions: Durrell Analysis of Reading Difficulty* (New York: Harcourt, Brace and World, 1955), p. 14.

test batteries also contain an analysis of word attack skills; however, they heavily emphasize phonics.

Reading specialists generally want to see how well a child with specific word attack problems handles himself in a spelling test. A test of this nature should be given at the child's instructional level. Through an analysis of spelling errors, the reading specialist can extend his diagnosis and verify previous findings. A child who substitutes one consonant for another or one vowel for another indicates confusion in handling phonics (e.g., *perty for party*). If he confuses the order of the letters (e.g., *picinc* for *picnic*), he is indicating directional confusion. Of course, spelling errors can confirm suspicions of reversal tendencies (e.g., *was* for *saw*). An analysis of the child's performance on these tests, combined with the diagnostic data previously available, should lead the reading specialist to a thorough evaluation of the type of word attack skills with which the child is having his basic problem. It bears repeating that if a child does not know his letter sounds, one must evaluate whether he has the *auditory discrimination skills* necessary for learning them.

The reading specialist is cautioned that many children have learned to attack words adequately in isolated drill-type exercises but are not capable of performing the same task when they see these words in context. It would be erroneous, therefore, to conclude that a child does not have a word attack deficiency simply because he performs successfully on diagnostic tests of word attack skills. Evaluation must be made in an oral reading situation where the child is faced, not with the single unknown word, but with the unknown word in a group of familiar words. Here, too, clues to meaning have as much importance as do clues to proper pronunciation.

If the tentative hypothesis identifies the *comprehension* area as needing further diagnosis, attention must again be directed to those questions asked in classroom diagnosis (see Chapter 4). Clinical diagnosis will be extended to review the history of the basic types of approaches used in the child's reading instruction. From this type of analysis, it often is possible for the reading specialist to understand gaps in areas of instruction and to suggest remedial programs to fill these gaps. In the area of *comprehension*, the specialist should establish the answers to four additional questions before proceeding to remediation.

1. Is the child's poor performance on a comprehension test due basically to weak comprehension skills, or is it more closely related to inadequate vocabulary? One technique for determining the answer to this question is to make a careful comparison between word meaning and paragraph meaning scores. Poorer performance in word meaning usually indicates that a child's vocabulary skills are prohibiting maximum performance in comprehension.
2. Is there a need for further comprehension testing to verify scores upon which there is conflicting evidence? It may be necessary to administer a test which has more items, one which has a better variety of items, or one which measures a certain type of comprehension skill not measured in the previously administered silent reading test. When children have basic comprehension difficulties, the reading specialist seldom will find one silent reading test capable of satisfying all of the child's diagnostic needs. If another test is administered, the results of that test should undergo the same diagnostic scrutiny as did the previous test. Scores of such tests should not be averaged, however. When more than one test of silent reading is used to diagnose skill strengths and weaknesses, analysis of all the responses to types of questions rather than a composite score is critical to clinical diagnosis.
3. Is the child's poor performance on a comprehension test due basically to reading speed? In classroom diagnosis, the ability to complete the reading assignments in a specific time period was considered; in clinical diagnosis, equal consideration must be given to the child who fails to complete reading tests in the allotted time. There is no possibility of obtaining this information from the grade scores on silent reading tests; rather, a careful inner test analysis will reveal the amount of material covered by a child in a given test. A test now is available to determine the flexibility with which a child attacks print designed for different purposes. The *EDL Reading Versatility Test** is designed to provide this type of information when speed of reading is being considered as a limitation to the child.
4. Is the child's poor comprehension on specific text exercises caused by a different field of experiences than those of the author? It is easy to understand that a city child unfamiliar

with farm life might score poorly on a story test about farming yet be quite capable of comprehending a similar story about city life. Diagnosis, however, is not so easy. While broad areas of experience may be identified, a child's background of experiences is quite personal and involved. A child who can pronounce the words of a passage yet fail in comprehension may have a weak experiential background in that topic. Therefore, he cannot form the concepts that the author's words indicate.

If the tentative hypothesis identifies *reading habits and attitudes* as the problem area, the reading specialist has found that the child has the basic skills to read adequately but does not care to read. This diagnosis involves a careful consideration of the information from the areas of emotional and physical diagnosis. The child may indicate either that he has a poor attitude towards school-type tasks and books or that he is physically uncomfortable to a point that he does not pursue the reading act eagerly. Further evaluation is needed of past efforts made by the school to encourage the child to read, the availability of books in the school and at home, and the general atmosphere which may either encourage or discourage reading in these situations. A child who can read but doesn't normally is not considered in need of a specialist's attention; rather, he is a classroom teacher's responsibility as long as the difficulty is educational in nature. The reading specialist's obligation, therefore, is to make specific recommendations to the classroom teacher to assist him in encouraging the child to read. It will be helpful, therefore, for the reading specialist to use a measure of the child's interests in his diagnosis. Fully aware that interests are of-the-moment and ever-changing, the reading specialist nevertheless will attempt to assess the child's interests either formally through an established interest inventory or informally through interest inventories and/or a personal interview with the child, his parents, and his teacher. We have found, for example, that many children, although they are reading as well as can be expected, are placed in frustrating reading situations daily in school. It does not take a specialist to realize that reading is not much fun for these children and that they easily might have developed a negative attitude toward reading. Information gleaned in such a manner will be important to include in the diagnostic report of a problem reader.

Diagnostic Batteries

There are available for clinical diagnosis a group of tests which, used in a single unit, constitute a diagnostic battery. These tests are designed for use as a rather complete educational analysis of a given child. The more prominent of these batteries are the *Durrell Analysis of Reading Difficulties,** Gates-McKillop Reading Diagnostic Test, Diagnostic-Reading Scale,** and *Monroe-Sherman Group Diagnostic Reading Aptitude and Achievement Tests.** The first three are individual in nature, while the last is a group test. A careful examination of these diagnostic batteries is essential for an appropriate selection for clinical diagnosis. The only items that all these tests have in common are measures of silent or oral reading and word attack skills. Some tests also include word recognition, oral reading, arithmetic, spelling, auditory and visual discrimination, and auding.* The main advantage of using a diagnostic battery is that the scores of the subtests are more comparable since they are standardized on the same population. Another advantage is that there is one manual and one test to learn to administer and interpret; one does not have the overwhelming job that occurs in some other types of testing combinations. The resulting information will provide an individual analysis of how a student is reading and how his skill development is related to his total reading scores. These diagnostic batteries are not without limitations; some are too brief and some are standardized on very small populations, thereby causing reliability problems. Most important, possibly, the reading specialist will find that the test does not measure the types or quantities of skills that he wishes to measure, thus causing validity problems. Therefore, in clinical diagnosis, it is unlikely that any one of these diagnostic batteries will be adequate for a complete diagnosis. Note that subtests of diagnostic batteries have been recommended for use in specific areas of diagnosis — not for precise scores — but for indicators of strengths and weaknesses which might be studied in more depth.

Sample Diagnostic Teaching Lesson

As the reading specialist begins to formulate his diagnostic hypotheses, he must realize that his findings are limited to testing situations. He must realize that testing alone can produce distorted findings. It is here that we suggest a short session of diagnostic teaching designed to see how the child operates in the areas hypothesized as strengths and weaknesses.

Specifically, the reading specialist should provide a lesson which would check his findings concerning reading level, major skill strengths, and major skill weaknesses. For example, if the diagnosis supported an instructional level at 3-1, skill strengths in beginning consonants and directly stated recall, and skill weaknesses in vowels and problem solving, a lesson should be designed to see how the child operates in each of these areas. Several books, one at the 2-2 level, one at the 3-1 level, and perhaps one at the 3-2 level can be selected with silent reading followed by questioning in the area of strengths and weaknesses. A short phonics lesson can be developed to see how well the child handles consonants and vowels.

If the hypotheses are confirmed, the diagnosis becomes both more certain and valid. However, if the child can perform during instruction, new hypotheses will need to be formulated and tested. It is our experience in clinical diagnosis that rarely are all hypotheses confirmed. Clinicians who skip the step of diagnostic teaching place themselves in the position of drawing faulty conclusions. Preparing a report on a child which contains faulty conclusions has serious consequences. If specialists expect teachers to use their reports to adjust instruction, they should test their findings in instructional situations. In the Reading Center at the University of Maryland, we have found diagnostic lessons which follow testing to be of the utmost value. These lessons usually take about fifteen minutes and frequently modify the report significantly.

DIFFICULT DIAGNOSTIC PROBLEMS

The So-called Nonreader

Unfortunately, not all diagnosis falls into neat packages of specific skill deficiencies. A small number of children appear unable to profit from even the best instruction in any of the skill areas. They cannot learn to read by conventional methods. The diagnosis of this type of child is the responsibility of the reading specialist.

Commonly referred to as dyslexic, neurologically deficient, minimally brain damaged, or as possessing a specific reading disability, the nonreader has disabilities complicated by multiple factors. The child is almost always emotionally involved in his gross failure. He is likely to be physically deficient and may appear to be dull. Trying to please the teacher often is no longer of interest to him. Diagnosis has failed to identify a consistent pattern of errors. Educators have attempted to teach him by all known methods; each of these methods has failed to teach him to read.

Effective diagnosis calls for an interdisciplinary approach to this child. All diagnostic facilities, educational and noneducational, must be used. Every effort should be made to seek out the sources of this child's difficulties. It is often necessary that this child be diagnosed in clinics which have been established to work efficiently with him. Diagnosis and initial remediation will be accomplished most effectively in these clinic-type situations. Many school districts are establishing special schools for such children. Carefully trained teachers work in coordination with personnel from other disciplines to establish meaningful educational programs for these very troubled learners.

In some cases, despite all our efforts, these children continue to fail. Multi-disciplinary efforts are continuously explored in hopes of establishing new areas of diagnosis and remediation for them. Schiffman has initiated major efforts to establish communication lines between the disciplines.[9] As a result, better understandings of the role of each discipline have been established and communication lines have been identified. When such cooperative efforts are not available, we can at least be sure that early identification is established. Any educator who finds such a child must refer him without delay to a specialist who is equipped to handle this type of child. When extended into the secondary schools, remediation is extremely difficult, time-consuming, and expensive if, in fact, the child has not become a dropout by that time.

The Culturally Different

Another group of children who appear to be experiencing severe difficulty in traditional programs are those who come from culturally different backgrounds. Their language and their experiences are not likely to correspond to the instructional materials which they are expected to use. Mismatching children from poor income homes with books designed for middle and upper class children has been common. When inferences are made concerning the intellectual power of poor children, "mismatching" must be viewed as potentially harmful.

---

[9]Gilbert Schiffman, "Program Administration within a School System," in *The Disabled Reader,* ed. John Money (Baltimore, Maryland: The Johns Hopkins Press, 1966), p. 241.

Language differences can appear as errors in word recognition and oral reading tests. Of course, these differences are not errors. The examiner should know which distortions are due to the language of the child and which are actually errors in oral reading. Otherwise, he will be penalizing the child because of his language; such a practice is not a useful diagnostic technique.

Finally, diagnostic instruments which use stories based on middle-class concepts (Dick and Jane going on a vacation in the suburbs) put poor children at a disadvantage in the testing situation. Interpretation of low reading and intelligence scores must be in terms of the different cultural backgrounds of the children.

Aside from considerations such as these, culturally different children should be diagnosed using the questions suggested in this chapter. Strengths should be noted and taught too. Deficiencies should be worked with through the child's demonstrated strengths. The accept and challenge philosophy is extremely important for establishing good diagnostic and remedial relationships with these children.

LEVELS OF CLINICAL DIAGNOSIS

Initial Screening

The reading specialist will find that an accurate diagnosis of reading disabilities will take much time and effort. It is unfortunate that time is wasted in clinically diagnosing large numbers of children who do not have reading problems; these children are referred to reading specialists who have no means of knowing the child until the entire diagnosis or a major part of it is complete. It seems advisable, then, that the reading specialist have a technique which will permit him to screen children prior to the administration of the entire diagnosis. Thus, the reading specialist can eliminate the long waiting lists of children actually in need of diagnosis.

For these reasons, the concept of "initial screening" is introduced. An initial screening should be a brief, concise evaluation of the child's reading skills, taking approximately one hour. We recommend the following:

1. A test of verbal ability (such as the Peabody Picture Vocabulary Test)
2. A test of word recognition (such as Botel Word Recognition)

3. A test of word meaning   (such as Botel Word Opposites) (Reading)
4. An oral reading test   (such as the Gilmore Oral Reading)
5. A phonics test, if necessary   (such as Botel Phonics)
6. A test of silent reading   (such as informal measures)
7. Information from the parents   (such as parental interview)
8. Information from a diagnostic lesson

We have found that approximately one-fourth of the children referred for clinical diagnosis can be eliminated from complete diagnosis on the basis of an initial screening because their problems are not basically ones of poor reading. Many children are referred by parents who have not accepted their children as average students and are anxious to see them earning A's and B's in school. Some children are referred for poor grades in school for which there appears, as a result of initial screening, to be no blame on reading skills. We find that the screening often provides us with enough information to outline an instructional program. The amount of examination time and effort saved by the early identification of these children can be used for more thorough diagnosis of those children in real need.

Classroom teachers who have had the opportunity to use initial screening techniques in college courses have found them usable in classroom diagnosis; however, initial screening is recommended as a classroom diagnostic technique only if the teacher has had supervised experience with the administration and interpretation of the specific instruments suggested.

Selective Study

Selective studies can be conducted for one of two reasons. First, during instruction a reading specialist often finds a child's responses to be conflicting. It may appear, for example, that the child's silent reading comprehension has been underrated by the screening. Selective testing is advised. Second, selective testing may be necessary if diagnostic results in one area or another are conflicting. For example, if the school reports that the child has low average I.Q. but the verbal ability test finds him to be high average, further testing is advised.

In neither situation did the initial screening provide enough information for accurate diagnosis. However, the reading specialist was able to identify the area in need of further testing; he became selective about how much further testing is needed. Selective testing follows the principle of maintaining efficiency (i.e., not over-testing a given child).

Since selective testing generally involves only a test or two, no special form is recommended for reporting such results. However, since reporting is important, the reading specialist should prepare a report on the selective testing. Such a report should include the reasons for testing, the test scores, and a test interpretation. If the testing results in a changed instructional prescription, that also should be included in the report.

Case Study

Occasionally a full case study seems necessary to complete a diagnostic evaluation. To develop a full case study, in-depth testing is required in the areas of intelligence, verbal performance, auditory skills, visual skills, word recognition, oral and silent reading comprehension, and word attack skills. To these are added medical reports and a developmental history as well as detailed information from both the school and the home.

The decision to proceed with a full case study will stem from lack of information on the child and failure of the initial screening to identify satisfactorily the child's strengths and weaknesses. Every aspect of the child's educational development, along with an evaluation of his intellectual, emotional, and physical development, is needed for the specialist to attempt to identify the causes of his problems.

Case Reporting

As in classroom diagnosis, the information accumulated in a clinical diagnosis is useless unless it can be organized so that it is readily understood. This organization must differ for the various recipients of the report — the reading specialist, the classroom teacher, or the parents.

A case report is the typical approach to preparing diagnostic information for clinical use. Although the precise form may vary, the following format should be used so that persons unfamiliar with this child can make optimum use of case information:

1. The first page should contain a concise summary of the essential data included in the report (i.e., name, age, address, and school of the child, degree of reading retardation, and a summary statement of the diagnostic findings, including intellectual, physical, emotional, and educational diagnosis).

2. The first page should be followed by as many pages of explanation as necessary. The explanation should include all test scores, the dates upon which they were administered, and the name of the test administrator, as well as diagnostic interpretations of the test performance and evaluations of the child's responses. It also should include noneducational data from screening tests and referral reports. It is here that the relative importance of each piece of data is evaluated and interrelated and that causative factors may be identified.

3. A page or two of complete description of the successes of the diagnostic lesson should be the contents of the third section.

4. The last page of the case report should be reserved for specific recommendations and referrals. Recommendations should include those to the clinic, the classroom teacher, and the parents specifying preventive as well as remedial procedures.

Reports to the classroom teacher generally are not effective in case report form; however, they should contain the more important test scores and a concise, readable, usable set of recommendations for corrective action. This report does not preclude the classroom teacher examining the case report if he so desires. The main purpose of the report to the classroom teacher is to enable him to understand the child's reading in order to facilitate proper classroom adjustment. We have found it useful for the report to contain a page or two of written material which is explained to the teacher in a face-to-face interview. Teachers nearly always have questions about the report which can be answered during the interview. It is more likely that the report has been understood by the teacher if it has been discussed. Prior to talking with the teachers about the reports, we had simply mailed them. A follow-up investigation indicated that many teachers never read the reports and that many more had studied them but had not understood them.

In reporting diagnostic findings to parents, we recommend neither the use of the case report nor the reporting of precise scores. Reports to parents can contain a general statement in each of the four areas of diagnosis and, most importantly, recommendations for parental action and referral. Test scores without careful explanation tend to be taken as absolutes, thus causing many problems among the parents, the child, and the schools. It is desirable to discuss diagnostic results with parents so that questions can be answered and emphasis placed on certain conclusions. Considerable effort should be made to stress the child's strengths with the parents and to urge them to look for strengths in the child. Parents who view their child as weak and deficient are likely to communicate these views to the child. By looking for and commenting upon his strengths, parents assist in the development of the child's positive self-concept. Chapter 11 covers the parental roles and the problem reader more thoroughly.

PITFALLS OF DIAGNOSIS

Both clinical and classroom diagnosis may be plagued by certain pitfalls. They are:

1. Overgeneralization: The tendency to use total test scores without examination of the pattern of test scores; the tendency to draw conclusions before all facts are in; the tendency to rely upon the first significant symptom; and the tendency to hazard guesses outside the professional field are all examples of overgeneralizing in diagnosis. Overgeneralizing can be controlled, in part, by making couched statements when all data is not available. For example, instead of saying that a child has a poor home life, one might say that from the data available the home conditions bear watching as a possible cause of the child's educational development. More than merely playing with words, couched

statements protect the educational diagnostician and lead to more accurate reporting of diagnostic results.

2. Overextension of diagnosis: Extending diagnosis beyond that which will help arrive at an accurate picture of the child may cause the child to become overconcerned about his problem and is a waste of time. In commenting on the disadvantages of extended diagnostic periods, Strang concludes, "He may feel more strongly than ever that something may be wrong with him."[10] Overextension of diagnosis occurs more commonly in the clinic than in the classroom, for it is in the clinic that the most careful study of the child is conducted and a wide variety of tests are available. Some clinics suggest that each child receive a complete diagnostic analysis regardless of his needs. This can only be justified in the interest of gathering research data; however, the expense to the child must always be considered, for not all children can accept large quantities of diagnosis. Nevertheless, every effort must be made to arrive at a true picture of the child's problem. Through the use of initial screenings, selective studies, and in-depth case studies, diagnosticians have choices available and can avoid overextension of diagnosis.

3. Abbreviated diagnosis: We often find that abbreviated diagnosis does not investigate a given child's reading problem properly. Insufficient diagnosis is most common in the classroom where lack of time and materials exert constant pressure upon the teacher's efforts. Regardless of the limitations of the classroom situation, the teacher must use all available data to insure that the information obtained is reliable and valid. Through abbreviated diagnosis, it is common to jump to wrong conclusions and, in effect, to waste large amounts of time which would have been saved through a more thorough diagnosis. If diagnosticians include the diagnostic teaching lesson as part of their diagnosis, the chance of an abbreviated diagnosis is lessened, for in a diagnostic lesson unknown factors come to light.

4. Overstepping profession boundaries. There is a tendency for educators to make statements which are beyond the

---

[10]Ruth Strang, *Diagnostic Teaching of Reading* (New York: McGraw Hill Book Co., 1969), p. 8.

professional boundaries of their preparation. The diagnostician must refrain from playing psychiatrist or medical doctor; instead, knowing the signs of referral, he must refer willingly. As in the first pitfall, couching terms in a diagnostic report that goes beyond the field of education will help avoid overstepping professional boundaries. For example, if a telebinocular examination indicates the need for referral, the clinician might write that poor performance on test four of the telebinocular indicates the need for a professional visual examination. That type of statement is more appropriate than one stating that the poor score on the telebinocular indicates visual problems which need professional attention.

5. Unfounded statements of fact: In direct relation to the preceding pitfalls are positive, factual statements made by educators based on evidence which does not justify that strong a statement. The couching of terms to indicate areas of suspicion where more testing may be needed, or areas where referral is necessary will be beneficial to all those who are attempting to arrive at a child's problem. An examiner must be certain that positive statements concerning a child's problem are backed by highly reliable data.

6. Isolation of factors: Isolated pieces of diagnostic data, test scores, and the like must not be examined without consideration for their relationship to the entire diagnosis. It is not unusual for the significance of particular data to be lessened when it is placed in the total picture of a child's reading problem. A single piece of data or a single test score used in isolation is likely to lead to a distorted picture of the child's problem. Even in the classroom, where time and materials are at a premium, this pitfall should be avoided.

7. Previous bias: The examiner must be alert to the possible interference of data which is tainted by bias. Bias is often found in the remarks of parents or teachers and can have a definite effect on the direction the diagnosis may take. To circumvent this effect, the examiner may intentionally avoid the evaluation of data from the parents and teachers until his tentative hypotheses are reached.

SUMMARY

It is through mutual awareness of the specific diagnostic responsibilities of the classroom teacher and the reading specialist that both can perform diagnosis most efficiently. The difference between working with the child in a classroom group and working with a child individually outside the classroom calls for quite different diagnostic responsibilities and approaches. The realization of these differences enables educators to diagnose problem readers effectively.

Following the observation of the child in reading situations or following testing, diagnosis takes the form of questions which are designed to lead the classroom teacher and the reading specialist to adjustments in instruction in terms of the child's needs. The fact that clinical diagnosis goes further than the classroom teacher can go must not deter the teacher from doing what he can for the child in the classroom.

Diagnosis, to be most useful, must be recorded and interpreted accurately to the individuals concerned, whether they are teachers or parents. All diagnosis need not culminate in an in-depth case study. The choices among initial screenings, selective studies, and depth studies places the reading specialist in a flexible diagnostic role.

Finally, diagnosis does not terminate within a given period, but continues as long as an educator is working with the child. The continuous nature of diagnosis enables the educator to determine the precise program which will best help the child toward improved reading.

SUGGESTED READINGS

Betts, Emmett A. *Foundations of Reading Instruction*, pp. 438-85. New York: American Book Company, 1946. In this section of his book, Betts presents in detail the concepts and techniques involved in the conduction and interpretation of informal reading inventories. The student who desires to use this technique should check this source.

Bond, Guy L., and Tinker, Miles A. *Reading Difficulties, Their Diagnosis and Correction*, Chapters 4, 5, 6, and 7. New York: Appleton-Century-Crofts, Inc., 1967. Another of the basic texts which must be considered required reading for those who are involved with the diagnosis of reading problems. The chapters recommended refer particularly to the diagnosis of educational problems.

Buros, Oscar K. *Reading Tests & Reviews*. Highland Park, New Jersey: Gryphon, 1968. Listings of all available reading tests available as of 1968. Most tests receive critical reviews. An essential book for those selecting testing instruments in reading.

Dechant, Emerald. *Diagnosis and Remediation of Reading Disability*. Parker, New York: Prentice-Hall, 1968. Chapters 1, 2, and 3 present an excellent position on the uses of educational diagnosis.

Farr, Roger. *Reading: What Can Be Measured?* Newark, Delaware: International Reading Association, 1967. Chapters 2 and 3 discuss the use and misuse of available testing instruments in reading. Readers are encouraged to study Farr's discussion.

Harris, Albert J. *How To Increase Reading Ability*, 4th Ed. New York: David McKay Co., Inc., 1970. Chapters 7 and 8 present rather interesting discussions of the topics discussed under educational diagnosis. Harris' book is considered required reading by all those seriously interested in the diagnosis of reading problems.

Kolson, Clifford J., and Kaluger, George. *Clinical Aspects of Remedial Reading*. Springfield, Illinois: Charles C. Thomas, 1964. Chapters 3, 4, and 6 discuss diagnosis of reading problems from the most difficult to the not so serious. This book limits itself to clinical diagnosis and would be most interesting to the reading specialist.

Strang, Ruth, *Diagnostic Teaching of Reading*, p. 8. New York: McGraw Hill Book Co., 1964. In Chapters 3 through 7, diagnostic techniques are presented which have application to classroom as well as clinical situations. There are specific suggestions for working with older children in diagnostic situations.

6.

Remediation—A Place to Start

Remediation of reading problems is not, as many believe, based upon mysterious techniques which are impossible for the classroom teacher to understand. Rather, remediation is based upon sound instructional principles focused upon the needs of the children on the basis of careful diagnosis. Since remediation calls for skillful teaching, it is assumed that anyone who works in a remedial program is a skilled teacher who keeps up-to-date by reading and study.

As previously discussed in diagnosis, there is seldom *one* cause of reading problems; therefore, there is seldom one approach to the solution of such problems. On this point, the public has often been led to believe the opposite, thereby causing pressure to be placed upon educators to teach by certain methods. That there is seldom one satisfactory remedial approach, however, in no way justifies using a little of all known teaching techniques; this is called the "shot-gun" approach. Rather, remediation must be in direct response to diagnostic conclusions, necessitating the use of the most suitable educational techniques as solutions to the diagnostic conclusions. These conclusions contain information concerning the child's skill strengths as well as his weaknesses. With this philosophy as a base, the principles of remediation are viewed with reference to the diagnostic findings.

PRINCIPLES OF REMEDIATION

Certain aspects of remediation may be considered principles to guide the educator. The first three principles of remediation apply equally well to both the reading specialist and the classroom teacher. They are to be considered unalterable, for without them the remedial program is likely to be inefficient.

Remediation must guarantee immediate success: In the remedial program, the child's first instruction should culminate in a successful, satisfying experience. In this way, the child who has experienced frequent failure in reading begins the remedial program with the attitude that this educational experience will be both different and rewarding. Without this attitude, the best remedial efforts are often ill-spent. Successful learning situations also are assured by directing activities toward learning experiences which the diagnosis has indicated are the child's strengths and interests. It is generally recommended that all the early lessons be directed toward the child's strengths. As remediation progresses, the percentage of time devoted to strengths is likely to decrease. When the child starts to ask for instruction in the areas of his weaknesses, rapid changes in instructional strategy can take place. However, it is recommended that throughout the entire program, a large portion of every lesson be directed to strengths. If instruction to strengths drops below the 50 percent mark, one should question effectiveness of the program.

Remedial successes must be illustrated to the child: It is not enough that a child be started at the right level and experience a successful situation; for him, successes must be real and must be presented so that he is acutely aware that *he has been successful.* Real successes involve instruction which helps the child become effective. As the child progresses, charts, graphs, word files, and specific teacher-praise comments can be used to illustrate successes. This principle remains in effect during the entire remedial program, for we shall always be interested in accentuating the child's growth and success.

Remediation must provide for transfer to actual reading situations: There will be occasions in a remedial program where isolated drill in various areas will be required; however, drill activities should always come from contextual reading material and should always conclude in contextual reading situations. The overlearning of all skills takes place best in actual reading situations.

Remediation should result in skill development: It is not unusual to hear of remedial programs which are tutorial in nature, implying that the instruction is designed to enable the child to be successful with a given material in a given classroom situation. Although we are interested in the child's success in the classroom, the remedial program should be designed to develop the reading skills in which the child has demonstrated a deficiency, not merely to help him get through tomorrow's class session. The child should not become solely dependent upon remedial sessions for his daily school success. Of course, remediation is likely to affect attitudes as much as it does reading skills. As attitudes toward reading and school improve, teachers can expect to notice changes in daily classroom performances.

Remediation should be flexible: While applying the remedial program prescribed by the diagnosis, the teacher should remain willing to adjust to the occasionally changing needs of the child. For example, his original procedures may be less effective than desired, creating a further need for flexibility. Since diagnostic findings are not completely formulated until after remediation has begun, flexibility is required.

Remediation should be conducted in terms of established goals: Clearly established goals should be developed for each lesson and for the entire remedial program. Instructional goals might best be stated in behavioral terms, indicating the behavior which is expected as a result of the instruction. Goals which reflect attitudinal changes also should be used. Children should be alerted to the daily instructional goals; indeed, we have found it beneficial to involve them in the development of goals.

Remediation involves cooperation: The remedial program is seldom the responsibility of one person. More commonly, it requires an interaction among the reading specialist, classroom teacher, medical personnel, specialists outside the educational field, parents, and school officials. One-man programs, particularly for the severely retarded child, are unnecessarily limiting.

TYPES OF REMEDIATION

Remediation falls into the same three categories as does diagnosis. The reader will find his remedial role more clearly defined as he gains an understanding of each category.

On-the-Spot Remediation

The type of adjustment made daily by a teacher to the needs of his children is on-the-spot remediation. Based upon informal diagnosis, its characteristics are: it is conducted immediately; it is pinpointed to a directly observable reaction to instruction; and it does not involve major adjustments in classroom instruction.

The following examples of on-the-spot remediation illustrate its importance.

1. Following a period of silent reading, the teacher identifies two children who are unable to respond to questions involving literal understanding. The teacher works with those two for a few minutes to clarify their misunderstandings.
2. A child is having difficulty working through a beginning exercise in syllabication involving the identification of the number of syllables in words. The teacher spends a few minutes with him on auditory discrimination of syllables in familiar words.
3. A child has been absent two days. The teacher assigns another child to work with him for several days to assist him when learning becomes confusing.

Such on-the-spot remediation techniques are an integral part of effective teaching. While specific attention will not be given to it in this chapter, many of the suggestions for classroom and clinical remediation will provide insights into on-the-spot remediation. Teachers should use them when they can.

Classroom Remediation

Educational adjustments in the classroom resulting from classroom and/or clinical diagnosis are included in this type of remedial program. Although instruction is directed to the child with an established problem, the child remains in the classroom during remediation and continues to participate in normal classroom activities, although instruction is often individualized. It differs from on-the-spot remediation in that it is a more formal, directed effort.

The following examples of classroom diagnosis illustrate its importance.

1. Three fifth grade children consistently have made spelling errors when attempting to spell words involving consonant blends. The teacher utilizes activities, such as *Speech to Print Phonics,** which stress consonant awareness and lead into activities using consonant blends.
2. A first grade child exhibits consistent patterns of poor concept development. The teacher plans several lessons such as those found in the *Peabody Language Kits** which, though interesting for many children, stress listening and speaking skills to which the target child can respond.
3. After many attempts to remediate on-the-spot, two children fail to respond. The teacher conducts a classroom diagnosis and determines strengths and weaknesses in the area of concern. Instruction follows which permits the children to demonstrate strengths and work toward needs.

Clinical remediation

Clinical remediation involves one of two alternatives: working with the child outside of the classroom environment; or working with the child in the classroom permitting the teacher to observe clinical techniques. Of the two, the latter seems preferable. Clinical remediation assumes small group or individualized instruction, pinpointed to specific skill strengths and weaknesses. As discussed, clinical remediation follows clinical diagnosis and normally is not conducted by the average classroom teacher. Clinical diagnosis is likely to involve other specialists, such as doctors, psychologists, and the like. One should note that clinical diagnostic techniques are not the province of reading specialists alone, but the intensiveness of the work implies treatment by specialists for individual children.

Clinical remediation is viewed by some as involving removing the child from his assigned building and reassigning him to a school designed to handle special cases. Such conditions as brain damage, severe hyperactivity, and severe perceptual disabilities are typical of such schools. Indeed, many such schools do meet the needs and special abilities of such children; however, these schools must not be considered "dumping grounds" for all those who do not "fit." For example, the Learning Center High School in Anne Arundel County, Maryland, meets the needs of severely disabled learners. Children who have rebelled against the system of education are provided learning opportunities designed to their individualized needs and interests. The school's purpose is to assist the child to become a functioning learner. Such a school, were it designed merely to accommodate discarded students, would be difficult to justify.

REMEDIATION — HOW TO BEGIN

While remediation is based on diagnostic findings with special consideration in the skill areas, initial efforts in remediation must concentrate on the child's interest and his sense of worthiness. Specifically, the program should start with highly interesting activities which aim at his diagnosed strengths. We have found the following types of activities highly effective in initial remedial sessions:

> Building model cars and airplanes
> Science experiments followed by language experience stories
> Short field trips in the area of the child's interest followed by language experience stories
> Reading of headlines and picture captions in sports magazines, auto magazines, newspapers, and so on.

No direct attack on the child's weakness is recommended. All of the time is spent working on challenging, but interesting activities which permit the child to demonstrate his strengths. He needs to show the teacher, his parents, and himself that he is a worthwhile learner.

Generally, every effort should be made to avoid materials and instructional activities which are similar to those with which he has met failure. Teacher-made activities and materials from the real world of children his age are preferable.

Most children approach the new remedial situation with a certain amount of fear and hesitation. Many are uncooperative and refuse to try. Others refuse to remove their coats. Still others openly defy attempts at instruction saying, "I can't" or "I don't want to." Therefore, initial instruction must work to develop self-concept and willingness to work prior to any instruction which might further threaten the child.

As attitudes begin to change — and they will — many teachers immediately move to instruction on diagnosed weaknesses. Sudden changes from instruction aimed at strengths to instruction aimed at weaknesses can disrupt the learning severely. While no rules exist, the following suggestions are offered for making the switch tolerable for the child.

Begin and end every lesson with activities that guarantee results (i.e., teaching to strengths).

In an hour session, spend no more than ten minutes on areas of weakness, using strengths to get at weaknesses.

Involve the child in planning his activities. He will start to ask for activities which will get at his diagnosed needs.

Instruct children in small groups and search for ways for each child to succeed in the group every day.

Provide opportunities for extra reinforcement through constant contact with parents and other teachers, emphasizing your approach and stressing the student's successes.

Provide options for the child so that he either can choose or ignore certain activities. Keep notes on his choices and develop more worthwhile activities of the type that he chooses.

Provide rewards for successful work in new areas. Special trips, ice cream cones, notes home, and simple praise (when earned) can make some extra effort on the part of the student worthwhile.

Provide situations in which the child can work with other children as a working partner. At times the other child may have advanced skills with which he can assist his partner. At other times, a child's specific strengths can be used to assist another child who is in all other ways a better reader.

In beginning remediation, success is a necessity. Success and feeling better about one's self are tied to one another. The teacher will feel better about himself too because good teaching is highly enjoyable.

A specific example may be helpful. Children are encouraged to contract with the teacher at the outset of each lesson or each week. The learning activities to be engaged in and the quality of the work to be done are determined by mutual agreement. Some of the work may be teacher-directed; other portions may be self-directed. The child should work at his own pace and should determine the order in which he wants to tackle the various tasks. His only limitation is the availability of the teacher. We use the following type of planning sheet for contract development.

Activity† 　　Study all your sight words 　　with _____	Activity† 　　Read your last experience 　　story to the teacher.
Activity† 　　Play consonant game with 　　_____	Activity 　　Helper
Activity 　　Silent Reading	Activity
Activity	Activity

†Required

The use of the contract sheet is as follows:

1. Required activities are those which the teacher feels must be accomplished within the time allotted.
2. The quality and quantity of the work is written in the box.
3. The small box is checked by the child when the work is completed. Younger children might place a ⌣ or a ⌢ in the box to indicate how they feel about their work. Others may place an S for Satisfactory or a U for Unsatisfactory in an effort to self-evaluate their work.
4. Blanks and blank boxes are filled in from the contract session. Such selection allows the child to determine much of what he is to do. Note: A contract means both the child and teacher have negotiation possibilities.
5. When the sheet is finished, more work is *not* assigned in the time period. The pay-off for getting done must not be more work.

In this book, the emphasis will be on doing away with un-needed labels and the inferences which go with them. Instead, diagnose for strengths and adjust programs so that all children can profit from reading instruction. With culturally different children, accept and challenge may be a most useful philosophy.

SUMMARY

It should be remembered that the teacher's first responsibility is to educate all of the children in his classroom as effectively as possible, reading problems notwithstanding. He most effectively fulfills this responsibility by: examining observable symptoms; evaluating the child's difficulty through this pattern of symptoms; adjusting the educational climate; and considering the possibility of referral. In contrast, the reading specialist's first responsibility is to upgrade the effectiveness of the reading instruction of all the children through diagnosis of reading problems within and among the various classrooms. Furthermore, he is responsible for the accurate diagnosis of seriously retarded readers. Herein lies the basic difference between diagnosis using a pattern of symptoms and more thorough diagnosis for causation, both of which are acceptable and proper when dealing with problem readers in the schools.

SUGGESTED READINGS

Bond, Guy L. and Tinker, Miles A. *Reading Difficulties, Their Diagnosis and Correction.* New York: Appleton-Century-Crofts, Inc. 1967. The reader will find Chapter 4, "General Nature of Reading Disability," of particular benefit under this topic; it is quite thorough.

Harris, Albert J. *How To Increase Reading Ability.* New York: David McKay Co., 1970. Chapter 5 (III) provides a broad outlook to supplement students' reading under this topic. The more inexperienced reader will want to examine this reference closely.

Strang, Ruth. *Diagnostic Teaching of Reading.* New York: McGraw Hill Book Co., 1969. Chapter 2, "The Role of the Teacher in Diagnosis," is an excellent discussion of diagnosis in the classroom. The student will find this a handy reference for both this and the following chapter.

Waetjen, Walter R. and Leeper, Robert R., ed. *Learning and Mental Health in the School*. Washington, D.C.: ASCD, 1966. Several chapters by diffierent authors illustrate the necessity for consideration of a theory behind your instructional strategies. Of particular value to the Accept and Challenge motto are the writings of Syngg.

Introduction to Diagnosis

Regardless of the educator's professional position (i.e., classroom teacher or reading specialist), diagnosis is essential to good teaching. Diagnosis implies that the educator will actively search for clues to assist in evaluating the present state of the child's skill development and the developmental history of the child's attitudes and habits toward reading and learning.

Strang has developed a model to use in explaining the reading process. This model clarifies the role of diagnosis in instructional situations.

o = the child or children being taught.
s = the learning situations into which these children are placed.
R = the responses of these children to the learning situation.
T = the impressions or traces from the response left upon the nervous system.

---

[1]Ruth Strang, *Invitational Addresses* — 1965 (Newark, Delaware: International Reading Association, 1965).

P = the perceptions which develop as a result of many such experiences.

That a child and his perceptions cannot be separated illustrates the cyclic nature of the learning process. Teachers can teach better when they have information about previously developed perceptions. They should attend to responses during and after the learning situation for effective diagnostic teaching. Therefore, diagnosis can take place prior to instruction, at the o level, to assist the teacher in the selection of the learning situation, s. Also, it can take place at the response level, R, where the teacher can evaluate the effectiveness of the learning situation which was developed for the children.

The classroom teacher should enter diagnosis with as much accuracy and confidence as possible. The day is past when the diagnosis of reading problems could afford the aura of mystery which once surrounded it. Since diagnosis is most useful if the person conducting it also interprets the results and institutes the instructional adjustments, teachers must become skilled at diagnostic teaching. The failure of teachers to develop these skills may be attributed to three myths which have developed about diagnosis.

1. Diagnosis requires the use of specially designed tests. On the contrary, the best diagnostic procedures rely upon observing the child in the learning situation. When tests are called for, many of the single purpose tests, either commercial or teacher-constructed, are the most worthwhile.

2. Diagnosis requires a highly specialized, well-trained person. As in all educational areas, there are levels of competency. Some diagnosticians are highly competent and well trained. However, every teacher who is willing to adjust instruction for his students can use diagnostic teaching procedures. These procedures are not reserved for specialists; most teachers use them regularly. They can be improved with but a little effort and knowledge. Therefore, one function of the reading specialist in today's schools should be assisting teachers to become effective diagnostic teachers.

3. Diagnosis calls for a case-study write-up. College and university reading training programs traditionally have included case development in their programs. While case development is an extremely useful educational experience, diagnosis does

$$(\frac{140}{100} \times 2.0) + 1.0 = 3.8$$

Their research shows that this formula is much more realistic than formulas using mental age, such as that mentioned above.[11] In using this formula, consideration must be given to three factors. First, it must be understood that the term "years in school" does not mean the child's grade placement, but rather, the actual number of years that he has attended school. Therefore, for a child who has a grade placement of 4.8 and who has not accelerated or repeated a grade, the appropriate entry would be 3.8 for "years in school." (For this formula, kindergarten does not count as a year in school.) Second, the teacher must have accurate data concerning the grades repeated or accelerated. Third, the examiner should understand that the addition of 1.0 years in the formula is to compensate for the manner in which grade norms are assigned to tests, 1.0 being the zero month of first grade. Despite its obvious advantages, most teachers, lacking complete understanding of it, refrain from using this formula.

Cleland[12] prefers to average four factors, giving equal weight to each, in arriving at a reading potential score which is compared to reading achievement. In this formula, he computes the grade equivalents of chronological age, mental age, arithmetic computation, and the Durrell-Sullivan Reading Capacity Test:

$$
\begin{aligned}
\text{C.A.} - 5 &= 6\text{--}5 &&= 1.0 \\
\text{M.A.} - 5 &= 8.4\text{--}5 &&= 3.4 \\
\text{Arith. C.} & &&= 1.5 \\
\text{D/S Cap.} & &&= 2.5 \\
& && \overline{8.4} \div 4 = 2.1
\end{aligned}
$$

This formula has several advantages: first, although mental age is used without the compensation that Bond and Tinker give, it is equalized somewhat by the use of chronological age; second, the use of reading capacity adds auding as a factor (we have used the Peabody auding age as a substitute for the Durrell-Sullivan); and, third, the use of arithmetic computation provides measures of the child's ability to do nonverbal school work. It is important to note that grade equivalents of M.A. and C.A. are obtained by subtracting 5,

---

[11]Bond and Tinker, *Reading Difficulties*, p. 94.

[12]Donald L. Cleland, "Clinical Materials for Appraising Disabilities in Reading," *The Reading Teacher*, XVII (March 1964), p. 428.

for the 5 years the child did not attend school. (Harris recommends subtracting 5.2). This formula, or variations of it, is commonly used in clinical diagnosis. We find that it compares much more favorably to the Bond and Tinker formula than to the mental age formula and is preferable to either of these for a precise clinical diagnosis.

To compare the child's score on a test of auding with his achievement test performance is another relatively easy way of determining the degree of retardation. In this case, the auding score is an estimate of reading potential and may be obtained from tests such as the *Peabody Picture Vocabulary Test* and the *Botel Listening Test*. On the Peabody, the auding age equivalent may be converted to grade equivalent by subtracting 5 years.

The classroom teacher in his diagnosis will first use symptoms observed in the classroom to determine which children appear to have the potential to read better. In comparing the child's reading achievement with observable estimates of the child's potential, he will have made the initial identification of the child in need of diagnosis.

How large the difference between reading potential and achievement must be to be considered serious will vary with the grade placement of the child. There may be many children who fall slightly short of full reading potential, yet would not be considered problem readers. In fact, it is rare for children to reach their full potential. Older children can manage a larger variance between potential and achievement without the severe ramifications that occur with younger children.

The scale in Table 2 may be useful in selecting a cut-off point between a tolerable difference and one that is sufficient to interfere with the child's progress in reading and other subjects. Tolerable differences are presented in this table by individual grade level in Column 1 and by groupings for primary, intermediate, and junior and senior high school levels in Column 2. A child in the primary grades retarded .9 of a year has exceeded the minimum tolerable difference, while a child in an intermediate grade with this same difference has not exceeded his tolerable difference. Although this scale should not be adhered to rigidly, it does provide reasonably useful limits. However, since diagnosis includes considerably more analysis than the estimation of potential and achievement, it would be folly indeed for the educator to evaluate a child's progress in reading by this technique alone.

TABLE 2

Degree of Tolerable Difference Between
Potential and Achievement

End of:	1	2
1st grade	— .3)	
2nd grade	— .5)	.5 of a year
3rd grade	— .7)	
4th grade	— .8)	
5th grade	—1.0)	1 year
6th grade	—1.2)	
7th grade	—1.3)	
8th grade	—1.5)	1.5 years
9th grade	—1.7)	
10th grade	—1.8)	
11th grade	—2.0)	2 years
12th grade	—2.2)	

†Tolerable difference ranges must be used as judgment points, not as absolutes.

When selecting the method for computing the degree of reading retardation, the following factors should be considered:

1. The number and type of children selected as retarded in reading will vary with the method employed.
2. Each method is only as good as the instruments used to obtain the scores for its computation.
3. A child with a specific skill deficiency may not be discovered by these types of formulas.
4. The ultimate selection of a method in reality may have more to do with availability of the data required than the inherent values of the system.
5. The confidence that a given examiner has found in the method and materials used has much to do with his ultimate selection. The examiner, after weighing the above factors, employs that method best suited to his situation.

The educator is encouraged to view scores from intelligence scales as indicators of potential for reading. Although intelligence per se is not to be considered the cause of a child's reading problem, assessment of intelligence remains basic to the diagnosis of reading problems to identify properly those who will profit most from a program of correction. The classroom teacher is encouraged to use techniques available to him to make estimates of reading potential, allowing the reading specialist or appropriate psychological personnel to make more precise identifications. An understanding of the limitations and advantages of the measures of intelligence will greatly enhance the educator's use of the resulting scores.

As valuable as the use of intelligence test scores may be for determining the reading potential of children, such data can easily be abused. When children are admitted or rejected from reading programs on the basis of their reading potential, an important factor can easily be overlooked, i.e., the ability of the classroom teacher to plan an effective program for a child. Perhaps the most valid criterion for screening those who need help is whether or not a teacher feels he can help a child. If he cannot help, efforts should be made either to help a teacher with educational adjustment or to help a child directly. Reading specialists who attempt to duck a responsibility of this nature are subject to criticism from teachers as well as from parents. When reading specialists are overworked and assigned to too large a student population, the screening of children according to potential becomes more frequent. And, while the problem of the reading specialists is easily understood, they should not curtail their efforts to obtain help for all children who need it. Again, the right of every child to the best educational opportunities which we can provide should not rest on his performance on an intelligence test.

PHYSICAL DIAGNOSIS

A physical limitation is considered a cause of a reading problem when it interferes with a child's potential and his performance. If a child cannot see a printed page adequately, he cannot be expected to read it as well as his potential indicates he should. Whose job is it to assess the severity of physical disability? Although physical limitations are recognized first in a classroom or clinical diagnosis, medical personnel or other specialists are responsible for specific identification, corrective measures, and recommendations. Both the

6. The child works with the activities in the order of his choice. Some children choose to do the least desirable work first; others save it for last.

7. The completed contract is returned to the teacher, and both the teacher and the child evaluate the quality of the work.

8. Occasionally, completion of the contract results in a bonus-type pay-off (e.g., a letter home, a special privilege, a prize, and the like).

9. Contracts completed are saved and become instruments for final evaluation of the child's progress; they are especially useful for parental conferences.

· Pupil and Teacher Plan Daily Work via Contracting

Getting Everyone Involved:

Many teachers lose opportunities to involve people who want to help the child but do not know how. Generally, the desire to help will result in some kind of attention — often negative — being paid to the goals and philosophy of the reading teacher. The answer to such a situation is to involve parents, other teachers, and the child's peers whenever it is possible and from the outset of the program.

Other teachers can reinforce strengths which the specialist knows will work with a given child. They can assist in reinforcement activities and make the work the child is doing with the specialist relevant to his total school day.

Parents, when informed, can also reinforce the work. They can ask the child to do tasks which they are told he can do well. They can develop pride in the child's accomplishments if the specialist will help them look in the correct directions. They can provide rewards and praise when they know the proper time to do so.

Peers can work with a given child by teaming with him on activities which he cannot do by himself. They can also conduct some of the time-consuming, drill-type activities; they too can profit from the child's strengths. For example, the author worked with a boy who always was the poorest in every activity. He always saw himself as a follower, never as a leader. As a field trip approached, he was taken on a "dry-run" to familiarize him with the features of the field trip. He became excited and served as a group leader on the actual field trip. The other children appreciated his leadership and assistance. By getting everyone involved, the teacher can change a child's life from one of failure and frustration to one of success and excitement about living.

SUMMARY

Once the classroom teacher or the reading specialist has the principles of remediation well in mind, he must formulate a remedial program. Once rapport has been established by working with the child in the area of his strengths, the remedial program will attempt to eliminate the child's skill weaknesses that have been indicated by the diagnosis.

SUGGESTED READINGS

Dechant, Emerald. *Diagnosis & Remediation of Reading Disabilities.* (West Nyack, New York: Parker Publishing Co., 1968), Chapter 4. Discusses the need for organization and implementation following a diagnosis. The reader will find the information useful and supplementary to the chapter just read.

Gates, Arthur I. *The Improvement of Reading.* (New York: The Macmillan Co., 1947). Gates devotes Chapter 5 to the establishment of a remedial program. The reader who desires more information will find this a suitable reference.

Kaluger, George, and Kolson, Clifford J. *Reading & Learning Disabilities.* (Columbus, Ohio: Charles E. Merrill Publishing Co., 1969). In Chapter 8 the authors suggest techniques for starting a child in a remedial program. With an approach differing from those suggested in this chapter, the authors explain the necessity for establishing rapport.

7

Remedial Activities in Readiness Skills

Because remediation of readiness skills is developmental in nature, children who lack the necessary readiness skills should be provided with experiences similar to those used in initial instruction in these areas. Classroom and clinical techniques should not be differentiated since the techniques used are the same. Clinical remediation, however, is likely to be more personalized and possibly more intensified.

Remedial suggestions are offered in the following chapter for each of the readiness skill areas (i.e., language, auditory discrimination, visual discrimination, and orientation skills). In all remediation, attention must be given to the skill activities which the child can demonstrate as strengths.

LANGUAGE

Language difficulties can result from three different causes: the language of the child does not match the language of the school; it is underdeveloped due to a limited experiential language background; or it reflects limited intellectual development. In discussions about language teaching, many writers tend to confuse these three causes and treat them similarly. The following suggestions will be discussed under the specific headings suggested above.

Language Mismatching

Children whose language differs from that used in school and in the materials of instruction are often found in remedial reading classes. Their difficulty lies in attempting to learn to read a language which is different from the one they speak. How seriously the problem of mismatching effects reading ability is uncertain; however, one might safely assume that it causes a degree of discomfort which, when coupled with other learning difficulties, can interfere with learning to read easily. On the other hand, of course, many children with mismatched language do learn to read effectively.

Instruction for these children must start with acceptance of their language by the teacher. Genuine respect for the language which all children bring to school is extremely important. Attacks and criticisms of one's language is personally intolerable, for such techniques attack not only the child but his family and his friends. Specifically, the teacher should demonstrate acceptance by:

Responding to the language without initial correction.
Responding to the child's thoughts with enthusiasm regardless of his language form.
Not repeating the child's response in a correcting effort.
Permitting the child to write his language without correction.
Using his own language. He should not try to mock or imitate the child's language.

The premise upon which such suggestions are based is that anyone can work better and faster with a child who feels comfortable and accepted. However, teachers demonstrate considerable concern about these techniques because they feel that they are responsible for improving a child's language. But the concept of "improving" in itself implies nonacceptance. The teacher must recognize the child's language as being good for him and acceptable for his purposes.[1] The teacher also can help a child to become aware of other language forms in addition to those more commonly used in school. Most importantly, we want the child to feel accepted so that he is affectively ready to receive further instruction. Specifically, the following instruction techniques are advised:

---

[1]Kenneth S. Goodman, "Dialect Rejection and Reading," *Reading Research Quarterly* (Summer 1970), p. 603.

1. When using prepared materials, accept the child's use of dialect. If the sentence is "I see two dogs," and the child says, "I see two dog," accept it without correction. By so doing, meaning is being stressed and language is accepted.

2. Use language experience stories which the child can dictate to you (see page 186 for specifics on the use of language experience.). In writing the child's contributions, be certain to spell words accurately (e.g., if he says, "da dog," write, "the dog"). Again, as the child reads the story aloud, he will probably say, "da dawg" and that should be considered acceptable. However, teachers should not change the child's syntax (e.g., if the child says, "I ain't got none," it should be written as he says it). To change his contribution to "I don't have any" is a correction and denies the principle of acceptance.

3. Structure numerous opportunities for the child to hear and to respond to language which is commonly found in books and is used in other segments of our society through the following methods:

   a. Read to him. Read every day. Read good literature. Talk with him about what you have read. Let him discuss it with you.

   b. Always serve as a model for the child. Enunciate precisely and use standard English forms. Teach the child to respond to your language. Use of tape recorders to provide stories and directions for activities can provide even more model opportunities.

   c. Provide structured lessons to develop the child's ability to use the language he will find elsewhere in society and particularly in school. Feigenbaum suggests the following three steps:[2]

      Auditory discrimination: Help the child to hear differences in language form: Take one type of difference (negation, for example) and say, "Tell me whether these two sentences sound exactly alike or different: 1. I ain't gone none. 2. I don't have any." As the child

---

[2]Irwin Feigenbaum, "The Use of Nonstandard English in Teaching Standard: Contrast and Comparison," in *Teaching Standard English in the Inner City* (Washington, D. C.: Center for Applied Linguistics, 1970), pp. 87-104.

develops auditory discrimination skills between his language and school language, move to step two.

Identification of school language: From the two sentences, help the child to pick the one he is most likely to hear the teacher use or to read in books. Auditory awareness of school language is not difficult to develop but is not to be assumed merely from the ability to discriminate auditorily.

Dialect transfer: Say one sentence and have the child respond in the other language. Such transfer should be practiced both ways (i.e., from his home language to school language and the reverse). For example, the teacher says, "I ain't got none," and the child attempts to put the expression into school language. Then the teacher uses school language, and the child responds in his language. When conducting structured lessons, the teacher should start with a structure common to the child's language and stay with one structure until dialect transfer is mastered before selecting another. All lessons must be conducted without reference to right and wrong or good and bad.

Once dialect transfer is mastered, the teacher should encourage the child to use school language as he responds in school but should not encourage him to use it in his informal conversations at play or at home. As children with language mismatch problems gain skill in dialect transfer, instruction with materials using school language can be used without fear of difficulty.

Underdeveloped Language

Children who come to school seriously deficient in experiences simply do not have the conceptual framework to work effectively in reading. Children from isolated rural poverty areas and those from severe poverty areas in large cities might be considered as representing these types of children. In the following discussion, it is assumed that this type of child lacks experiences but not mental ability. He may appear to be dull because he fails to understand situations which are comprehended commonly. He may not know about mountains, lakes, automobiles, airplanes, television, and so on. The school is obligated to provide instruction which will equip such a child to utilize his potential. Specific educational adjustments include:

1. Emphasis on the creation of language experiences. Everything that happens during the school day is discussed. Linking language directly to the experiences of children helps them to develop concepts for the things they are encountering. Trips, pictures, films, and tapes can be used in the development of language experiences. Activities within the classroom, special programs in the school, and visitors in the classroom also stimulate language. Every experience must be discussed, for language should be a constant part of the experience. For example, it is not enough for a class to make a trip to the zoo. The children should talk about what they are experiencing, and the teacher should bombard them with language explanations of what they are experiencing.

2. Starting with the language experience approach. As it does for children with different dialects, the language experience approach assures a successful start in reading since the language concepts a child encounters are those he has suggested.

3. Employment of available commercial programs. Several companies have commercial programs designed to facilitate language development.** Most of these programs involve stimulation with pictures, tapes, or films. Teachers are directed to help children explain what they are seeing or hearing. Vocabulary is developed as children listen to each other and to the teacher. Synonym and antonym activities also stretch the child's conceptual framework.

4. Continuous language exposure. Activities which permit children to talk with one another and to listen to the teacher make language improvement possible. Activities such as role playing in which children are encouraged to act out roles of story characters or persons whom they admire stimulate children to talk with each other. A telephone corner with toy phones can be used to stimulate talking. Perhaps an older buddy can come to the room to talk with a child about an exciting experience. Activities that stimulate one-to-one conversations are needed in abudance for many children with underdeveloped language backgrounds. Activities through

which the teacher can encourage children to talk include: a
question chair placed close to the teacher's work area (a child
with a question comes to the chair, and the teacher talks
with him); simple repetition games which call for the child
to repeat what the teacher has said; and eating lunch and
chatting with one or two children every day. Activities such
as these place value on language as communication and ex-
pose children to modeled language. However, since reading
is *not* withheld until large vocabularies are developed, it is
important to remember that the language bombardment
concept must continue for several years.

Intellectual Development

There are some children who have language problems which stem
from slow intellectual development. They may be six years old but
have slowed intellectual development so that they react to language
like four year olds. Many of these children have compounding problems, such as poor motor coordination or physical defects. Although
many find their way into programs for the mentally retarded, many
others are in the classroom and teachers must learn how to work
with them.

As a first suggestion, every teacher is encouraged to look at
each child as a developmental human who is as much as he can be.
Therefore, the teacher should work with him from where he is in
his development. Accept him. Categorizing him through name calling or special grouping does not indicate acceptance and is of limited
value. At the same time, expectations in terms of rate of learning,
quantity of learning, and retention ability should be realistic. Programs must be adjusted for these children in order to utilize their
strengths. Patience and many rewards for successful performances
should be predominant. Successes must be highlighted, and failures
must be minimized or ignored.

Regardless of the type of language deficiency, the child's education must continue. No excuses, no "cop-outs." Starting points
must be identified and progress should be documented. The teacher
should keep in mind that all children can learn and that all can
profit from reading programs if the programs are adjusted to their
strengths.

The classifications for language deficiencies suggested in this
chapter are not as clear-cut as they might seem. Many children

might be handicapped by two or by all three types of language limitations. But these children can and must learn. Educators cannot use language development as an excuse for not teaching; students cannot use it as an excuse for not learning.

The developmental nature of language is obvious. That these children have language indicates that they have developed their language to some degree. Schools simply must start with what the children have, make them feel comfortable, illustrate to them that learning is possible and fun, and be pleased with whatever successes occur.

In each instance, the use of the language experience approach as a technique for initial reading instruction holds considerable merit. Any teacher who plans to work with children who have language limitations *must* be skilled in the use of the language experience approach.

AUDITORY DIFFICULTIES

Numerous children enter school without the necessary auditory skills to profit from normal instruction. When ignored by the teacher, these auditory skills can remain undeveloped, thus causing considerable discomfort to the struggling reader. For this discussion on remediation, auditory skills will be classified in two general areas: hearing problems and auditory discrimination problems.

Hearing Problems

While the teacher can do nothing to correct hearing problems aside from referring the child to a hearing specialist, he can make temporary classroom adjustments to facilitate a comfortable learning situation for the child.

1. He can arrange the child's seating so that he is close to the teacher during group instruction. The child's better ear should be toward the group, his poorer toward the wall.
2. The teacher should stand close to the child's desk during group instruction and should increase his volume so that the child with a hearing problem can hear the instructions. He can also face the child, thereby providing opportunity for lip reading.

3. Creating a buddy system for a child with a hearing problem is helpful. When the child does not hear the teacher or the other children, his buddy can repeat the information and help him to understand it.
4. When possible, visual learning activities (i.e., reading instead of listening) should be stressed. Instruction for independent work should be written, as should rules, regulations and announcements. The writing can be on the board, on chart paper, or in personal notes to the child with the hearing problem.

The child who comes to school with hearing problems can learn and should be put in learning situations which permit him to function as comfortably as possible.

Auditory Discrimination

It is not uncommon to find school children with normal hearing skills but underdeveloped auditory discrimination skills. These children have difficulty distinguishing one sound from another. Their difficulty is likely to be easily recognized by one of the following symptoms: speech impairment or difficulty with phonics. That children come to school with most speech skills developed would lead one to believe that their auditory discrimination skills are also developed. However, for those with underdeveloped articulation skills and for those who are not in the habit of listening carefully, the following suggestions can be of value.

1. Request the assistance of a speech therapist who either will work with the child, help the teacher to diagnose the child's difficulty, or offer suggestions for classroom adjustments.
2. Serve as a speech model for the child. Enunciate distinctly and read to the child with articulate speech patterns.
3. Provide exercises which stress gross auditory differences. For example:

> Tell me whether the words which I repeat are the same or different:
>
> catch   —   catch
> big   —   dog
> many   —   some
>
> Tell me whether the first sound you hear in the words which I repeat are the same or different:

big	—	big
butter	—	lettuce
boy	—	sail

4. Gradually provide exercises involving finer auditory discriminations. For example:

Tell me whether the words which I repeat are the same or different:

catch	—	catch
corn	—	scorn
can	—	tan

Tell me whether the first sound you hear in the following words is the same or different:

big	—	pig
bite	—	tight
best	—	best

5. Provide exercises which demand longer auditory memory. For example:

Listen to the first word which I give you. Then tell me whether the following words are the same word or different:

pig: pig — small — big — pig — dig

Listen to the first sound in the word I give you. Then tell me which of the following words have the same beginning sound:

pig: bite — pick — pencil — dig — picnic

6. Provide exercises which call for listening for sounds in different parts of the word. For example:

Listen for words which end in the same sound as the word *pig*.

dig: ditch — park — twig — dog

7. Provide exercises which indicate the ability to hear rhyming words. For example:

Listen to the first word I give you, and tell me whether the following words rhyme with that word:

cat: rat — sat — pot — pat

8. Provide a stimulus word and ask the child to say some
words which rhyme.

cat: _____   _____   _____   _____   _____

Techniques for conducting drill lessons such as those suggested
above can include: placing items on tape and having children do
the exercises independently; having an aide or a skilled child read
what you have prepared; calling the children who need such work
to your desk while the others are working independently. The point
is that the children need daily practice to assist them in the development of the auditory discrimination skills. As the skills are
mastered, periodic review is necessary. It is also necessary to review
the skills prior to the development of phonics lessons.

Auditory discrimination skills are easily developed. Skills
which have been taught can be reinforced through game activities
(see Russell[3] and Heilman[4]).

VISUAL DIFFICULTIES

As is true of auditory problems, visual problems also can be
grouped into two categories: those dealing with the skills and
functions of vision and those dealing with visual discrimination.
Numerous children find giving visual attention difficult either as the
result of a physical disability or of a developmental lag.

Problems in Vision

A child's visual problems can be adjusted and corrected by visual
specialists. The teacher, in the meantime, must work with the
child daily. Several suggestions are offered for helping children
with vision problems:

1. Arrange seating so that the child has the best light, the
least glare, and the optimum distance for his difficulty. A
far-sighted child can sit in the back of the instructional
area and a near-sighted child can sit in the front.

---

[3]David Russell and Etta E. Karp, *Reading Aids Through the Grades* and
Listening Aids Through the Grades (New York: Teachers College, Columbia
University, 1951).

[4]Arthur Heilman, *Phonics We Use. Learning Games Kit* (Chicago: Lyons
and Carnahan, 1968).

2. Supplement writing on the board or on chart paper by providing auditory reinforcement (i.e., he simply reads what he
   has written). Also, increase the size of his writing on the
   board, making it as heavy and bold as possible.
3. Use the buddy system. By working with a child who has
   normal sight, a child with visual difficulties can seek help
   when his vision keeps him from getting needed material.
4. Stress auditory learning. A child with visual problems might
   respond better to a phonetic approach or at least to sound
   reinforcement. Tracing also helps, for it develops within the
   child opportunities for reinforcing his weak visual skills.
5. Make visual activity periods of short duration. As a child
   shows signs of discomfort (e.g., rubbing of eyes and inattentiveness), he should be released from the visual tasks involved in reading.

Adjustments such as those suggested above are not the answer
to the child's basic problem but are adjustments which can make
learning both possible and comfortable for a child who usually is
expected to perform under normal, competitive situations.

Visual Discrimination

Difficulties with visual discrimination skills are usually the result
of either a lack of experiences or a failure to attend to the task. In
either case, it is obvious that successful experience can develop comfort in visual discrimination skills. The following suggestions can
be of value in developing visual discrimination skills.

1. Start with the language of the child. As he talks, write down
   what he says. Visual discrimination drill exercises will evolve
   from material which has meaning for him and which he
   would like to be able to read. For example, if the child
   wanted to talk about what he saw on his way to school, the
   following story might develop:

   I saw a big dog.
   His name was Rex.
   The dog frightened many of us.
   But I picked up a stick and scared the dog.
   Everyone thinks I am very brave.
   Do you?

Once the story is written, two copies are prepared, one to work on and one to save for reading. The following are visual discrimination activities which can be done on the copy which the child can mark; this copy ultimately either will be placed in his folder or destroyed.

a. Ask the child to pick a word which he knows. Write the word on a card then have him find it in the story. He does not need to say the word (although he might as well), but he does have to match it.

b. Write the letter S on a card and ask the child to underline that letter every time he sees it in the story.

c. Ask the child to circle all the words that begin with the letter A. (Give him an A card.)

d. Write a phrase on a card. Have the child find it in the story and draw two lines under it.

e. Ask the child to draw a box around every word that ends with the letter E. (Give the child an E card.)

From story copy which has been duplicated have the child cut out words and phrases and match them with the story on chart paper. Such an activity enhances transfer from activities at the board to activities at his seat. Depending upon the story, there are many visual discrimination activities which can help children to develop the required skills. Matching, seeing letters in words, finding letters in specific parts of words, and finding groups of words in a certain order are but a few examples. By asking the child to do something different in each activity (i.e., underlining, circling, drawing a box, and so on), the teacher can see easily how well the child has done. A major advantage of working with a story for visual discrimination is that you are asking the child to perform the types of tasks he will do when he reads. Therefore, transfer possibilities seem to be enhanced. As is true with auditory discrimination, start with gross discriminations and move to fine discriminations. For example, beginning with the letter S is easier than starting with D. Finding a word is easier than finding a letter, although finding a letter or a group of letters in a certain position in a word is even more difficult. Discover where the child is in the development of his abilities and work from there. It is also important to give a stimulus with which the child is to work visually. Auditory reinforcements are fine, but the activities must be visual to visual (i.e., the child sees a word on a card and matches it with a word on the board).

2. The child's word cards (i.e., cards on which he has written words he has mastered) can be used to develop visual discrimination skills. For example:

   a. Find all the words that end in *e*, like at*e*.
   b. Find all the words in your file which end in *ing*, like walk*ing*.
   c. Find all the words that have double consonants, like te*ll*.

   The suggestions for such activities could be endless, but two points about them are important. One, you are working with visual clues and from words which the child knows, and two, through teaching from strengths, children can develop strong visual discrimination skills.

3. Provide an area in the room where several magazines are collected. Instruct the child to look through the magazine ads for examples of certain kinds of words (e.g., words about people, words which describe things, etc.). Provide a visual stimulus, a pair of scissors, some paste, and a place to post his findings. Checking is simple; look at his product. Two or three children working together on such a reinforcement activity can check the others' work.

4. Game-type activities hold considerable merit in developing visual discrimination, just as they do in developing auditory discrimination. Suggestions can be found in Russell[5] and prepared games are available from sources such as Heilman.** For example, give the children a set of cards with letters on them. Start with a small group of letters, such as *S*, *T*, and *W*. Hold up a letter and have the children hold up the same letter. Then hold up two letters and have the children hold up the same two letters in the same sequence. Such an activity gradually can be increased in difficulty, thus developing the attention to detail and visual discrimination skills needed for reading. Once the game idea is developed, students can play the game without direct teacher supervision.

---

[5]Russell and Karp, *Reading Aids Through the Grades.*

5. Commercially prepared materials are available in several forms. Workbook-type activities, spirit duplication master sheets, and pencil-paper activities are common. Many such activities start with form identification. For example, five balls are placed on a sheet; four of them are green and one is red. The child is to mark the one that is different. However, such activities, in our opinion, should be reserved for only the most severely handicapped and even then seem to be of questionable value in the reading process. Several of the more popular commercial materials are listed in Appendix B. Our finding is that teachers themselves can make materials which are more relevant and more related to the reading process with relatively small committments of time and energy. We also have found that children respond very well to such "homemade" materials.

While making materials for children to use in visual discrimination activities, several precautions are necessary:

1. Printing should be done very carefully; however, typing is preferred.
2. Only printing should be used on working copies. These copies should contain no art work, pictures, or other types of distractions.
3. At first, small amounts of print should be used on a page. Do not smother the child with too many words and sentences.
4. Make activities short and, if possible, self-correcting. Provide answer keys or models of marked copies.
5. Make the print of beginning activities look like that which the child is accustomed to seeing. For very young children, each new sentence should start a new line. With older children, material can appear in paragraph form. To make the material too much like a pre-primer is insulting to older children.
6. Always end the activity with a reading of the story. If the children cannot read it, read it to them. Always bring the activity back around to reading for thought. Discuss the story and its meanings with the children.

7. When the child does well, tell him that he has. Praise for legitimate successes is important in all drill work, but do not praise incomplete or inaccurate work. Instead restructure the activity so that the child can complete it and then praise him.

Continue with visual discrimination activities as the child begins to read. Review as well as more advanced activities should be part of the child's visual discrimination program until he is operating with comfort.

ORIENTATION

Orientation difficulties are reflected by an inability to follow visually the print in words or sentences. Orientation skills are commonly listed under visual discrimination; however, difficulties in this area seem to be peculiar enough to justify separate classification. As has been stated, visual discrimination skills are related to seeing likenesses and differences, while orientation skills are concerned with the left-to-right controlled visual movements necessary for effective reading.

It is generally acknowledged that children's orientation errors cannot be corrected by simply calling the errors to their attention. Remedial procedures in the area of orientation skills are most effective when they help the child to feel the comfort and success that accompanies correct orientation and when they provide practice to extend the skill into a habit.

Four specific questions were asked in the discussion of the diagnosis of orientation problems in Chapter 4. The framework of remediation will involve dealing with those four questions in terms of instruction.

1. Does the child exhibit visual difficulty in following the print from left-to-right?
2. Are the errors basically habitual reversals?
3. Are words habitually omitted without destroying context?
4. Does the child habitually lose his place?

The reader will recall that the symptoms suggested by these four questions are closely related at times for they all pertain to directional attack on the printed page. As a result, remedial techniques are often quite similar. However, we have differentiated these areas in an effort to make remediation as precise as possible.

The failure to move left-to-right.   This is a problem that normally can be traced to a faulty habit and, therefore, is usually alleviated by concentrated practice to correct the habit. Many suggestions for improved left-to-right movement across the printed page are available in the manuals of the basal readers. The following specific suggestions have worked well with children who need more practice than that suggested in these manuals:

1. Utilize opportunities for writing experience. It is through writing that a child can clearly see the necessity of the left-to-right formation of words across the line. The child should observe the teacher as he writes on the board, and those children who are able to write should be given every opportunity to do so.
2. Illustrate that sentences involve a left-to-right progression of words. An initial approach would be to have the child reproduce sentences containing his own sight words, thereby actively involving him in developing effective left-to-right sequence. An understanding of this concept is demonstrated when the child is able to create his own sentences from his resource of sight words. The Rolling Readers,** which present basic sight words in a game-like situation, are readily adaptable to this technique.
3. Have the child point to words as he reads. In this respect, the finger is used as a crutch until the *habit* of left-to-right eye movements can be developed more fully.
4. Utilize choral reading activities. A dividend added to the obvious advantages of choral reading is the child's opportunity to experience in a group a feeling for the flow of words from left-to-right. Reading orally in unison with the teacher or with another child or two also is helpful in the same way. There should be one good model of oral reading in the group. Sentences from experience stories can be cut into word cards and reassembled to match the original sentence.
5. The Michigan Tracking** program has been useful in working with children who come to us with severe orientation problems. These materials are constructed to teach the child

1. **The man walked.**

She This The Them
me may mad man
talked waked walked walled

2. **Joe ran here.**

Jim Joe John Jack
run ray ran ram
there then head here

3. **Dad is big.**

Day Dad Dab Dog
it at as is
bag bug big bog

4. **Boys play ball.**

Bugs Bays Buys Boys
plan play park page
bill pull ball balk

5. **I saw birds.**

A I It As
was say way saw
bids birds burst birch

Fill in:

Boys _____ ball.

Joe _____ here.

The man _____.

_____ saw birds.

Dad is _____.

Min_____Sec_____.

6. **Girls, go home.**

Grills Girls Guys Goods
go got get golf
house horse home come

7. **Look at him.**

Cook Lake Took Look
it as at is
his her him hem

8. **Are you there?**

Car Are Far Tar
one your you once
here then were there

9. **Who was that?**

Why How Who What
saw was way wash
this then that they

10. **Call her up.**

Came Tell Tall Call
him her has his
up on down in

Fill in:

Who was _____?

Call her _____?

Girls, _____ home.

_____ at him.

Are _____ there?

Min_____Sec_____.

From *Word Tracking* by Donald E. P. Smith. Reprinted by permission of the author.

to move from left to right and from the top of the page to the bottom. The children must complete the entire activity in order. If they miss one item, the materials are constructed so that they cannot finish.

The concept of tracking can be adapted to any materials. For example, take any unit of print and provide a sentence to look for:

> Look for: See the dog run
> Unit of print: I have a dog. You can *see* him on Satur-
>   day. He can run into *the* house. My *dog*
>   can *run* very fast.

6. Mechanical aids are available to help children with orientation skills. Tracking, for example, can be reinforced by the use of the Controlled Reader.** The child watches a story from a film, which is paced either a line at a time or by a left-to-right exposure control and which can be regulated for speed. Both the Leavell Language Development Service** and the Delacato Stereo-Reader Service** feature binocular hand-eye coordination and self-paced reading. Many schools also have tachistoscopic devices which can be used to present flashed material to children in order to develop both speed of perception and left-to-right reinforcement. Mechanical aids can help motivate the child to attempt activities which are otherwise rather dull. However, when one considers the costs of such devices and the excitement that can be created with teacher-made materials, it would appear that the use of machines in remedial reading is of a seriously limited value. First, they all place children in reading situations which are unreal. Reading is not a mechanically paced activity; rather, it is a stop-and-go activity. The reader stops to use word attack skills and to reread certain passages; he then goes quickly to other sections. That all words and phrases deserve the same amount of reading time can be seriously questioned. Machines which claim to have the pacing feature must be evaluated carefully to determine their worth in a reading program. When mechanical aids are used, they should be followed by practice with normal reading materials without the use of the aid. In such a way, the child may be assisted in transferring from practice situations to real reading situations.

The tendency to reverse letters, words, and phrases. While normal for some beginning readers, the tendency to reverse letters, words, and phrases is one of the common orientation difficulties, particularly with young problem readers. Different from following left-to-right across a line, reversals involve inappropriate left-to-right progression in words and phrases within a line. The child not only must consciously attack words from left to right but must develop this attack into a habit. After awareness is developed, the problem can be solved by specific practice.

1. Kindergarten and first grade teachers should emphasize directional progression both directly and subtly. Through writing on the board in front of children and calling their attention to the direction that the letters flow to form a word, the teacher can give the children opportunities to grasp this concept. The children may also write on the board, for there is less tendency to make directional errors when doing board work. The correct response may be reinforced by permitting the child to write very large letters at his seat. It should be noted that this is a more difficult concept for some children to grasp than is the left-to-right movement across a line of print, especially when whole word techniques have been stressed in initial instruction. The writing of easily confused words either at the board or at the child's seat reinforces with a sense of touch the left-to-right progression within words. When individual language experience stories are being written, the teacher should sit beside the child so that the child can watch the words being formed. By sitting across the table, the child watches the words being formed right-to-left instead of left-to-right. If the teacher types the story, he should let the child sit at the typewriter to watch the word form.
2. Phonics lessons also provide opportunity for the reinforcement of proper progression through words, particularly in initial and final consonant substitution activities where the position of the letters in words is emphasized. In phonics lessons, where stress is being placed upon the initial sounds in words, it is often possible to place words on the board to illustrate the similarities or differences in the initial sounds. This practice, of course, emphasizes the left-to-right concept as it applies to word attack.

3. Spelling class, where the concept of the position of the letters in each word is of primary importance, is an excellent time for reinforcing the proper image of the word. Through the spelling of confused words, the teacher is able to reinforce the proper sequence of letters in a silent situation.

4. Children also may be encouraged to trace the words that are missed so that they may feel the left-to-right progression. When groups of children display this difficulty, imaginary tracing of the letters in the air can achieve much the same results. As the children trace the word, they are expected to pronounce it correctly; if they cannot do this, the problem is more likely one of inadequate sight vocabulary. Specific instructions for the *Kinesthetic Technique*[6] follow:

    a. The child is exposed to the word symbol and its pronunciation. (That these words are usually taken from the child's experience stories implies that he knows their meanings.)

    b. The child is directed to trace the word while saying it. (This tracing procedure is to be repeated until there appears to be confidence within the child that he actually has mastered the word. The teacher demonstrates as often as necessary when beginning this approach.) Fernald notes that finger contact with the letters is essential, especially in these early stages.

    c. The child next writes the word with the copy in sight. Again, he is instructed to say the word as he writes it.

    d. The child then is directed to reproduce the word without the copy, again pronouncing it as he says it. With a situation involving an experience story, the child returns to attack the word properly in his own story. It should be noted that this technique is not one in which the child spells the word or sounds the letters; rather, it is a whole word technique in which the child pronounces the word as a unit. The advantages of the tracing technique are not limited to orientation skills; other uses will be noted under sight vocabulary and word attack where a more detailed explanation is presented.

---

[6]Grace Fernald, *Remedial Techniques in Basic School Subjects* (New York: McGraw Hill Book Co., 1943), Chap. 5.

The reading specialist will find several variations of the *Kinesthetic Technique* in the literature. Some prefer that all tracing be done in sand; some prefer the use of a blackboard; others feel that tracing the word in large copy is entirely adequate. Some suggest that the word be printed, providing the best transfer to actual reading. Others prefer that the word be written in script to reinforce the flow and connection between the letters. Regardless of the system, the left-to-right progression of the words is reinforced, and the child, sensing the total results of his efforts, does learn to pronounce words properly.

5. Three-dimensional letter blocks are available commercially or can be made in a woodshop. The blocks should have one rough surface (the top side) made of sandpaper or the like. The child is told to examine the block letters and build words from printed copy, then trace them, and pronounce them, thus having the reinforcement of touch added to his learning skills.

6. *The Delacato Stereo Reader Service*** has a set of prepared cards which are of particular value when used with children who have a combination of mixed dominance and reversal tendencies. In this situation, the reading specialist places the appropriate card on the side of the Stereo Reader which corresponds to the child's hand preference. The child then reads the card, indicating his knowledge of the placement of abstract symbols in various left-to-right positions and the placement of words in their proper left-to-right pattern.

The reading specialist, as does the classroom teacher, will find many opportunities in other reading activities to reinforce left-to-right progressions through words. It goes without saying that every opportunity should be utilized.

Tendency to omit words without distorting context: Omissions are generally made unknowingly. Therefore, the first remedial activity is to call the child's attention to the fact that although his error has *not* interfered with his comprehension, his reading has *not* been accurate. It should be understood that, in these cases, we assume that the children have read the words prior to pronouncing them and, while not distorting the context, have failed to recall the precise words of the author.

1. Effective utilization can be made of a tape recorder for children with this type of difficulty. Having taped an oral reading selection, the child listens carefully to the tape while following the story with his eyes. He then marks each word that he discovers he has omitted. (Children are generally surprised to find that they make the many omissions that they do.) The child then attempts to reread the story without omitting any words; again, he listens to the tape while following the story; again, he marks his errors. We often find that once alerted to this type of error, the child is able to make conscious corrections, although this technique may need to be repeated several times to develop satisfactory performance.[7] Self-diagnosis helps to emphasize to the child his reading strengths and errors. Self-diagnosis followed by practice and reevaluation tend to correct most omission errors.

2. If using a tape recorder does not seem to develop the desired understanding, the teacher can read and have the child follow in a book. In this case, the teacher makes intentional omissions and the child marks them. The taping of this reading provides an opportunity to go over the child's markings, calling his attention to specific errors. Listening stations designed to permit several children to listen to oral reading on one tape without disturbing others have been used to great advantage for these purposes.

3. The reading impress method[8] has value for children who make many omissions. With the impress method, the teacher and the child read in unison. The child is reinforced by the teacher's voice. Obviously, older children and better readers can be used to assist children using the impress method, but the peer tutor must receive precise instructions. Many children who commit omissions read unusually fast, perhaps in

---

[7]Robert M. Wilson, "Oral Reading Is Fun," *Reading Teacher* (October 1965), pp. 41-43.

[8]Paul M. Hollingsworth, "An Experiment With The Impress Methods of Teaching Reading," *Reading Teacher* (November 1970), pp. 112-14.

an effort to conceal their errors. The classroom teacher may urge such children to slow their reading speed in an effort to be more accurate. This is one of the few situations in remedial reading in which children are asked to read more slowly.

4. Phrase flash cards, used in sight vocabulary development, have application to this difficulty in that a child is taught to become aware of the order of small groups of commonly used words. These cards, having a left-to-right aspect, enhance the child's orientation skills even when used for other purposes.

5. Prepared *Tachistoscopic Slides* based on Dolch's list** of the most commonly used words are available in phrases and may be used with children having this specific deficiency. Flashed at rates of 1/5 or 1/10 of a second, the slides give the child practice in accurate word identification of common groupings. An omission in this area calls for more practice, followed by transfer of the learned skills to the printed page.

6. Silent reading with controlled exposure devices, such as the *Controlled Reader,*** are useful in these cases also. By controlling the amount of print exposed, the eye-voice span is controlled as well, thus facilitating emphasis upon the words as they appear sequentially in the story. Omission errors will usually decrease with the use of these materials; however, activities again must be developed to provide transfer from these types of devices to normal reading situations. Children also make omissions because they do not know the world about which they are expected to read. Omissions not of an orientation nature can be corrected by directed study of vocabulary and word attack techniques. (See Chapters 8 and 9).

Habitual losing of one's place: This weakness might be a visual problem; therefore, it first would be advisable to check for signs of ocular difficulty manifested by other symptoms (see Chapter 3). If there is no indication that the difficulty is visual, the child should be given instruction in techniques to help him maintain his place while reading.

1. Many children who habitually lose their place are aware of having done so; however, if the child remains unaware of his difficulty, instruction probably will be ineffective. A child's failure to maintain his place while reading may be illustrated by the use of the tape recorder as it was used in noting omissions.

2. There is a tendency for children who have this difficulty to point to the words while they are reading. Normally, this practice is considered an undesirable crutch; however, if it keeps the child from losing his place, it is better than allowing him to flounder. The classroom teacher should assist the child in trying to stop *unnecessary* finger pointing. First, he can have the child point to each line in an attempt to lessen the emphasis on words. Second, he can suggest that the child hold the line with a card until he develops the habit of reading through the line without losing his place.

3. Pacing devices, which control the child's exposure to the page, have some usefulness with this type of problem, for they give the child a feeling for fluent, uninterrupted reading. For older students, films such as those provided with the *Controlled Reader*** and *Iowa Films*** also are available. Using these, the student is able to concentrate more fully on the concepts in the story because the controlled exposure lessens the possibility of his losing his place. The limitation of both of these types of devices is that, in the actual reading act, the child alone is responsible for keeping his place; he will not have a mechanical instrument to assist him.

4. Pacing devices can be used with the child's books by regulating his reading through the movement of a shield down the page to cover the print. It should be remembered that these machines basically are designed for speed reading exercises, and since speed is not the objective in this case, the rate of operation of the machine should be at an easy pace for the children to handle. The *Reading Accelerator*** and the *Rateometer*** are two popular examples of pacing devices.

5. A modified pacing device, the *Delacato Stereo Reader*,** may provide the child with a similar type of controlled experience. The modification in this case is the child's control of the pacing device. He can stop it, reread the passage,

and practice the type of reading he eventually will be expected to do in other reading situations.

EXTENDED REMEDIATION IN THE AREAS OF READINESS

Adaptations of instructions that have been suggested in this chapter are among the types of activities that classroom teachers and reading specialists might conduct when readiness skills appear to be lacking. When the child is so severely handicapped that he is referred by the classroom teacher for clinical remediation, the reading specialist can operate in several ways:

1. He can intensify the remediation to include the ideas already presented on a regularly scheduled basis. If several children have been identified, he can meet with them several times a week and enrich their experience, thus freeing the classroom teacher from the specific training activities which the children might need. However, he should keep in touch with the teacher and help him make instructional adjustments. But, for example, the reading specialist might conduct the specific visual discrimination activities for the teacher. He can do this in the classroom or in a separate facility.
2. He can train one teacher to work with him so that ultimately his work is assumed by the teacher. Thus, where there are several third grade teachers, one might work with the reading specialist to become skilled in working with children who have readiness problems. While the teacher is being trained, the children also are receiving the help that they need. Many authorities now feel that the reading specialist always should be working with teachers to upgrade their skills so that in coming years, the trained teacher will need less and less of the specialist's time for working with children.
3. In certain activities, specialists can train paraprofessionals while they work with children. In the training of paraprofessionals, reading specialists assist with the identification of the children and with the planning. They supervise the work and conduct lesson critiques. Much of the work can be conducted by paraprofessionals when it is carefully planned

for them. Activities, such as stimulating language stories, making word cards, supervising games, and reviewing children's work, can be done by paraprofessionals, freeing both the reading specialist and the classroom teacher to work with more children.

4. Some school systems establish special learning facilities for children with serious perceptual handicaps. Those who are so active that they have limited ability to function in the normal classroom, for example, are provided with special schooling staffed by teachers and specialists skilled in working with the perceptually handicapped. When it is possible, classroom teachers should be freed to work in such such facilities to gain skills for adaptation to the classroom. The primary goal of any such school is to prepare the child to return to the classroom as a functional learner.

5. Cooperation with community and school resource personnel is often possible to arrange. Medical personnel, for example, may be made available to the reading specialist to assist in diagnosing strengths and weaknesses in order to establish the best program for children with serious limitations. Psychological personnel, nurses, vision specialists, and home-school visitors all can be involved in working with the child. Visual perception activities, for example, might be directed by medical personnel through some stages of the program.

6. Specially trained consultants might be included in programs for children with serious deficiencies. Experienced nursery school and kindergarten teachers might have highly useful instructional suggestions. Persons trained in the use of the Gillingham[9] technique also might be called upon. Local college and university personnel who operate clinics and who work with seriously handicapped children might offer program suggestions and work with specially identified children.

In effect, when children cannot learn to read because of readiness limitations, the entire resources of the school and the community should be utilized. Every effort should be made to prepare these children for normal classroom instruction. Schools cannot afford to leave any children without the help they need in order to

---

[9]Anna Gillingham and Bessie W. Stillman, *Remedial Training* (Cambridge, Mass.: Educators Publishing Service, Inc., 1960).

learn. No time limitations and no budget limitations can be tolerated. When classroom teachers know that the entire program is designed to help them with those children they are not equipped to help themselves, the entire atmosphere of the school improves and more children do learn to read.

SUMMARY

The activities involved in readiness instruction are not limited to primary grade teachers. Teachers at all levels must be skilled in identification and treatment of the types of problems discussed in this chapter. Reading specialists must know how to obtain maximum help for teachers who cannot reach children because of readiness limitations. In most cases, there is no reason why reading instruction, directed to the strengths of children, cannot proceed while readiness programs are being conducted. Of course, the effort must be to assist the child in becoming the most successful learner possible.

SUGGESTED READINGS

Fernald, Grace. *Remedial Techniques in Basic School Subjects*, Chapter 5. New York: McGraw Hill Book Co., 1943. The advantages and specific techniques of the tracing technique are presented in these pages. The reader will find this presentation interesting and complete.

Hall, MaryAnne. *Teaching Reading as a Language Experience*. Columbus, Ohio: Charles E. Merrill Publishing Co., 1970. This book provides a basic background for those unfamiliar with the possibilities for using the language experience approach in remediation. Chapter 7 deals specifically with the teaching of prereading skills through the language experience approach.

Hymes, James L., Jr. *Before the Child Reads*. New York: Row, Peterson & Co., 1958. Hymes presents the point of view of an experienced educator of young children. His chapter "You do not have to 'Build' Readiness," while concerned with preschool children, should be considered required reading.

Kephart, Newell C. *The Slow Learner in the Classroom*. Columbus, Ohio: Charles E. Merrill Publishing Co., 1971. The reader will find interesting reading covering completely the motor readiness needs of youngsters. Particular attention is given to motor skills which the author sees as being related to success in learning.

Monroe, Marion, and Rogers, Bernice. *Foundations for Reading*, Chapters 1-5. Chicago: Scott Foresman and Co., 1964. The author's have presented a series of chapters relating to the beginning processes of reading. The educator who is attempting remediation without a thorough understanding of this initial process will find this reading very profitable.

8

Remedial Activities for
Vocabulary Skills

Vocabulary remediation falls into two broad categories: sight vocabulary and word attack. In both cases, the objective is to assist the child to decode words (and groups of words) in order to get meaning from them. Remediation in the area of vocabulary is likely to receive major emphasis in any remedial program since for most children it appears to be the greatest block to effective reading.

REMEDIATION IN SIGHT VOCABULARY

Sight vocabulary involves the skills of instant word pronunciation and word meaning. While the remedial approaches in the area of sight vocabulary problems are presented in terms of the questions asked in diagnosis, it must be remembered that the end goal of sight vocabulary is the decoding and association of the word in a line of print, in a sentence, or in a paragraph rather than in isolation, for word meaning depends on relationships with other words.

Remedial procedures will be developed in direct reply to the questions asked under the diagnosis of sight vocabulary difficulties. Specifically, those questions are:

1. Does the child miss small, similar words or does he falter on words that are obviously different?

2. Do the words missed represent concrete or abstract concepts?
3. Does he know the word in isolation but not in context?
4. Does he pronounce the word properly but fail to associate it with the correct meaning?
5. Is the error one in which the child eventually pronounces the word but not without due hesitation?

These deficiencies seldom appear alone; rather, they are interrelated. The purpose in establishing the answers to the questions is to determine in which areas the interrelationship has taken place and to emphasize these areas in remediation. Through examination it can clearly be seen, for example, that words of minimal meaning differences are often words with abstract meanings which require dual remedial considerations.

THE LANGUAGE EXPERIENCE APPROACH

Of first priority in remediation of vocabulary problems is common agreement about how the language experience approach fits into a remedial situation. Use of the language experience approach includes the following possibilities:

Following Direction Activities Can Come Naturally
from the Language Experience Approach

1. Following an experience with one child or a group of children, the teacher generates a discussion concerning the experience. The children are encouraged to talk about what they saw or did, about how it made them feel, and about the meaning the experience had for them.
2. Following free discussion, the teacher tells the child, or children, to write a story about the experience. The teacher asks for contributions and writes before the children exactly what they say. While words are always spelled correctly, the teacher does not change the children's sentence structure as he writes. Some guidelines for writing stories are:

   a. Encourage all children to contribute.
   b. In the beginning, use some type of identification for the child's contribution (i.e., "Donald said, 'I see a big dog ' " or "I see a big dog (Donald) ").
   c. Read what has been written immediately following the writing of each sentence. Next, have the child who gave the sentence read it; then, the entire group.
   d. For very young children, start every new sentence on a new line. For older children, write in paragraphs.
   e. Begin by making stories rather short. If the children have more to say, write the story on two pages with only a few lines on each page. Children with serious reading problems can become discouraged with too much print on a single page.
   f. Have children watch as the story is written. Call attention to the formations of words as they are written.
   g. As children develop skill with beginning consonants, invite them to help with the spelling of words (e.g., "How would I begin the word *boy*?").

3. After the story is written, have the children read it in unison several times.
4. Duplicate the story as soon as possible, making at least two copies for each child. One copy can be placed in a folder to become the reading material for the children. The second copy can be used for skill development.
5. Skill can be developed from language experience stories in a variety of ways. In Chapter 7, visual discrimination, auditory discrimination, and orientation skills were discussed. Skills in vocabulary can be developed as follows:

    a. Have the children mark all the words which they know. Then have them put several of these words in a private word box or word bank. The child's word bank provides a natural opportunity for meaningful word drills.

    b. Children can practice their known words in pairs or in small groups. They can match words in their word bank with words in their stories. They can select words for classification as action words, as naming words, as people words, as words beginning with specific letters, and so on.

    c. Once a group of words is developed, children can use their word banks to help them with spelling activities. They can use them to build sentences, make crossword puzzles, and many other activities.

    d. The teacher can add words to the child's bank occasionally. When the word *and* or *the* occurs again and again in a child's story, but he chooses not to place the word in his bank, the teacher can call it to his attention and place the word in the bank. Service words will be needed in future reading and in vocabulary activities.

6. Comprehension activities can also be developed from language experience stories (see Chapter 9).

    The suggestions listed above in no way cover all the possibilities for uses of the language experience approach in remediation. Additional specific suggestions are provided under various remedial areas in this and other chapters. Those unfamiliar with the language experience approach will want to study the books of Stauffer and Hall listed in the Suggested Readings at the end of this chapter.

Does the child miss small, similar words?

Or does he falter on words that are obviously different? Quite often, problem readers will miss small words which are minimal in configurational differences (e.g., *when* and *where*) while effectively attacking larger and more obviously different words (e.g., *elephant* and *Christmas*). The latter is considered a problem of sight vocabulary, while the former is normally a problem in word attack, especially if the large words missed are at or below the instructional level. The major point is to work from the child's strengths. If he can work with words of maximal differences, the teacher should provide more exercises with those types of words, moving cautiously to words that are more similar until skill is developed. Then, he should move to words even more alike until he develops skill with words which have minimal differences.

Classroom remediation: The child ultimately must receive instruction in the discrimination of words that are minimally different. These exercises should be conducted in phrase and sentence form so that the child realizes that the minimal difference distorts not only the pronunciation but the meaning of the words as well: "We took the dig (instead of *dog*) for a walk." To clarify these similarities and differences in minimally different words, it is sometimes feasible to pull these words from context for study (*dig-dog*). Any exercise, however, which concludes with the word in isolation is in error for drills should always be followed by return to context.

Using words from the child's word bank (i.e., words which are already known) illustrates teaching to strengths. Locating words which look very much alike, pronouncing them, noting meanings, using them in sentences, and noting how they look alike and different is extremely useful.

Programmed materials which are particularly adaptable to the classroom for use in remediation of this type of skill deficiency have been prepared by qualified persons. These materials can lead the child to observe differences made by particular words which are alike except for minimal differences (e.g., *hat* and *bat*). As an example of these materials, *Programmed Reading*** contains a series of exercises through which the child can develop skill with a minimum amount of teacher supervision. Note the sample on page 190. The child must look at the pictures, read the sentence or partial sentence, and use closure to obtain the correct code and message. These exercises progress from the elementary type seen here to complete stories. The forced-choice closure concept is maintained at all levels (i.e., the child selects from a limited number of appropriate responses).

The child is reinforced further by the correct answer after each frame or after each page, depending upon how much material the teacher feels the child can handle without reinforcement. The skills developed in the workbooks are transferred to reading in prepared *Storybooks,*** containing stories with minimally different words. Although it is unlikely that these materials will satisfy the total

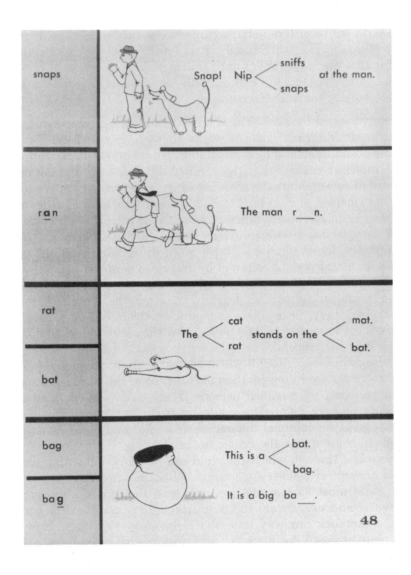

Sample Page of a Programmed Reader (Photograph
with Permission of Webster Division, McGraw Hill)

reading needs of the child, they are particularly useful when working with minimal differences.

In the early grades, the teacher may use experience charts to illustrate the need for careful visual discrimination of minimally different words. In these situations, the teacher should take every opportunity to emphasize how words of similar configuration actually differ in both form and meaning, using the child's own language contributions as examples. For instance, when he writes a child's story, the teacher should look for opportunities to demonstrate how certain words look alike or different. Children can grasp the need for careful word examination when they see how minimal changes actually change their contributions.

Clinical remediation: Due to the adaptability to individualized instruction, it should be obvious that the techniques utilized in the classroom are equally usable in clinical remediation.

For children with this deficiency, strengths that are inherent in the linguistic approach can be utilized with word banks which add a personalized factor. Adaptations can be developed to almost any type of material; for example, the programmed materials mentioned above illustrate adaptations of the linguistic approach. The *Let's Read Books*** and *The Merrill Linguistic Readers*** are carefully prepared linguistic materials for beginning reading, appropriate for individualized instruction of children with serious reading problems. Both of these approaches have in common a controlled vocabulary of minimally different words; the controlled initial presentation of words with consistent vowel and consonant sounds; and an absence of pictures which requires correct visual perception for accurate decoding. A similar approach, *The Linguistic Readers,*** varies somewhat from those mentioned above but does maintain the necessity for visual perception of minimal differences. Even if the use of these particular materials does not appeal to the reading specialist, it still should be obvious that the *concept* of the linguistic approach has advantages for certain children and adaptations of it may be made. Use of the term *linguistic approach* in these cases refers to the materials produced for reading instruction by linguists such as Barnhart and Fries.

Do the words missed represent abstract concepts?

It is common for children to find it particularly difficult to remember words which represent abstract concepts (e.g., *when, these, if, those*). Emphasis in remediation for children with this type of difficulty should focus on the word as it appears in context, for it is from context that the function of these words can be understood. Furthermore, since there is seldom a reading situation in which these words are used in isolation, they should not be taught in isolation.

Classroom remediation: Once again, experience story approaches are of particular value in the development of this type of reading sight vocabulary. Children use these words to formulate their experience stories, providing a natural opportunity for instruction in the service and function of these words as the child uses them. Although the experience story approach will probably be used more frequently with the younger problem reader, considerable success with this type of approach has been found with older students as well. It is in experience story reading that we can be certain that all words used have meaning for the child since they are his contributions. Through these materials, the use and nature of abstract words can be effectively illustrated to the child.

Again, word bank words which carry little meaning of their own (*and, the, of,* and the like) are known to children and can be developed into meaningful activities. For example, using *and, the,* and *of* from a child's word bank, ask him which word would fit in the blank: bread _____ butter, I see _____ man, and on top _____ the table. The use of such modified closure activities develops skills in the use of abstract words.

Due to the nature of these words, it is advisable that the initial introduction take place in a contextual situation. Applicable to the teaching of all children, this phase of classroom remediation will not require that the child be instructed alone.

Sight vocabulary drills with abstract concepts are most effective when the words are used in phrases (e.g., *in a good spirit*). Prepared phrase cards with the more commonly used word combinations are available in the *Dolch Game*** series. There is little or no justification for sight word drill with these words in isolation, for when they are extracted from context, any meaning the word contains is lost.

Clinical remediation: In clinical remediation, individualized emphasis will be placed on the same techniques as those used in the classroom. A particularly useful technique for clinical remediation with this type of child is the experience story; the resulting activity is used as it is in the classroom. However, in clinical remediation, opportunities are available for more personalized attention since clinicians are usually working with children individually or in small groups.

After a certain amount of sight vocabulary has been developed, children with more serious reading problems may build sentences from word cards. Here emphasis should be placed upon the function of the abstract word as created by the student. With this activity, the unknown word is not placed in a definition situation; rather, it appears in a functional situation, the sentence. Intentional distortions of these types of words in context may be used to illustrate their importance. Here a child also is directed to substitute in order to distort the author's meaning and then to indicate an awareness of how the author's flow of meaning and ideas have been changed.

Such word games as Word Lotto, which use abstract words, can be used successfully to reinforce words which have been pre-

By Placing Word Bank Words on a Checker Board, It Is Possible to Make Drill Exercises an Enjoyable Activity for Children

viously learned (i.e., words from children's word banks). Word games are highly motivating to children and tend to take the drill atmosphere from reinforcement activities. Games such as checkers can be used with words taped on each square. As the child moves or jumps his opponent, he is expected to pronounce the word or words on the spaces involved. Children become so enthusiastic about such activities that they ignore the drill nature involved.

Does the child know the word in isolation, but not in context?

A word which appears in isolation on the chalkboard may be recognized more accurately than is the same word when it appears in context surrounded by other words.

ran

The child ran to the store.

While the opposite is more normally true, certain children do tend to be distracted by a full page of print. In oral reading, for example, we often find children scanning the page for words which they know or do not know. Others, having been taught to use context clues, do not look carefully at the word which is causing difficulty. The reading act, however, requires use of words in context. With this type of problem, remedial approaches in the classroom and in the clinic do not differ, for the emphasis is on placing sight vocabulary in context. Whether through the use of experience stories, sentences obtained from prepared materials, or sentences created by the teacher, *all* drill for children with this deficiency must begin and end with the word as it appears in context. Children who are seriously crippled by this deficiency may have the word in question highlighted or emphasized in some manner; for emphasis, the word may be framed by the hands, underlined, marked in a different color, or some such technique, but since the word remains in the sentence, the child is ever alert to the function of the word. Only the exception would justify taking the word from context to develop sight vocabulary, for it has already been established that the child knows the word in isolation. Most of the difficulty with this type of reading problem can be prevented by the application of all drills to context, even in the earliest reading instruction. If, from the beginning, the child grasps the concept that words are learned to be used in sentences, this difficulty is less likely to arise. Start with words in phrases or short sentences. Help the child to master discriminations in small quantities of print. Then add more sentences and longer units.

A group technique for these children can be of value to all. Each child uses a given word in a sentence, printing the sentence on the back of a card. These cards are collected and redistributed, providing each child the chance to read another's response. Such activity develops an active feeling for the use of the word in context.

When the problem is a severe one, special learning conditions may need to be developed. Books without pictures (natural distractors from the print), areas in the room which are fairly stimulus free, three by five cards to screen out all but the line of print on which the child is working, and reading in unison can create the feeling for pronouncing all of the words in a sentence. Remember, in cases such as these, we are not concerned with teaching the word, but rather, simply with making the child comfortable so that he can see the word in order to read it in context.

Can he pronounce the word he sees in print but fail to associate it with the correct meaning?

Remedial instruction in this very important area must be precluded by the following two considerations:

1. There are situations in which children, for one reason or another, fail to develop a background of experiences which permits them to associate properly the meaning with the word they have pronounced. If this deficiency is chronic, remediation of necessity will consist of experiential language development rather than instruction in sight vocabulary.
2. We find numerous children who have little trouble pronouncing the words they see in print. Although they know the meaning of the word and can use it in a sentence, these children fail to associate the word with the correct meaning, apparently because of preoccupation with word pronunciation. Remedial activities with these children, then, should be in the area of sight vocabulary where they must be taught to be conscious of what the word *says* as well as how it *sounds*.

Classroom remediation: As has been stated previously, every word drill should end with the word in context. In this way, the precise meaning and function of the word are best understood; children with this deficiency must have context emphasized even more precisely.

The child begins by reading easy material which allows him to demonstrate his knowledge of the word in question by paraphrasing the author's words. Specific mention of this technique will be discussed under the answer to the question (Chapter 9) of paraphrasing in comprehension remediation.

It is often useful to establish whether the child knows the meaning of the word through definition. If he does, it is not the meaning of the word as such that is causing the problem, but the use of the word in a particular contextual situation. The presentation of the word in various settings is then appropriate.

Since children already understand the meaning of the pronounced words, experience stories using the child's own wording again play an important role in remedial efforts. We hope that teachers of elementary school children will provide numerous opportunities for group experience stories in which there is an association between the experiences of the group and the words which represent those experiences. This is a golden opportunity to create the situation in which children learn from other children better than they do from adults. Frequently we find other children reacting better to the responses of their peers than to teacher efforts. Competition must be held to a minimum; although children will learn from each other, one must be certain that during remediation there is peer group rapport and that differences between the children do not become the issue.

There are numerous opportunities for the classroom teacher to provide directed exercises in word meaning through a study of synonyms and antonyms. Drills of this type usually involve the collection of lists of synonyms and/or antonyms and their usages. Emphasis, of course, is placed upon the similarities in the meanings of the words, and children with association skill deficiency will find this drill particularly profitable.

Although frequently not included as a remedial technique, the dictionary is of particular assistance to older students. Their knowledge of the correct pronunciation of a word in print permits them to use the dictionary to find meanings efficiently; it may, incidentally, develop a habit of consulting the dictionary for unknown words. Techniques for use with the dictionary are discussed under the heading of word attack skills.

Although it is fine to talk about building experiences to develop listening and speaking vocabularies, it is another thing to build such a program (refer to Chapter 7). The *Peabody Language Development Kits*** contain programs for 180 lessons in language development. The teacher may find this type of program a guide for the entire school year. Among the experiences included with these kits are: following directions, brainstorming, critical thinking, memory, rhyming, and listening. Pictures, objects, and tapes are used to enrich the child's experiential background.

The *Ginn Language Kit A*** provides the teacher with another program for language development. The Ginn Kit consists of pictures through which vocabulary can be stimulated, synonyms developed, and language experience stories drawn.

Clinical remediation: For the child seriously handicapped by the inability to associate, the *Non-oral Reading*** approach may contain the requisites for initial clinical instruction. This approach by-passes completely the vocalization of the printed word and emphasizes instead the word's association with a pictured concept. The child's task is to match the printed symbol with a picture representing the concept for that symbol. This direct association from print to concept minimizes the importance of pronunciation for children who have been overdrilled in it.

The reading specialist will also find it useful to have the child respond directly through physical activity to such printed word commands as "jump up," and "shake hands." This approach also minimizes vocalization of the printed word, emphasizing again the meaning of the word through the child's response. The *Nichols Tachistoscope Slides*** developed for this purpose appear to be effective in establishing the importance of the concepts covered by words.

Collecting words from the word bank in categories can help to stress word meanings. For example, to collect action words, the child must think of word meaning, not just pronunciation. Words which are names of things can be matched with the action words to make short sentences (e.g., *dogs run, ducks talk, horses jump*). Children can look at the sentences which they have built to determine which make sense. This is an extremely meaningful activity. Stimulating children with incomplete sentences, such as "I like to _____" makes the learning personal and, therefore, more interesting.

The reading specialist also may use initial sight vocabulary exercises consisting of nouns, adjectives, and verbs which can be pictured. The *Dolch Picture Word Cards*,** containing 96 of these types of words, may be used. Several matching-type games involve a child by having him physically match a picture with a printed word, thereby indicating his understanding of the meaning of the word in a game-like activity which is self-motivating. *Picture Word Puzzles*** provides similar reinforcement with children having association deficiencies.

Active participation can be achieved by having the child build sentences from the words which he knows. After known words are placed on cards, the cards are scrambled and the child is asked to build a specific sentence or to build a sentence of his choosing. The *Linguistic Block Series*** can be used in the same manner with the blank block for words in the child's personal vocabulary.

Is the error one in which the child eventually pronounces the word but not without undue hesitation?

The important point here is that the child did pronounce the word. Why did he hesitate? Was he distracted? Did he stop to use word attack skills? Was he searching for context clues? If the child was working to pronounce the word, it is unwise to devise activities which would rush him. Perhaps he needed the time during the hesitation. He is saying that he can pronounce the word but that he does not know it well enough for it to be called a sight word. In such cases, reinforcement activities that aid the child in overlearning the word are appropriate; speed activities with flash cards are not. Directed lessons about the appearance and meaning of the word can be conducted and games and short drill activities can be used. Almost any suggestion in this chapter can assist the child to master the word. But most importantly, a child should not be hurried with word pronunciation when he is using the word attack skills that are important to him in order to be an independent learner.

Other children are, of course, simply sluggish and slow in their reading. The following activities can be developed to help them recognize words more quickly.

Classroom remediation: The major emphasis in the classroom is likely to be in the use of flashcards containing the sight words either alone or in a phrase. The classroom teacher, assured that the word is already known, can assist the child to realize that the word can be recognized without undue hesitation. When instant recognition has been accomplished in flash card drill, the use of the word in contextual situations is again desirable.

Many children appear to be hesitant when they are, in reality, not making a serious, concentrated effort as they work. With these children, reasonable time limits for the completion of the task should be set and adhered to whenever possible. It is often possible to set short term goals which will enable the child to see his way more clearly to the end of the established goal, thus permitting him to work more efficiently. Here, of course, our goal is not speed reading; it is merely the efficient use of time in the act of reading.

Clinical remediation: The reading specialist is likely to use mechanical devices such as the *Tachistoscope*** or the *Flash X* to accomplish the same ends as the classroom teacher. This does not preclude the use of flashcards in any clinical situation, but we have found that children seriously limited in word recognition seem to enjoy the motivation provided by machine-type devices. With both of these devices, it is possible to make slides from lists of words with which the child has demonstrated difficulty. These homemade slides are preferable for children with this deficiency. Again, it is best to place the words used in these techniques into context for quick recognition at the end of every lesson.

Because of the nature of clinical remedial situations, it is often easy to identify the child who is not working efficiently. This child must realize the need for efficiency in his use of working time. Proper emphasis here may be placed upon the completion of a reading task in a reasonable time period rather than upon the number of words read per minute. It can be noted that children who are working to meet a words-per-minute criterion often make *that* their major goal and de-emphasize comprehension. The *SRA Laboratory*** (rate builders), in which a story must be read and questions answered in a relatively short period of time, provides useful practice of a desired type. Using easy material, the child should adhere to established time limitations.

When mechanical motivation is desired, another use for the *Controlled Reader*** is found; however, the child must work with material he can recognize if he is to perform within reasonable time restrictions. It is essential, therefore, that the use of the *Controlled Reader* to increase speed of recognition must be at recreational reading levels (note limits of mechanical devices in Chapter 7).

One advantage of working in contractual situations (see Chapter 6) is to develop the self-pacing abilities of the children. As they see what they are to do in a given amount of time, they can adjust the contract to be certain to finish. Working efficiently becomes more important and more realistic when the child has some control over the quantity of work he is expected to complete in a given amount of time.

Additional Considerations in Sight Vocabulary

The following aspects of remediation in the area of sight vocabulary should be carefully understood by any person conducting remediation in this area:

The need to tell the child the word: The teacher will find many situations in which it is advisable to tell the child an unknown word. Although we normally would not suggest that teachers provide unknown words, a child will often be in situations where he simply does not have the skills needed to attack unknown words. In these cases, telling him the word will permit him to move along with the context of the story, focusing his attention on those words he has the skills to attack effectively. In such cases, the teacher need not feel guilty about telling children words, nor should he make the child feel this way. In other situations, the remedial teacher is justified in being reluctant to tell children words.

The need for overlearning: The very nature of sight vocabulary (instant recognition and meaning) implies that it must be overlearned. Overlearning, not to be conducted in isolated drill activities, is most effective when the child has opportunities to use the word again and again in context. Many remedial efforts fail because they do not provide for the overlearning of sight vocabulary words in context. Experience stories, trade books, and similar materials are available to facilitate transfer for children with serious limitations.

Reinforcement of word attack skills through the use of word banks exemplifies the concept of accept and challenge and meets the need for overlearning. Several suggestions for the use of word banks as reinforcers are:

1. Find all the words that begin like _____ or end like
   _____.

2. Find all the words that rhyme with _____.

3. Find all the words that are one syllable words or two syllable words, and so on.
4. Find all the words that are examples of _____ (a given generalization).
5. Find all the words that contain silent letters or blends or digraphs and so on.

Competitive Games Add Enrichment to Otherwise
Boring Phonics Activities

Likewise, games, either commercially developed or not, make overlearning exciting and fun-filled. Games which follow the pattern of a race track and involve the spinning of a wheel or the rolling of dice can be used. Each block on the race track can require the child to demonstrate a skill, initial consonant substitution, syllabication, or vowel knowledge.

Every remedial session should provide opportunities for the children to read materials of their own choosing. Perhaps as much as 25 percent of the remedial time can be wisely spent in such activities. It is through a great deal of reading that children become comfortable with words which they will meet over and over again. Overlearning is often interpreted as a drill-and-grill type activity. Obviously, the more motivation an activity has, the less it will be viewed as a chore.

Motivation Techniques

The often subtle development of power in sight vocabulary needs to be illustrated to the problem reader so that he may be encouraged by his progress. The following techniques have been found to be particularly helpful in motivating certain types of children:

1. Transferring every lesson to contextual situations illustrates that the work the child is doing in sight vocabulary is, in effect, making him a better reader. Particularly with older children, this in itself is often ample motivation.

2. Recording experience stories in booklet form is of interest to younger students, for they can see progress merely by the quantity of the material they have been able to learn to read. The sight vocabulary implications of that quantity can be pointed out if need be to the child.

3. Charts illustrating the goals toward which the child will work in sight vocabulary seem to trigger some children's efforts to achieve better performance. Ultimately, it is desirable that intrinsic motivation fulfill the function of such charts. An illustration of success through the use of charts must be carefully planned. Objectives must be short term and within the realistic grasp of the student. Charts which emphasize long range goals can discourage as well as encourage students. During a recent moon shot, our clinicians raced their students in vocabulary development against the astronauts. The moon shot lasted eight days and the students won the race. The short term nature of the chart made it worthwhile.

4. Sight vocabulary cards maintained in a file or on a ring illustrate visually to the child that he has accumulated a number of useful words through which he can become a better reader. These words should not be listed in isolation; rather, they should appear in a sentence with the word highlighted. This use of word banks illustrates the concept of acceptance and challenge and teaching to strengths.

In several of the techniques above, games and mechanical devices have been suggested for teaching purposes. These appear to hold the child's interest and to establish a degree of motivation, while assisting the child to develop his sight vocabulary.

As has been mentioned, the use of contracts through which children regulate their learning to some degree are of particular value. The completion of a contract is motivation in itself. Of course, specially constructed rewards and motivational devices can be built in. For example, contract completion can result in an immediate reward through free-reading time, praise, and other encouragement. The motivation to strive for future efforts is built-in and automatic.

REMEDIATION IN WORD ATTACK

Word attack skills include those techniques which enable a child to decode an unknown word in order to pronounce it and to understand it as it is used in contextual situations without teacher assistance.

Difficulties in the area of word attack are the most outstanding weakness of problem readers. Consequently, there are many commercial materials available and many approaches recommended in the professional literature; the resulting abundance has often served to confuse rather than to clarify the preciseness of approaches in the area of word attack difficulties.

Children need word attack skills in order to read words without depending on teachers or parents. Remedial programs in word attack, then, should be designed to foster independence in reading, not merely proficiency in word attack drills.

Because there are various methods for attacking words not known at sight, educational focus should be on those word attack skills which assist the child in attacking words most efficiently in terms of time and most consistently in terms of application. Once overlearned, efficiency in word attack should have the same aim as did sight vocabulary (i.e., to decode the word and associate its meaning instantly to the context in which it occurs).

As indicated in the diagnosis of the problem reader, word attack falls into three major categories: phonic clues, structural clues, and contextual clues. The dictionary skills, the fourth category of word attack, which normally are not considered of remedial necessity, at times need development in remedial programs.

Discovery Technique

It must be assumed that most children referred for remedial help have had instruction in word attack skills. That those skills have not been mastered indicates clearly that the instructional efforts have failed. Therefore, part of the reason for failure in learning word attack skills must be attributed to the technique of instruction. Throughout this chapter, the *discovery technique*[1] will be mentioned as a solution to specific problems. A brief review of the *discovery technique* and some of its possibilities are included as a preface to the discussion of remediation in word attack.

1. The teacher presents word patterns which contain the visual clues desired for instruction.
   For example, (using known words)

   > index   picnic   pencil   chapter

2. The teacher directs the children to observe, visually, the patterns in the words. For example:

   a. place a v above each vowel.

   v v
index

   b. place a c above each consonant between the vowels.

   vccv
index

   c. divide the word into syllables.

   vc cv
in/dex

3. Have the children form generalizations in their own words. For example, one child might say, "vc/cv"; another might say, "When you have VCCV divide between the *c*'s," concerning the patterns and the syllabication above. Any appropriate response from a child is acceptable. The teacher should avoid forcing his wording on the children.
4. Have the children turn to material which they are reading to collect words which fit the pattern. For example, the teacher might refer to a specific page in a book on which he knows there are five words which fit the pattern. The children might also find words in their word banks which fit the pattern.

The major advantages of the *discovery technique* include the active response needed by the children, the acceptance of their wording for the generalization, and the impact which results from forming a generalization through the use of visual clues. Teachers

---

[1]Morton Botel, *How to Teach Reading* (Chicago: Follett Publishing Corp., 1968), p. 64.

may choose to vary the approach at times; in fact, Botel suggests that steps three and four be reversed from the way the technique is described above. Other variations might include: a discussion of exceptions to the generalization; help in beginning the wording (e.g., "When a word contains the pattern . . .") ; and directed activities from word lists to determine the ability of the children to discriminate the visual pattern. Although the *discovery technique* will take more time than would simply telling the children, the lasting effects of the learning should be extremely valuable.

Phonic Analysis

Remedial efforts in the precise area of phonics will, again, be in terms of the questions asked following the establishment of word attack as the area of skill deficiency.

1. Is the problem basically the child's inability to discriminate auditorily?
2. When the child mispronounces or substitutes words, is there a pattern of vowel or consonant errors?
3. Does the child need instruction in the usage of known sounds?

Although in diagnosis the skills of phonics have been delegated to three precise areas (sound of letters, syllabication, and blending), it is necessary that the remedial program combine these areas for instructional purposes. The functional use of phonic skills involves the ability of the child to divide the word into syllables, sound the letters, blend the sounds into a recognizable word, and check the derived pronunciation in the context from which the word was taken. Essential to the sounding of letters is the ability to discriminate auditorily the differences in the sounds. Remedial suggestions will deal with each of these areas in terms of questions presented in Chapter 4.

Is the problem basically the child's inability to discriminate auditorily?

Classroom remediation of auditory discrimination should be considered. This technique is discussed in full in Chapter 7.

Clinical remediation: Children with severe phonic disabilities quite often need an auditory discrimination program which is related clearly to the phonic technique to be used. It therefore is recommended that the child with severe auditory discrimination problems be instructed with a phonic technique which has auditory discrimination as an inherent part of the program. Then it can be assured that no child is introduced to sounds which he cannot discriminate auditorily. *Speech to Print Phonics*** and *Phonovisual*** are examples of these types of materials.

The use of visual clues and kinesthetic reinforcement is essential for children with severe auditory discrimination problems. We do not mean that phonics instruction should be withheld; rather, the child should use visual clues, relying more upon sight than sound. Here too the sense of touch is added to the other senses used for learning.

Games can provide exercises in auditory discrimination. As in other cases, games can provide the reinforcement needed for the overlearning of skills without the negative aspects of routine, monotonous drill. The games in auditory discrimination require considerable teacher supervision with problem readers for there is no point in having the child reinforced by his errors. Under teacher supervision, errors can be turned into valuable learning situations. Commercially available games include the *Dolch Games,*** *Spelling Learning Games Kit,*** and *Phonics We Use Learning Games.***

When the child mispronounces or substitutes words, is there a pattern of vowel or consonant errors?

Diagnostic conclusions should have established whether the child's problem is basically one of total unfamiliarity with the sounds of letters or whether there is a specific vowel or consonant pattern in the error. This pattern should be precise enough to establish the position of the error (i.e., initial, medial, or final), assuming, of course, that the problem is not one of auditory discrimination.

The process of teaching the child the unknown sound will not vary in classroom or clinical remediation in most cases. The decision whether to teach this sound from whole words or in isolation basically is reserved for the teacher. In either case, the major decision concerns which approach best suits the child's strengths. Both will call for providing ample opportunity for the child to demonstrate his skills rather than his weaknesses, and the suitability of either approach will depend upon the following:

1. The teacher's familiarity with a given technique combined with the availability of materials and results obtained through its use. Although we recognize that teachers generally work best with familiar techniques and materials and we encourage them to do so, new methods and ideas should not be overlooked. Inflexible and inappropriate teaching can result from the failure to adapt. It is therefore very important for the teacher to be as objective as possible in his assessment of the materials and techniques which he can use most effectively.

2. The child's previous experience and his reaction to that technique. If, after good instruction, a child fails with a given technique and develops a negative attitude toward it, another approach may be more desirable.

Approaches to teaching vowel and consonant sounds: If available information concerning the child's initial introduction to phonics (a whole word method, for example) determines that this instruction was of satisfactory quality, it is correct for the teacher or reading specialist to select the other approach (sounds in isolation), for it can be assumed that, even with good instruction, the first technique was not effective. This type of selection requires an awareness of the techniques used in both approaches. Again caution is advised, for if the child has profited by a previous method, it is justifiable to build upon what the child has learned (i.e., his strengths). In these cases, a reteaching of a previously taught method may be called for or it may be appropriate to use the same method with minor modifications. Assessments are often difficult and can best be made only by placing the child in instructional situations and evaluating his performance. Reference is made to the suggested readings at the end of this chapter for several sources of recommended techniques for the teaching of the sounds of the various letters and letter combinations.

Regardless of the approach employed, each lesson should be concluded with the child's being placed in a situation where he can attack the sound in a word and words containing the sound in a sentence. The difference between clinical and classroom approaches likely will be due to the type of material appropriate for follow-up activities which facilitate overlearning. A conscious effort on the part of the teacher and reading specialist should keep the child alert to the fact that each time he decodes a word the sounds which he utters should be associated with a meaningful concept. As part of each phonics lesson, techniques must be used to facilitate this alertness. The child should be required to put the pronounced word in a sentence or the teacher might present words in which classification is possible (e.g., things we do at school and names of animals). In either case, the child's attention is called to the fact that the pronounced word has meaning as well as sound.

Classroom remediation: Classroom remediation logically should start with the discovery approach. Emphasizing the child's strengths and helping him to recognize that much of what he has to learn is already known to him helps greatly with his self-concept. In using the discovery technique with instruction in letter sounds, the patterns presented can come from word bank words or from words which recently have been learned by the child. It facilitates learning greatly if the child can pick words from the second category, for example, from his word file. We often find that such procedures result in generalizations about sounds without any further formal instruction. Obviously the use of key words selected from his own bank of words can remind the child of letter-sound associations.

Materials have been designed to provide systematic follow-up for the instruction mentioned above. Such materials as *Phonics Skilltext*** and the workbooks of various basal series can be adapted to meet this need. It is indefensible in remediation, however, to start a child on page one of such material and force him to work through the book; rather, those activities which effectively will reinforce the sound which has been taught should be selected and utilized.

We have found that the *Speech to Print Phonics*** materials develop high motivation, place the child in an active learning climate, and put the new learning into a substitution activity with every lesson. Even older children find such materials useful and pleasant.

Placing children in game situations for the overlearning of these skills has proven effective. In these situations, children work together without the pressure of scholastic failure toward the overlearning of the desired sound. The *SRA Word Games Laboratory*** and *Phonics We Use Learning Games*** have particular usefulness in these classroom situations, for they have game attractiveness and do not require constant teacher supervision. Included in this material are ample reinforcement exercises needed for the various consonant and vowel sounds and sound combinations.

Consonant Lotto** and *Vowel Lotto*** can also be used to provide reinforcement activities in game-like situations. These games may be used best after the sounds have been taught to reinforce the learned skills; they are of little value in the initial instruction of a sound.

Clinical remediation: The reading specialist will provide follow-up activities which are either commercially available or are of his own design to comply appropriately with the basic approach he has decided to use. He may, as a result, choose one of the techniques listed under classroom remediation. He also must be aware of the packaged programs which are commercially available and which have found popular acceptance with reading specialists. The following annotated list may serve as a guide:

1. *Speech to Print Phonics*** provides for auditory discrimination; teaching of the names of letters, sounds of letters, and letter combinations; and the application of these learned skills to word attack situations. Context and meaning as well as sounds are stressed. It is structured for group work by way of every-pupil response cards.
2. *Phonovisual*** carefully presents initial sound identification followed by final sounds and leads to the "tucking in" of vowel sounds for whole word identification. Consonant and vowel picture word charts are included for initial instruction.
3. *Gillingham*** presents a system of teaching and reinforcing the sounds through kinesthetic techniques. Spelling and phonogram identification cards are featured.
4. *Phonetic Keys to Reading*** provides techniques and materials starting with prebasal reading with continued reinforcement and more advanced skills as basal stories are brought into use. These materials are in workbook form but differ from other workbooks in that they are designed to be used at specific times during the basal program.
5. Workbooks: A variety of workbooks are available to guide the child through the various sounds of the letters. Not directly related to any basal series, these programs are intended as suitable replacements of the skills taught in the basal program. The *Phonics Skilltexts,*** *Phonics We Use,*** *Diagnostic Reading Workbooks,*** *Working with Sounds,*** and *Herr Phonics*** are examples of these materials.

Vowel and consonant exercises designed for use with secondary school students are not as plentiful. For the most part, these students are expected to profit from the materials used with elementary school children. It is not uncommon, however, to find that these students do not care to work with elementary materials. The specialist will find materials such as *Tactics for Reading*** more acceptable to secondary students. Of course, if the student has no phonic skills, he will find little satisfaction from the use of materials designed with the assumption that the basic skills have at least been developed to a small degree.

Clinic work in the area of teaching sounds should constitute a very small portion of the tutoring time. Instead of long, boring sessions, reading specialists should concentrate on short practice periods of high impact followed by reading opportunities in which the skills learned are used. The death of many otherwise effective remedial programs comes as a direct result of excessive grill and drill which may produce some skill development but which carries the side effects demonstrated by a steady decline of interest in reading.

Does the child need instruction in the usage of known sounds?

In other words, does the child know the sound-letter correspondence but seem to have no system for using it? Remedial efforts in answer to this question include instruction in syllabication, blending, and pronunciation. The child may have an awareness of sounds but no system for applying this awareness to the attacking of larger words.

Many children find their way into remedial programs with initial diagnosis listing knowledge of letter-sound association as a major problem. Upon working with these children, it quickly becomes obvious that they know their sound-letter relationships but have not developed a system for putting them into use.

Syllabication: It is imperative to remember that the child will need to use syllabication when he comes to words of two or more syllables which he cannot pronounce at sight or through the use of other word attack techniques. An illustration of the difficulty of this task may be seen when an adult looks at the following nonsense words and attempts to pronounce them:

sogtel	sog-tel
akot	a-kot
sognochest	sog-no-chest

It should be realized that when a child attacks words which he does not know at sight his procedure is likely to be to divide the word into syllables and to pronounce the syllable without intensive phonic analysis because of his ability to associate a given syllable with a familiar syllable. A highly valuable word attack technique which meets the goal of efficiency, syllabication is of particular value to older students. The teaching of the generalizations necessary for accurate syllabication is similar for the classroom and the clinic.

For children who have had this instruction in their normal classroom situations and have failed to respond to it, we would suggest the use of the *Discovery Techniques*.

The effectiveness of this technique depends primarily upon the teacher's preparation of patterns from which to work and his understanding of the generalizations to be made, including their exceptions (see *Suggested Readings*). The number of generalizations necessary may vary with the needs of the child in relation to the types of words he meets at his instructional level.

The following three generalizations are *essential* for all children in learning the syllabication of words.

1. The vowel-consonant-vowel generalization: When a word has the structure v-c-v, syllable division is usually between the first vowel and the consonant.

$$v \quad cv$$
Example: (over = o/ver)

   However, vowels which are followed by a consonant "r" form an exception to the v/cv generalization, the "r" going with the preceding vowel.

$$vc \quad v$$
Example: (carol = car/ol)

2. The vowel-consonant-consonant-vowel generalization: When a word has the structure v-c-c-v, syllable division is usually between the consonants.

$$vc \quad cv$$
Example: (picnic = pic/nic)

   However blends and digraphs are treated as one consonant.

$$v \quad cv$$
Example: (achieve = a/chieve)

3. The consonant —le generalization: When a word ends in the structure consonant plus "le," those three letters form the last syllable.

c-le
Example: (ankle = an/kle)

Once the generalizations are made, it remains necessary to reinforce the learning through activities in which the child can use syllabication for word attack. This reinforcement is most effectively conducted through activities designed by the teacher to correspond to the material from which the child is reading.

Again, it is possible to reinforce introduced skills through game-like exercises. Some of the *Dolch Games*** and the *Phonics We Use Learning Games Kit*** are useful for reinforcement of this type. These games will help the child to realize that words can be divided into syllables rapidly and effectively. Once this awareness has been developed, he should be placed in situations where he is expected to use this skill when he meets words in a line of print.

For children who fail to understand syllabication at this point, the *Fernald Technique*[2] with a modification for emphasis on the syllables of words may be used to direct the child to substitute the pronunciation of *syllables* in all steps that require him to pronounce the *word*. Although this technique will not teach the child how to divide words into syllables, its value is in assisting the problem reader to grasp the concept of syllabication.

Blending and pronunciation: Once the word has been dissected, either through syllabication or through the actual sounding of each letter of the syllable, the child must be able to blend these sounds and to obtain a pronunciation with which he can associate a meaning. Again, classroom and clinical techniques are similar.

When difficulty with blending arises, the child must be given ample opportunity to divide known words into syllables and then to blend these sounds in order to obtain a feeling for blending. It is clear that the blending of sounds and syllables is an inherent part of each lesson in which the child learns the sound or divides the word into syllables. Again, the stress in remediation should be on giving the child material which will permit him to use his newly developed skills and to overlearn them until they become a reading

---

[2]Grace Fernald, *Remedial Techniques in Basic School Subjects* (New York: McGraw Hill Book Co., 1943), Part II.

habit. In phonics instruction, functional use of phonics cannot be accomplished without practice in syllabication and blending.

There are several phonics approaches which simplify the problem of blending and pronunciation by teaching the sounds as units rather than in isolated pronunciation. In the following case, for example, the sound of "*b*" will be taught in the initial position as it relates to the various vowels: ba, be, bi, bo, bu. This then is immediately substituted in word-building exercises:

bad	bit	but
beg	boss	

Cordts† presents in detail the techniques and philosophy of a blending approach to the teaching of phonics.

Structural Analysis

Do the words which are substituted or mispronounced contain prefixes, suffixes, or compound words?

After having experience in diagnosis, a teacher probably will note that the most serious difficulty occurs in the use of suffixes. Deficiencies in the ability to attack compound words are generally not too serious, for children easily can be taught to pronounce the words if they know the parts. If they do not know the parts, the problem is inadequate sight vocabulary. Although prefixes cause more difficulty than compound words, the fact that they are at the beginning of the word; usually a separate, easily pronounceable syllable; and concerned with a meaning which directly alters the base word makes them easier to learn and causes less difficulty in remedial reading. However, in the case of suffixes, where the above three factors are often missing, many children experience difficulty. It is with suffixes that the service of the base word is most likely to change, even though a precise difference in meaning is not evident. Note that in the following words when the suffix is removed, the spelling and configuration of the base word is distorted, causing an additional complication in the study of suffixes.

run	running	runn-ing
hope	hoping	hop-ing

---

†See Suggested Readings and Appendix B.

Classroom remediation: Basal series teacher's manuals contain specific suggestions in the area of structural analysis which, if followed, will be of great assistance in classroom remediation. These manuals generally are followed by recommendations for specific skill activities in the accompanying workbooks.

For a child who fails to respond to these techniques, the *Discovery Technique*[3] is again suggested for its advantage in making the child generalize structural patterns from known words. This technique is equally applicable to difficulties with prefixes, suffixes, or compound words. In teaching the decoding and interpretation of the prefix *un*, for example, it may be best to follow a procedure similar to this:

1. Present the word happy in a sentence.   *John is happy.*
2. Change the word to unhappy.   *John is unhappy.*
3. Have the child generalize the difference in meaning.
4. Present several other words in a similar manner.
5. Have the child generalize by answering the question, "What does *un* generally do to the meaning of a word to which it is prefixed?"
6. Collect word patterns of this type and see if they apply to the generalization.
7. Note that *un* has a sound which is consistent and that it changes the meaning of the words to which it is attached.
8. As the child reads, his attention should be called to words prefixed by *un*. He should determine if these words fit the generalization.

Word wheels which contain the base word easily can be made; as he moves the wheel, the child adds either the prefix or the suffix to the base word. Suggestions for these can be found in Russell's *Reading Aids Through the Grades.*[4] The teacher is cautioned in the construction of such reinforcement devices to be certain that the problem is not one of the child's not knowing the base word and to be alert to the spelling changes which occur when the suffix is added. Prepared exercises of this type are found in materials such as the *Classroom Reading Clinic.*** In this kit, word wheels, upon which base words are altered by prefixes and suffixes, provide ready-made reinforcement exercises.

---

[3]Botel, *How to Teach Reading*, p. 40.
[4]David H. Russell and Etta E. Karp, *Reading Aids Through the Grades* (Bureau of Publications, 1951).

Clinical remediation: Assuming that the child has been exposed to instruction in structural analysis and that the results of that instruction were, for the most part, unsatisfactory, the child is led to make the basic generalizations necessary for attack upon unfamiliar words. Through the *Discovery Technique*, the child is encouraged to make generalizations and become an active learner.

The reinforcement of instruction quite often is done in connection with instruction in other areas; for example, when an experience story is formed to aid sight vocabulary or comprehension, words which have possibilities for structural analysis can be attacked by using learning in word structure. Similar reinforcement can be applied during the free reading the child will do during remediation.

Children find the game approach an easy way in which to over-learn these skills. The *SRA Word Games Laboratory*** has several well-developed games for the reinforcement of the initial instruction in prefixes, suffixes, and compound words. These are usually interesting to the child and contain an inherent motivational advantage as well as the peer group learning advantage which has been previously discussed.

Supplementation of instruction can be accomplished by the use of the film-strips *Goals in Spelling*** which have been carefully prepared to present the concepts of structural analysis in a meaningful, motivating manner. Further reinforcement can be provided, especially for older students, with the materials from *Tactics in Reading*** and *Basic Reading Skills.*** Note that these materials direct older students to structural analysis exercises designed to encourage the student with more mature interests.

Contextual Clues

When the child made his contextual errors, were contextual clues available which, if observed, could have prevented the error?

Contextual clues are clues having to do with the relationship of words to their use in phrases, sentences, and paragraphs.

This difficulty is twofold: first, the child may not know what a contextual clue is and may need basic instruction to make him aware of the function of such clues; secondly, the child may recognize such clues when directed to them but does not normally anticipate them. For contextual clues to be useful in word attack, the child must anticipate the author's use of them. Finding that the child's difficulty is in not knowing the clues, the teacher must provide instruction in how to anticipate the clues besides simply teaching them. However, if the child already knows the clues, instruction may be limited to developing awareness of the clues.

Classroom remediation: Necessary for the anticipation of contextual clues is experience with various types of literary styles; therefore, remedial efforts should include free reading in the various types of contextual situations (i.e., the novel, the biography, and so on). Based upon these experiences with various types of literature, the child is more able to anticipate the type of context that a style normally presents and, therefore, to have better opportunities for using context clues when they are available.

Another step in anticipation of context clues is to assist the child in the techniques of previewing material before reading. Previewing helps him to determine the type of literature and the general direction of the author's writing as well as possibly locating some specific context clues prior to reading. Again, the classroom teacher will find use for directed activities in the manuals of basal series which will show, within the material the child is using, the classroom techniques for the use of context clues. Specifically prepared exercises such as *Using the Context*** provide the child with experiences in drill type situations which require the type of thinking necessary to use context. Using a forced-choice incomplete sentence arrangement (closure), these exercises require the child to justify his choice in terms of the available information. One of the early exercises reads as follows:[5]

> Dick's picture was very funny. The children looked at it and began to
> 1. _____
>
>   1. find   laugh   little

Removing the pure contextual guess from reading and replacing it with a process of contextual inferring helps the child develop the proper attitude for using contextual clues. Exercises of this type help to establish attitude and habit, but the ultimate effectiveness of the use of context must be in normal reading situations, rather than drills.

---

[5]Richard A. Boning, *Using the Context, Book A* (Rockville Centre, New York: Barnell Loft, Ltd., 1962).

Clinical remediation: An emphasis on free reading in a variety of types of materials must precede direct instruction with attention to the author's style and use of context clues. Drill activity has not proven to be useful with children who are seriously limited in this skill; in fact, it appears that excessive drill may be one of the reasons that such a child does not make use of contextual clues. Because drill activities are normally taken out of context, overuse of drill places the child in a situation which denies him the use of context and sabotages our aim in remediation for children with this deficiency. Therefore, although not outlawed in clinical remediation, drill type activities should be limited.

In place of drill, it is best to use the contextual situations in which the child is placed at his instructional level and to teach the use of context in directed activities while striving for other desirable goals. This may be done more easily in clinical remediation because of the individual nature of the program. Suppose that a child is working in a Directed Reading Activity (DRA) with the purpose of looking for the main idea. The child can be directed to contextual clues which will assist him to develop the main ideas of the story. In this manner, the child is not so likely to obtain the impression that the skills being presented are isolated and are to be used one at a time.

Closure activities should be extremely useful in clinical remediation. They call for the child to *fill in* words which are omitted by the teacher. For example, if the sentence has several words of usual difficulty, the teacher will rewrite the sentence and ask the child to read the easier words and fill-in the blanks. "Seven men were on a fishing trip. The _____ waves were extremely severe. Several of the men were washed _____. As others attempted to _____ the drowning men, they, too, were washed overboard. Alas, the ocean _____, and all seven were saved." Closure activities designed to aid comprehension call for meaningful substitutions, although not necessarily for the author's exact words. In the first blank above, *huge, large,* and *ocean* are all acceptable. The point is that children can be placed in situations calling for thinking about meaning and using context.

For older students, stressing the importance of context may be done through the use of books which they are expected to study in school. More attention to this aspect of the use of context is discussed under the comprehension skill area. *Tactics in Reading*** and *Basic Reading Skills*** provide directed activities with context clues for these older students.

Did the child's error result from failure to observe punctuation clues?

Punctuation errors are often due to the frustration level of the material rather than failure to observe punctuation. If this is true, directed activity to observe the markings will be useless and time may be spent more wisely on other skill areas with materials of the proper level. However, if the error is due to the child's lack of knowledge about the use of punctuation marks, instruction is needed.

Classroom remediation: Choral reading or reading in unison is again found to be an effective, subtle way for the child to obtain a feeling for punctuation marks. Following group oral reading, the child's attention should be called to the fact that punctuation marks have different functions and call for different inflections. Listening to good oral reading placed on a tape recorder will also assist in helping the child to become aware of the need to observe punctuation marks in his reading materials.

Opportunities for the child to follow the teacher as he reads in order to determine whether or not he observed punctuation marks properly also may be used effectively. When the teacher intentionally distorts the punctuation, the child can be directed to explain what this does to the ideas of the author. When used sparingly, this technique works well with youngsters having trouble hearing their own punctuation errors.

Clinical remediation: The above mentioned procedures may be supplemented by the experience story approach which puts the child in the author's place and makes him more aware of the need for punctuation to express how he feels and what he says. Generally, the reading specialist will add the punctuation necessary to indicate the expression which the child has made. Procedures can be varied by asking the child to indicate the appropriate punctuation and then by intentionally distorting the punctuation to change the meaning of the child's contribution. The child must then recognize the error and correct it. Note that both of these techniques place the burden upon the child for awareness of correct punctuation.

Extended Remediation

Due to the thoroughness of clinical diagnosis, several additional considerations must be made when the child begins remediation. Again, these considerations are in terms of the diagnostic conclusions.

Are the child's errors made when he knows the proper word attack skills in isolation but not when they are needed in context?

This particular diagnosis conclusion should be reached in clinical diagnosis. It is accentuated in clinical remediation because readers with severe problems have this difficulty in common, thus further complicating other weaknesses. In these cases, the child has been exposed to at least one system of instruction in phonics and has learned the phonic skills involved. It becomes important, therefore, for the child to be placed in a reading situation where the skills can be applied and, through individualized instruction, directed toward their most effective use. Of course, these children will have all isolated word attack drills discontinued since drill is not needed.

Techniques for the application of word attack skills to context have been mentioned under each skill category. Children with this deficiency will be placed in many situations in which a word attack skill will help him to approach unfamiliar material. Since each is a highly individualized instructional situation, the child must be provided with direction as to the effective technique. Gradually, he will develop the ability to attack unfamiliar material with less and less teacher direction.

Special Considerations in Word Attack

Several comments will further the teacher's understanding of his total role in the area of word attack. First, dictionary skills are excellent, indispensable word attack techniques. Children with reading problems may benefit from dictionary instruction; however, asking for special help for problem readers usually does not result from a limitation of dictionary skills alone. Work in programming has produced two publications which may be of use in either classroom or clinical remediation, *Lessons for Self Instruction in Basic Skills*** and *David Discovers the Dictionary*.** The appeal of these programs to remediation is their individualized approach, which requires a minimum of teacher supervision to assist the child in acquiring the skills necessary to use the dictionary.

Secondly, although many children can be taught the various word attack skills and know how to use them in context, the efficient use of these skills must be understood. Specifically, which word attack skills should be used first? A child comes upon an unknown word (e.g., *debating*) and must make a decision about how to attack it. Should he start with sounding the first syllable "duh-eh," should he first detach the suffix, or should he start elsewhere? The following suggested procedure is based upon the belief that the child should start with the largest unit in the word so that he can attack it quickly and with the least possible distortion. The child follows this procedure to the point at which he pronounces the word. The procedure is:

1. Look carefully at the word from left to right. Although this step may appear to be elementary, it is often all that is necessary.
2. Examine the context for contextual clues.
3. Examine the word for structural characteristics: prefixes, suffixes, and compound words.
4. Divide the word into syllables and try to pronounce it. As stated earlier, this technique is often sufficient for older readers.
5. Establish the vowel sounds and attempt to pronounce them.
6. Sound out all letters and attempt to pronounce the word.
7. If at this point the student still is unable to derive the word pronunciation or meaning, he should: first, be referred to the dictionary; second, be directed to use word attack skills which will unlock the word; or third, be told the word.

Although certainly not an unalterable approach to unknown words, the above system enables the child to practice efficient word attack techniques and generally leads him to the quickest, most satisfactory pronunciation and meaning of the unknown word. Now when the child comes to an unknown word (e.g., *debating*) the teacher can direct him through the steps mentioned above. The handy placement of these steps in printed form in a place easily available to the child will facilitate quicker independent usage. Reinforcement activities in context will be necessary for the child to develop such a technique and to retain it as a habit.

Motivation

By far the strongest motivation for the child in the study of word attack skills is being able to see how this knowledge and skill enable him to become more independent in his reading. It is essential, therefore, for the child to be put in the situation of transferring learned skills to context in every lesson if possible. Game type activities, as suggested above, make the reinforcement of these skills more informal and pleasurable. The child should be assured of an opportunity to win the games, for it is obvious that constant failure with these games will discourage the child. The motivation inherent in the pleasant and successful interrelationship with children supplies the desired outcomes.

The *Discovery Technique* has motivational appeal, especially to some of the older students who need work in word attack. The idea of generalizing the concepts of word attack with a minimum of teacher supervision usually becomes a highly motivating situation.

Graphic illustrations of a child's progress usually help to motivate. Teacher-made materials designed to illustrate established goals and the child's achievement within the scope and capabilities are effective motivating devices too.

Programmed materials with immediate feedback are interesting to children and contain inherent motivational appeal. These materials, designed to reinforce correct and alter incorrect responses, establish situations in which the child eventually will be successful — a desirable outcome in all types of remedial programs. A special section has been included at the end of Chapter 9, p. 259 for discussion of the child who, in spite of having no specific skill deficiencies, for all practical purposes may be labeled a nonreader. Included in this discussion will be a combination of word recognition and comprehension techniques.

SUMMARY

The remedial techniques to be used in the area of vocabulary deficiencies, whether sight vocabulary or word attack, are based on precise diagnostic findings. Once these are determined, the educator has a variety of approaches in remediation from which to choose. Starting with those which he believes will serve the child's needs most adequately, the educator remains alert during instruction to the possibility that his original approach may need to be modified as instruction continues. The goal of diagnosis is to make efficient use of instructional time; therefore, changes should be made only to insure maximum effectiveness.

Constant awareness of the value of incorporating skill activities into contextual situations is the responsibility of both the teacher and the reading specialist. Continued drill, without well-developed transfer opportunities, is of little value.

SUGGESTED READINGS

Botel, Morton. *How to Teach Reading,* Chapters 3 and 5. Chicago: Follett Publishing Co., 1968. In this well-written book, Botel presents the "discovery" and "spelling" mastery techniques for use in sight vocabulary and word attack lessons. The reader will find this a practical guide to developmental as well as remedial activities.

Burmeister, Lou E. "Usefulness of Phonic Generalizations." *The Reading Teacher,* January, 1968, pp. 349-59. This article reviews the research on phonic generalizations. A reading of this review is essential prior to work with children in a program which concentrates on phonics and the use of phonics.

Clymer, Theodore. "The Utility of Phonics Generalizations in the Primary Grades." *The Reading Teacher,* January, 1963, 252-58. This article discusses how functional the generalizations commonly taught to children are in terms of the number of times the generalizations hold true and the number of words to which they apply.

Cordts, Anna D. *Phonics for the Reading Teacher.* New York: Holt, Rinehart and Winston, 1965. This entire book is devoted to a description and explanation of a method of teaching phonics which reduces the necessity for extra blending of isolated sounds. The reader will find this technique valuable in working with many problem readers.

Fries, Charles C. *Linguistics and Reading.* New York: Holt, Rinehart and Winston, 1963. One explanation for the linguistic involvement in the teaching of reading can be found in this book. For those who have difficulty understanding the linguist, this book is a good introduction. Teachers of problem readers must acquaint themselves with the works of the linguists.

Hall, MaryAnne. *Teaching Reading as a Language Experience*. Columbus, Ohio: Charles E. Merrill Publishing Co., 1970. This book presents basic information for teachers concerning the nature and uses of language experience as an approach to reading instruction.

Heilman, Arthur W. *Phonics in Proper Perspective*. Columbus, Ohio: Charles E. Merrill Publishing Co., 1968. Heilman has combined an assessment of the place of phonics with a survey of the skills to be taught and has included examples and appropriate word lists. The educator who works with problem readers will find this book or one like it indispensable in working with phonics.

Herrick, Virgil E., and Nerbovig, Marcella. *Using Experience Charts with Children*. Columbus, Ohio: Charles E. Merrill Publishing Co., 1964. This booklet will provide the reader with many suggestions concerning the construction and use of experience charts. The classroom teacher should find these suggestions easily applicable to this group.

Lee, Dorris M. and Allen, R. V. *Learning to Read Through Experience*. New York: Appleton-Century-Crofts, 1963. A combination of philosophy and techniques, this book is a must for those who plan to work with seriously handicapped children. As we have indicated, this approach will be of particular value with many children, and the book will provide the educator with a thorough background from which to work.

Stauffer, Russell. *The Language-Experience Approach to the Teaching of Reading*. New York: Harper & Row, 1970. Chapters 1, 2, and 3 discuss the theory and uses of language experience approaches. Chapter 10 discusses special uses of language experience including clinical cases.

Wilson, Robert M. and Hall, MaryAnne. *Programmed Word Attack for Teachers*. Columbus, Ohio: Charles E. Merrill Publishing Co., 1968. This book presents the basic knowledge about word attack needed by teachers for instruction. The material is presented in a programmed format followed by tests which enable teachers to demonstrate their knowledge of word attack skills.

9

Remedial Activities for Comprehension Skills

All children, regardless of the severity of their reading problems, can think, and comprehension is a thinking activity. Comprehension in reading involves the skills of memory, the association of one's experiences with the ideas of another, and reflective thinking. Although children who can decode the printed words should be able to comprehend the material if the concepts involved are within their field of experiences, such is not always the case. Children need direction, encouragement, and specific instruction to learn how to apply their thinking skills to reading.

Comprehension is a difficult area for instruction. Terms and goals are not identified as easily as they are for the other skill areas of sight vocabulary and word attack. Suggested methods for instruction are vague; for example, many teacher's guides offer techniques for instruction in comprehension which are limited to asking the children questions. In practice, a child is asked a question; if he does not know the answer, one of his classmates is asked the same question. It would seem that such practices do not necessarily assist a child in developing comprehension skills.

Note that sight vocabulary and word attack are separated from comprehension, although all three areas are concerned with the meaning of words. This separation is made on the assumption that comprehension involves the meaning of words as they relate to each other and that it requires both sight vocabulary and word attack to be effective. Comprehension also involves reading as an active, thinking process. Even though pure memory will be an asset, comprehending involves purposeful reading during which the reader brings his ideas and those of the author together to form new meanings through the association of ideas.

Comprehension, being a complex concept, involves progressive experiences in the reading act. Therefore, the more a child reads, the better he is likely to comprehend. Since problem readers usually choose to read very little or not at all, they fall further and further behind. For this reason, remedial programs should be designed to allow many opportunities to read easy, interesting material of many varieties (fiction, science, biographies, animal stories, true adventure, and so on). It is partly through the awareness of authors' styles that a realistic feeling for comprehension can be developed. Without extensive reading in a remedial program, progress in the concepts of comprehension will be limited. We suggest that *at least* one fourth of all remedial time be devoted to silent reading of materials chosen by the child.

THE DIRECTED READING ACTIVITY

When teachers direct the comprehension of children, they usually use a form of the Directed Reading Activity (DRA). The steps of the DRA and several possibilities for its use are provided as review material.

1. *Readiness:* Motivation, purpose setting, and vocabulary development are the major features of the readiness step. Traditionally, the teacher directs the student at the readiness level. However, the child should be encouraged to motivate himself by selecting stories which he wants to read, sampling the story to see if he is interested, and contracting with the teacher to perform certain readings (see Chapter 6). The child should be encouraged to set his own purposes by making questions from the story title, looking at pictures in the story and forming questions about them, and skimming the story to obtain enough information to formulate questions about what is to happen. He should be encouraged to

anticipate vocabulary difficulties and be prepared, without teacher direction, to use a glossary, apply word attack skills, and call for assistance when unable to decode a word. As the child develops skills in the readiness step, he becomes an independent reader, the ultimate objective.

2. *Silent reading:* Children read to satisfy the purposes that have established for reading in the readiness step. Traditionally, teachers direct the silent reading step by determining the amount of material to be read silently (i.e., a paragraph, a page, several pages, or an entire story). As he directs the child in silent reading, the teacher asks questions to determine whether the reading has been meaningful, sets new purposes for the next portion to be read, and directs rereading when necessary. Ultimately, the child should direct his own silent reading. As he reads silently, he should stop at intervals of his own choosing to reflect on the purposes which he has set for himself, reform his purposes as the story develops, and reread when meanings are unclear. Teachers can develop independence by gradually increasing the amounts of materials to be read silently.

3. *Recitation:* A child is expected to talk with the teacher about what he has read. Traditionally, the teacher asks predetermined questions about the reading which he expects the child to be able to answer. Again, ultimately, the child should conduct the recitation step for himself. He should keep notes on the major points he has read, form questions on what he has read, ask those questions of the teacher or of other children, and demonstrate what he has comprehended through plays, art work, writing of summaries, and the like.

4. *Rereading:* When comprehension is not clear, concepts not fully developed, or portions of the story apparently not understood, teachers can direct a child to reread, either orally or silently. Of course, as a child gains maturity in independently working the first three steps, he can direct his own rereading as well. When he checks his own reading for purposes, he will know when certain portions need to be reread. He also might find passages which he wants to share with other children or with the teacher, thus creating meaningful oral reading opportunities. A child might choose to reread

an entire story several times when he enjoys it. Oral reading conducted with children reading to each other in pairs also builds independence and reduces pressure.

5. *Enrichment:*   When the child expresses interest in the ideas of a story, teachers can direct him to other materials containing similar content or style. It is not uncommon, for example, for children to become interested in bibliographies. When that interest is expressed, opportunities for reading bibliographies should be provided. Other children might find that they enjoy drawing or painting pictures about what they have read. Teachers should encourage them to do so. Still others might enjoy writing new endings to stories. Creative activities such as these should be permitted and encouraged as an important part of the remedial program. Once again, as a child gains comprehension skills, he should be encouraged to make his own decisions about the type of enrichment activities he wants to pursue. He might choose to do nothing more with the book, go to the library to look for a similar type of book, attempt a creative writing, or form discussion groups on stories of common interest.

The DRA should be used flexibly in remediation. The several alternatives mentioned above are only a few of the many alternatives that teachers use regularly. Two important points are being made: the activity should be lively and interesting; if the children are bored, the type of activity should be changed. The children should be helped to gain independence; everytime a child takes a step on his own, he should be encouraged, for if the child sees reading as interesting and if he strives for independence, remediation will be successful.

REMEDIAL ACTIVITIES IN COMPREHENSION

As in other skill areas, remedial efforts in the comprehension area exist in terms of the questions which led to diagnostic conclusions in the last chapter. These questions are:

1. Do the child's comprehension difficulties appear to increase as he encounters larger units of material?

2. Are the child's errors due to the type of comprehension expected?
3. Can the child recall the author's ideas, even though he remains unable to perform in content areas?
4. Is there a total failure to respond to comprehension situations?
5. Is the lack of response due basically to speed?

It is unlikely that a child will be limited in only one of these aspects of comprehension. Therefore, the merging of the following techniques is clearly possibly and highly desirable when the occasion demands.

Do the child's comprehension difficulties appear to increase as he encounters larger units of material?

The improvement of reading skills depends on the student's ability to respond to units of print of increasing length. In diagnosis it is easy to note whether the child's comprehension is limited basically to sentences, paragraphs, or to larger units. In these cases the problem is one of not being able to recognize the relationship between units of varying sizes and the flow of ideas created by the author.

Classroom remediation: All remedial approaches must start at the instructional or independent level. When the difficulty is related to the size of the unit, the instructional level is the largest unit the child can handle effectively. The DRA then is used by the teacher to help the child approach the next largest unit. The teacher must direct the child carefully toward desirable comprehension goals. When skill in comprehension has been attained, the child is then provided with experiences to enable him to set his own goals in the future. More material is then attempted by using the same general procedure to facilitate overlearning.

Many commercially prepared materials are available to assist the teacher in this effort. Note that the *SRA Reading Laboratory*,** for example, numbers the paragraphs in the easier materials for direct reference to small units of print. Many other materials take similar approaches to quantity of material expected to be understood.

The structure as well as the length of sentences and paragraphs causes trouble in textbook reading and in free reading, especially

with older children. *Tactics in Reading*** provides specific exercises
in sentence and paragraph meaning. Designed for students in the
secondary grades, these contain a variety of sentence and paragraph
structures and sufficient interest for motivation. *Basic Reading
Skills*** provides this reinforcement in workbook form with emphasis on shorter passages for older students.

Clinical remediation: Again, the approaches used in the classroom
are applicable; however, they are intensified and personalized in
clinical remediation.

   Highly motivating teacher-made materials easily can be developed to help children handle larger quantities of material. For example, a TV Guide from the Sunday newspaper can be used to help
children handle varying amounts of printed material and to respond
to tasks of varying difficulty. For example, the child can be asked:

1. What show is offered on Channel 4 at seven o'clock on Tues-
   day evening?
2. What sports events are offered on Saturday?
3. Select four movies you would like to watch during the week.
4. What shows are featured at eight o'clock each day?
5. Take 1½ hour per night and schedule your own television
   watching for the week.

   The use of newspaper articles, want ads, telephone yellow
pages, cookbooks, shop manuals, catalogues, encyclopedias, and dic-
tionaries can be developed similarly by starting with a specific activity requiring a minimum of reading and moving toward extended
activities requiring considerable reading. Children in remedial programs can relate easily and enthusiastically to materials such as
these, although they might tend to turn off book reading.

   Paragraph comprehension and understanding the interrelationship between paragraphs appear to be difficult tasks for many older
students. The reading specialist, therefore, must have materials
available for various reading levels and interests toward which to
direct the reading activities of these children. The *McCall Crabb
Standard Test Lessons,*** *The Reader's Digest Skill Builders,***
and the *SRA Reading Laboratories*** as well as a wide variety of
workbook type materials provide clinical remediation with a large
supply of appropriate materials of varying lengths.

Experience stories of increasing size may be used for the child who is limited in this area. The experience stories may appear as lines of print, short paragraphs, or larger units as the need demands. Again, it is the placement of the child in the role of the author that creates a receptive atmosphere for effective instruction in the concepts of comprehension.

Are the child's errors due to the type of comprehension expected?

All too often comprehension in the classroom is limited to questions on items for which there is but one correct response; consequently, such questions measure only the ability to recall details. However, in real reading situations, obtaining details is but one of several vitally important comprehension skills which must be developed. Instruction in these skill areas calls for specific changes in the DRA Readiness, Silent Reading, Recitation, Rereading, and Enrichment steps. These changes are explored under each type of comprehension skill.

The types of comprehension skills can be classified broadly as:

1. Literal understanding
2. Interpretation
3. Problem solving

The abilities to follow directions and to organize the author's ideas, atlhough they are also types of comprehension, will not be discussed here, although they will be discussed under the topic of study skills.

Remediation of comprehension deficiencies is based on diagnostic findings in relation to these five areas. Remediation presumes that the diagnostic conclusions were based upon an inner-analysis vide some measure of these different types of comprehension and that the diagnostic conclusions were based upon an inner-analysis of these measures to determine the precise nature of the deficiency. Comprehension, a thinking process, needs to be taught with an eye toward guiding and developing the thinking processes of the child to anticipate the type of comprehension desired.

Questioning

Teachers ask children questions to determine whether or not they have comprehended what has been read. The type of question and the expected response needs careful consideration prior to specific discussion of remedial activities. All too often, the type of question asked in commercially prepared materials is designed to obtain specific facts from the story (literal understanding). When working with large or small groups of children, questions at the literal level can be asked of the entire group at one time. Using Durrell's** idea of every-pupil-response cards, all children can quickly respond to literal questions. Each child, for example, has a card stating *yes* and one stating *no*. The teacher can select five or ten important details from the story and ask questions calling for a *yes* or *no* answer. Cards with names of story characters, dates, numbers to indicate choices in multiple choice questions, and so on also can be used. The teacher notes all of the children's responses and directs rereading or reformulates questions when responses are not accurate. Literal understanding can be checked in a short period of time, leaving more time for questions and activities at the interpretation and problem-solving levels. While comprehension at the literal level is extremely important, the time normally allocated for it is out of proportion to its importance.

When questioned at the interpretation level, the child is expected to respond in his own words, paraphrasing the ideas of the author. Such questions or activities as:

1. In your own words state the main idea of the story.
2. How would you summarize the author's major point?
3. Why did the major character lose his temper?

Questioning at the interpretation level requires that the child draw upon his field of experience to interpret the author's words. While we are interested in accurate interpretation, the teacher *must not* have a preconceived statement of the answer he is seeking. The child interprets in the best way that he can and his efforts must be accepted. If his answer contains inaccuracies, there is the possibility of inaccurate reading or of an inappropriate background of experiences. In either case, inaccuracy calls for reteaching rather than criticism. As the child grows more willing to discuss the ideas of the author and to express his feelings about what he has read, interpretation skills develop.

When questioned at the problem-solving level, the child is expected to think beyond the content of the story, applying either critical or creative thinking skills to the author's ideas through such questions as:

1. What would you have done if you were Jim?   (creative)
2. Did Jim make a good decision? Why?   (critical)
3. Can you think of a better ending for the story?   (creative)
4. What reasons can you give for father's actions?   (critical)

Obviously, questioning at the critical and creative thinking levels calls for even more openness on the part of the teacher. When the teacher asks critical questions, the child must have understood the author, must be able to interpret the author, and must apply his own experiences in order to analyze what has happened. The child's answer may differ from the one which the teacher has in mind and still may be accurate. If the child's reasoning is not clear, probing questions assist the child to seek alternatives.

A Learning Center Using Clothes Pins and Pizza Plate Provides Manipulative Activities Which Are Self-correcting

In creative thinking, any answer given by the child is acceptable and correct. He is being asked to create, and what he creates is good. Children tend to enjoy creative activities and, when their answers are accepted, tend to become more creative. For example, ask a group of children to think of a new title for a story with the idea of making the story into a television show. Tell them the title should attract attention. Children usually start with rather traditional titles but soon open up as they see the teacher accepting all of their responses.

The question asked by the teacher is important, but even more important, perhaps, is the teacher's response to the child's efforts. Accepting, probing, reteaching, and making reading activities exciting for children depend upon the teacher's attitude toward the responses of those children. Children also will learn to accept and to value a variety of peer responses as they see the teacher accepting them.

Literal Understanding

Noting important facts, recalling details, understanding sequences, and obtaining a feeling for the general mood and setting of the story are examples of literal understanding. Children generally receive considerable experience in reading lessons on literal understanding. They are accustomed to answering questions concerning details. Most children try to remember as much as they can about what they have read. Therefore, memory is a key ingredient to successful performance in literal understanding. Obviously, if one cannot remember what he has read, he cannot answer questions concerning it. It is in the first and fourth steps of the DRA that attention should best be focused to develop literal understanding. First, the child must always be aware of his purpose for reading particular material; and, second, if upon recitation the child is unable to understand the details, he should return to the specific section of the material in which the answer can be located. The problem, then, is twofold: finding what types of goal setting experiences are the most helpful, and finding what types of directed rereading best illustrate to the child a method for literal understandings.

The thought process involved in the recall of directly stated facts involves encouraging the child to pay attention to important details, to remember them, and to relate them to the larger ideas of the author. Names of people, places, dates, and major events should be emphasized during reading. Some prefer to underline or otherwise highlight the directly stated facts to be remembered; others accomplish this goal by taking notes. Regardless of the technique, the process is the same (i.e., the child is expected to indicate through action an awareness of the fact to be recalled, thereby triggering his mind to remember).

Classroom remediation: Besides normal reading exercises, many available classroom situations may serve to focus attention on literal understanding. With direction, the child can come to realize that details and sequences have definite importance in certain reading situations. To facilitate this realization, the teacher should start remediation with materials which are vitally interesting to the child, thus creating motivation for the effort which will be expected of him.

Pointing out the important information via italicized print, boldface type, information repeated for stress, and illustrated information highlights clues to important details to be remembered. Perhaps more subtle but equally useful are clues which words contain. Descriptive adjectives, proper nouns, action verbs, and the like all call attention to those types of details which should receive more careful attention. For example:

The *large house burned* in the middle of the *night*.

Most basal material is well designed to develop understanding skills. The classroom teacher using basal materials first must be certain that the child is working at the appropriate level and then select those lessons which appear to be most useful.

The reinforcement of these learned skills should occur daily in all reading situations; this task is more clearly the responsibility of the classroom teacher since he has these opportunities regularly, especially in the content areas. Although a child experiencing difficulty with literal understanding may have reading for details stressed to the exclusion of other types of comprehension, efforts should be made to call the child's attention to other types as soon as possible; otherwise, the child may have a mistaken impression of comprehension.

Recalling sequences causes considerable difficulty for many children. When deficient, the child is limited in his ability to handle content type materials and to fully appreciate reading of longer units.

The thought processes needed involve perceiving groups of items that are related in time (i.e., one comes first, then the next, and so on). Initially, children must obtain sequencing practice from such activities as following oral directions, doing work at their seats from oral and written instruction, or recalling events from a story which has been read to them by another.

During the DRA, the teacher will indicate to the child, prior to actual reading, that the material has sequential information in it and that a comprehension check will be in terms of sequences. When the child is deficient in this skill, it is normal to start with a sequence of two events and to advance to more involved sequences after that is understood. For example, begin with two events which are clearly representative of the beginning and ending of the story. When the children can perform with two events (i.e., when they can tell which one came first), add a third event, then a fourth, and so on. However, starting with many events to place in sequence tends to smother children with choices and does not lead to effective sequencing.

Asking children to place comics taken from the Sunday newspaper in sequence is a motivating technique for teaching sequences. Start with obvious sequences and move toward more subtle ones. If they are cut apart and pasted to cards, the comics are quite durable. Numbers on the backs of the cards to indicate the sequence make the activity self-correcting. Obviously, a teacher can build many sequence activities from comics in a short time and with little expenditure of school funds. Teachers can also develop sequence activities from newspaper headlines concerning space shots, world series games, elections, and the like. Children can read the headlines and place the events (recent to their experiences) in order. They can also match the headlines with newspaper pictures which they have placed in sequence.

Some experience stories can be cut into parts. When experience stories are stimulated by photographs taken during a trip, the photos can be arranged in sequence, topics can be written for each picture, and then topics can be arranged in order. Children can thus arrange the parts to make a sequential story.

Directing the child's attention to sequencing clues used by authors for emphasis on the importance of sequences is usually of some value. Items that are numbered, steps in a process, dates, the mention of time, and the use of sequence words (e.g., *afterwards, before, during*) are all indications that the author feels the sequence of events is of particular importance.

The development of consciousness of sequence often is done best by more subtle means. We might attempt to direct the child to the idea of making a movie in which three or four scenes are to be produced by asking, "What is the order of scenes so that the audience will understand the story?" Many teachers have used the technique of asking the child to retell the story successfully. However, it is important to realize that the child who is deficient in this skill may experience considerable difficulty in telling the story in sequence and may merely relate the details indiscriminately instead.

Clinical remediation: Using the same techniques as the classroom teacher, the reading specialist focuses his attention on the readiness, recitation, and reading steps in the DRA. During readiness, the child is assisted in obtaining certain types of interesting purposes which will prepare him for the information to be read. As the child develops skill in this step, there will be less and less teacher direction, until, finally, the child is in a position to direct himself to attack the passage purposefully. During recitation, some check will be made on the effectiveness of the child's attempt to recall directly stated facts. When recitation indicates that reading for details was ineffective, rereading is used for instruction. Here, the reading specialist directs the child to the section of the passage in which the desired information is contained. The child is asked to reread this section orally or silently and to locate the section which contains the desired details. The child is then redirected to the question and asked for the appropriate response. To reinforce the child's answering of this question, another situation should be created immediately requiring performance with the same skill on new material so that the child is aware of his ability to handle this step unassisted.

Due to the numerous test-like situations that call for the recall or recognition of details, the reading specialist, particularly with older students, will attempt to provide test-like exercises in which the preciseness of response depends upon the selection of the proper answer from several possible correct answers. Particularly useful in these cases is the multiple-choice question technique and, at times, the matching question technique. An awareness of the necessity for satisfactory performance on these types of questions is useful.

Although initial instruction in this area wisely is conducted at easy reading levels, it is necessary to move to the instructional level, for it is at this level that the child is most likely to see the necessity for concentration in order to reach desired goals. We often find that full attention is lacking when children are limited to working on easy material which does not require concentration. It is only with concentrated reading that directly stated facts can be recalled accurately. The *Reading Skilltext,*** *Reading for Meaning,*** *SRA Reading Laboratories,*** and the *Standard Test Lessons in Reading*** are examples of the types of readily available materials assigned for literal understanding. Most materials are used best for reinforcement since careful teacher direction and instruction are necessary in a child's initial efforts. It is a mistake to drill children in materials without immediate teacher follow-up to evaluate and redirect, since in the case of continued failure, materials can soon become burdensome and disinteresting to the child. By correcting errors immediately, the likelihood of reinforcing correct responses is enhanced. Of course, it is usually better to provide answer keys so that children can check their own work. When they check their own answers, reinforcement possibilities increase. They are more involved in the appropriateness of their work; their responses are reinforced immediately; and they can look for the correct answer when they cannot figure it out from the question asked. Self-correction is a highly desirable activity for children and saves teachers considerable time. It is important to remember that when a check exists in a learning situation (not a testing situation), the child can use several routes to answers. He can figure out the answer himself; he can ask someone else; he can look on an answer sheet; or he can look on someone else's paper. As long as he *learns* from his technique, he is *not* cheating. Obviously, if a teacher thinks a child is taking advantage of the opportunity to correct himself, he can change the rules for that student. Better yet, he can check the child's work occasionally, indicating interest in him and verifying his efforts. Such checking should be done in a conference atmosphere rather than in a "checking-up" atmosphere.

In clinical remediation, it is profitable to establish that the child is interested enough in the material to feel that the sequences are worthwhile and that he is reading material which is not too difficult in concept and vocabulary. For this reason, we often start with experience stories in which the child is asked to explain how to do something, such as build a model airplane, and then is directed to analyze the techniques which he used to indicate sequences. From this, of course, he will be directed to unfamiliar material of a similar nature to see how another author accomplishes the same task. When possible, the teacher can obtain funds to purchase car, ship, or airplane models and help children to see the importance of sequences by working with them in constructing models by using the sequential directions on the box. If model building is among the choices a child has when he develops his contract, he is likely to choose it. Recipes and sewing patterns have the same type of appeal for girls.

Again, the quantity of the material upon which the child is expected to recall sequences should be controlled carefully to keep the situation a potentially successful one. We want to be certain that the child's limitations are not due simply to poor memory.

Organization skills are closely related to the skill of sequence reading and should be considered remedial techniques. They are discussed more fully on page 235.

Older children seem to respond quite well to the materials in *Tactics in Reading*** which provides directed activities suitable for the reinforcement of sequence skills. The use of outlining to establish sequences has been used effectively as a means to develop this skill. The *Reading for Meaning*** exercises emphasize this technique for children able to read at and above the fourth grade level. A partial outline is suggested for children displaying serious difficulties with the concept of outlining. Completion of the outline develops the concept of what an outline should be as well as a feeling for the sequence of ideas. As competency develops, the child's contribution should constitute more of the outline; the ultimate goal is that the child will be able to construct an outline of his own unassisted.

The reinforcement of sequences quite often is not available in prepared materials, so it is necessary to draw upon every opportunity to correlate and reinforce sequence skills in the context areas.

Interpretation

The ability of the child to understand the relationship between the details and to draw one or two central ideas from a series of sentences or paragraphs is the skill of interpretation. Paraphrasing and drawing inferences are also examples of interpretation. Any activity which necessitates the child's relating to the author's ideas by using his own words and his own experiences involves interpretation. The key to remediation at the interpretation level is to accept and use the child's efforts for diagnostic teaching. If, for example, a child cannot relate to a mountain-climbing story, the teacher should find some pictures, a movie, or a television show about mountain climbing so that the child can have experiences relating to mountain climbing. At the interpretation level, the child should realize the importance of stating the author's ideas in his own words. Many children, when asked interpretation questions, respond at the literal understanding level (i.e., they parrot the author). Probing techniques, which accept the child's response but urge him to respond further, can help refine the thinking skills needed for interpretation. After experience stories are written, the teacher can write the same story while paraphrasing the children's stories. Children match the specific section of the teacher's story with their own. Once that skill is developed children can work in teams, paraphrasing their own stories.

Classroom remediation: Numerous opportunities are available to the classroom teacher for presentation of interpretation activities. Many teachers avoid activities in the interpretation area because the response must be individualized and the correctness of the response is difficult to verify. However, the importance of interpretation demands that considerable attention be given to it.

Since interpretation involves the child's ability to relate his thinking to that of the author, the first step of the DRA will need emphasis. Reading purposes will stress such activities as summarizing, reading between the lines, and determining the main idea instead of reading for details or facts. The first step of the DRA is also the place for building a background for the story. Pictures, discussions, film strips, and motion pictures might be used to assure that the children have experiences with the story's concepts. At other times, the simple procedure of using several of the terms in the story and of discussing situations using those terms assists the children when they meet the terms in the story.

Building a story into a motion picture by identifying the three most important scenes and then formulating a selling title for the movie is motivating to children and is a subtle way of stressing main idea. If interest is high, several children might develop a play or a movie from the story. When stressing interpretation, children must perform their roles without reading their lines from their books. Paraphrasing, inferring, and selecting the main idea will be essential. Many children demonstrate such skills in highly unique ways; for example, children might make a comic strip from a favorite story by creating both comic pictures and captions. Of course, acceptance of such efforts is the key to encouraging children to continue trying.

Analysis of the topic sentence in a paragraph can develop interpretation skills. The topic sentence contains the main idea. By stating the topic sentence in their own words, the children are studying both main idea and paraphrasing. An independent activity can involve children's matching cut-out topic sentences with appropriate paragraphs.

Open-ended questions which call for summarizing can be developed and can result in performances acceptable at many levels of refinement. For example, a summary could be a word, a phrase, a sentence, a paragraph, or several paragraphs. Summaries can be either written or oral and can be either drawn or acted out. By changing the activity, teachers can maintain children's interest levels while continuing to develop the same skill.

By grouping children so that readers having difficulty paraphrasing can work with children who are quite good at it, the children can learn from their peers. To involve those children having difficulty, all of the children can work in teams of two or three to come up with an answer to a teacher's posed question. By teaming children carefully, all will be able to make contributions to the final product. Pairing of children does not necessarily teach independence, but it often helps troubled children over the feeling of frustration, of giving up, or of simply not understanding what is going on. It also assists in making them active rather than passive learners.

With older children, questions can be written (e.g., multiple-choice questions) relating to the content of the story but changing the author's wording. In such cases, the teacher does the paraphrasing by means of the way in which he asks questions. The child's task is to match the paraphrased idea to the author's idea. Thus, children see that the same idea may be expressed in several different ways.

Sometimes a simple probing question can be helpful. For example, if a child answers with the precise words of the author, the teacher can respond, "Yes, that is correct. Now let's try to think of other ways to say the same thing." He might suggest changing one word or one phrase. So, if the author has written, "The general led a successful charge," the teacher might suggest that the children attempt to say the same thing using another word for *successful*.

When inferences are stressed as an interpretation skill, the teacher must be aware of two types of inferences. One the author provides intentionally, while the other is developed by the reader. For example, some authors lead the reader to a conclusion without actually stating it. Since inferring involves reading between the lines, the teacher should talk with children about it in exactly those terms.

Ideas such as mood, time, danger, and happiness are often only implied by the author. To draw inferences concerning such ideas involves a complete literal understanding of the author's message. Questions such as "How do you think the player felt after the game?" "When in history did the story take place?" and "Would you consider the people to be in danger?" are examples of questions which stimulate children to infer. Each question can be followed by probing, "What did the author say to make you think that?" The probing activity helps children to clarify their own thinking and understanding of how others have reacted to the same story they have read.

Cartoons can be used in activities for paraphrasing, obtaining the main ideas, and developing inference skills. For example, using three or four cartoons on the same subject (e.g., dogs), the teacher can have groups of children write captions for the cartoons and then let other groups try to match the captions with the pictures. As is true with comics, such an activity can be developed at many levels, all of which can be highly motivating.

Clinical remediation: Obviously, each idea suggested for the classroom can be applied to clinical remediation. In fact, most of the suggestions above were first developed in clinical situations.

When children have severe difficulty with interpretation of written material, the reading specialist should start with picture interpretation, help the child look at pictures which have story possibilities in terms of what they can see in the picture, and, then, move to interpretation. For example, the specialist can ask, "How do you think the children feel?" "How is that street different from the street you live on?" and "Make up a title for the picture." Once a child has skill in picture interpretation, his responses should be developed into experience stories.

When a reading specialist draws experience stories from pictures, both literal understanding and interpretation responses should be developed. To modify the language experience approach in order to develop interpretation, children can be asked to change a sentence without changing the meaning, change a word without changing the meaning, identify the sentences which describe the picture and those which interpret the picture, and discuss the main ideas. By moving from pictures to language experience stories, reading specialists can make a natural transition from vicarious experiences to reading. The next step is to move to stories written by others.

Perhaps several groups of children can write stories about the same picture. These stories can be compared using the above questions. When children are successful with the stories of other children, they are indicating that they are ready to start with other printed material.

In clinical remediation, when students first move from experience stories to printed material, they should start with small quantities of print. The specialist should attempt to make the activities as similar to those conducted with the experience stories as possible. One technique is to develop a language experience story from a picture in a book. Then, the students can read what the author has to say about the picture and compare the two stories for details, main ideas, inferences, and the like.

Another clinical technique is to select prepared materials such as *SRA Reading Laboratories*** and *Reader's Digest Skill Builders*** and identify the questions following the reading which deal with interpretation. The reading specialist should ask the children to read very easy stories and answer only those questions which he has identified. If no interpretation questions are asked, he can write several and tape them to the material. If he works with easy reading materials, the child can gain considerable skill at interpretation prior to attempting to interpret material at the instructional level.

After a group of children have read a short story, the reading specialist can draw inferences. The children are asked to find anything in the story that might justify the inference. In this way, the children become aware of the possibilities for making inferences without actually doing so themselves. To add interest to the activity, the reading specialist occasionally should draw unjustified inferences. It is as important for children to determine if an inference is justified as it is to find the justification. It adds considerable excitement to the activity as well.

We have found activities involving interpretation exciting and motivating to children and teachers alike. Often a child who has turned reading off will be turned on by activities at the interpretation level. The importance of interpretation demands considerable remedial emphasis, for without it the activities at the problem-solving level would be impossible.

Problem Solving

Children usually are not classified as being in need of remedial assistance if their only difficulty is in the area of problem solving. However, problem-solving activities ought to be considered necessary and valuable in remedial situations. Problem-solving activities involve the child in a reaction to the message of the author. The reaction takes on one of two forms, either critical or creative. A critical reaction calls for convergent thinking activities. The author's ideas are challenged, defended, and evaluated. Creative activities call for divergent thinking activities. The ideas of the author form a base from which new ideas can be developed. Children enjoy problem-solving activities, and such activities tend to make remedial programs relevant.

As is true with all comprehension, the teacher must be certain that the child is working with material that is appropriate to his reading level and his field of experiences. Problem solving involves both literal understanding and interpretation but is reflective in nature. Children cannot reflect on material which they cannot understand and interpret. Therefore, the student must be provided ample opportunity to perform on easy, interesting material in order to assure the development of the skill prior to moving toward material at the instructional level.

Once again, the type of question which is asked becomes important for instruction. Problem-solving questions are those which necessitate the child's using the author's ideas, comparing or contrasting, interpreting them, and applying them to a problem situation. Critical-thinking questions involve analysis of the author's ideas (e.g., Do you agree with the author's conclusions? Why? What reasons can you give for this story being true? Was the major character justified in his actions? Why or why not?). Creative thinking questions should involve projection and be open ended (e.g., If the story were to continue, what do you think would happen next? If you had been the victim in this story, how would you have acted? If we changed the events on page 3 of the story, how would it effect the ending of the story?). When questions are asked at the problem-solving level, teachers must be patient while children formulate answers. Gentle, probing questions can be stimulating to children, but the answers to the type of questions explained here are not always immediately available to the child. At times, the questions can be asked one day, worked on overnight, and answered the next day.

Classroom remediation: As is the case with interpretation, group work with children in pairs, threes, or fours is often helpful to start children on problem solving. In critical thinking, groups of children can take opposing sides, preparing arguments for their case, and discussing each point of view. In creative thinking, the creativeness of one child can stimulate creativeness in others.

Setting purposes which reflect problem solving is often useful prior to reading. However, it is often equally effective to set purposes during the literal understanding and interpretative steps, permitting problem-solving activities to be the purposes set for re-reading material.

The children often see problem-solving activities which are related to content subjects, such as history, as highly relevant. The classroom teacher has an opportunity to use content materials as reading instructional materials. Thus, the child is helped in two school subjects at once. It is also a technique to prepare children for lessons focusing on materials which they have difficulty reading.

Games involving figures of speech can be developed into both critical and creative reading activities. For example, the teacher can ask, "What does the expression *play it cool* mean? Rewrite the figure of speech using your own words while retaining the meaning."

Classroom games with analogies are also useful in developing problem solving skills (e.g., top is to bottom as front is to _____). To succeed in such a game, the child must know word meanings, determine relationships between words, and select the most appropriate answer from several alternatives. First, teachers might use analogies with an accepting attitude (e.g., if the answer can be defended, it should be accepted). Later, however, children should be expected to operate effectively enough to determine the correct answer or a synonym for it. A commonly used technique is to provide a multiple-choice response [e.g., top is to bottom as front is to _____ (middle, back, side)]. With the idea of moving from gross to fine discriminations, teachers should start instruction with analogies having distractors which are obviously wrong. As children gain skill, the distractors should be more like the appropriate response.

Myers and Torrance have developed a series of critical and creative activities for use at various classroom levels. Children enjoy working with these materials. For example, one activity involves asking the children, "What would happen if it always rained on Saturday?"[1]

Clinical remediation: Reading specialists are encouraged to use those techniques suggested for classroom remediation. In smaller groups, specific attention to desired skill development effects efficient results.

In clinical remediation, we turn once again to the progression of language development activities which were used at the interpretation stage. With picture interpretation, problem-solving questions are asked about action pictures (e.g., "How would you feel if you

---

[1] R. E. Myers and E. Paul Torrance, *For Those Who Wonder* (Boston: Ginn and Co., 1966), p. 1.

were there?" "What do you think will happen next?" or "How are these pictures alike or different?"). As children develop skill in responding to problem-solving questions concerning pictures, the reading specialist should use the language experience approach. Once several groups of children have worked on the same picture, stories can be compared, read, and discussed. The use of materials such as *Tweedy*** transparencies bring action and life to pictures. Even very young children find these transparencies stimulating and thought provoking. Older children respond to them equally well, and the reading specialist can move from discussion to writing activities using the transparencies as a basis for instruction. Then, moving to very easy reading material, the reading specialist can help the children develop problem-solving skills by using the writings of others. With older students, newspaper stories, advertisements, and television commercials are helpful to stimulate problem-solving-type thinking. The specialist can ask children what this written material is really saying. What words are used to influence? Is the article or the ad truthful? Why or why not? How would one rewrite the ad if he were a competitor? Basic to all of the above steps should be the teacher reading to the children. Children can watch the book, looking at words and pictures.

The reading specialist should determine the content areas which are being covered in the classroom. Borrowing those books and helping the children with problem-solving activities directly related to what they will be studying tomorrow is extremely motivating, especially to older children.

Role playing is also useful for children who have difficulty reacting to reading creatively. Children can be helped to respond creatively through materials such as *Teaching Reading Through Creative Movement*,** records containing both voice and music and stories which permit a considerable amount of action. As children become freer in creative expression, they can react to many things which they read. After the creative expression, discussions about why they feel the way they do make a logical transition to creative discussions.

Problem solving activities, like interpretation activities, tend to be extremely motivating to most children. As the teacher gets away from the tendency to hold the children responsible for large quantities of literal understanding, they tend to respond more willingly and at a higher level. Certainly problem solving activities should be included on a regular basis in a remedial program. When they are available, children will usually contract for them eagerly.

Can the child recall the author's ideas yet remain unable to perform in content areas?

Some children seem to perform in reading class but do not transfer those skills to their reading in content areas. The first consideration in such instances must be the readability of the material upon which they cannot perform. Often, there are extreme differences of readability between the books used in reading class and the books used in content areas. Content area books often are written at a level much higher than the graded reading books. On an informal basis, the teacher should note the differences in the size of the print; the length of sentences; the vocabulary load in terms of difficult words; and the difficulty of the concepts. If any of these factors varies noticeably from the reading class materials, the problem is probably one of material difficulty. *Yoakham,*[2] *Gunning,*[3] and *Spache*[4] present formal readability techniques which may be used to obtain a grade level of readability, although they do not evaluate the concept load of the material. The "cloze procedure" has been developed to enable teachers to determine the ability of the child to handle materials; it will also indicate the ability to handle concepts as well as word and sentence structures. Taylor[5] claims it is of value in determining readability. We have used this technique with the materials we expect children to read in the clinic and find it to be most helpful. It involves:

1. Selecting at random a passage containing an adequate sampling.

2. Retyping this passage, leaving out every fifth word. (Authorities differ on which word to omit, but we have found the fifth to be effective.) As a rule, neither the first word

---

[2]Gerald A. Yoakham, *Basal Reading Instruction* (New York: Prentice Hall Inc., 1955), Appendix I.

[3]William A. Jenkins, ed., "The Educational Scene," *Elementary English*, 37, no. 6 (October 1960), p. 411.

[4]Spache, George, *Good Reading for Poor Readers* (Champaign, Illinois: Garrard Press, 1968), Chapter 4.

[5]W. L. Taylor, "Cloze Procedure — A New Tool for Measuring Readability," *Journalism Quarterly*, 30 (Fall 1953), pp. 415-33.

in a sentence nor proper nouns should be omitted. An example of a clozure test on easy material would appear as follows:

Nancy was anxious to _____ her birthday party this _____. She had invited some _____ to her room at school. She _____ that they would all _____ able to attend.

3. Have the child read the incomplete sentences, filling in the missing words. To "close" properly, the child must know the words and understand the concept, thereby anticipating the author's ideas.

As the teacher gains familiarity with the clozure technique, he will find it a valuable aid in determining whether a child should read a certain book and how much help the child is likely to need with the book he has selected. For example, if the child scored well below his peers on a clozure test in a science book, the teacher has some clues to a child's difficulty. Science words can be stressed prior to reading. Conceptual background can be built through discussion, pictures, experiments, and so on, thus enabling the child to handle the material better.

Bormuth[6] has found that a clozure test score of 38 percent right is approximately equal to a test score of 75 percent right. Therefore, as a rule of thumb, clozure scores below 40 percent right should be regarded as danger signs for that child with that material. Either instructional adjustments are needed or easier material must be used for instruction. (For limitations of the 40 percent criteria, see Chapter 4.)

The second consideration is that reading problems in understanding content materials usually do not become pronounced until the child has reached the fourth grade. It is at this point that content reading becomes a regular part of the school program and the child with study skill problems is clearly handicapped.

Classroom remediation: The teacher should use the DRA with materials in content areas. The child who fails to see the need for a similar attack in unfamiliar materials must be directed to it in the same manner that we use in reading class. Each step of the DRA

---

[6]John R. Bormuth, "Comparable Cloze and Multiple-Choice Test Comprehension Scores," *Journal of Reading* (February 1967), p. 295.

must be used carefully in the development of skill in reading content materials, gradually permitting the child to guide himself through the steps.

Older children may find it beneficial to follow a specific study technique in their reading of content materials. Several of these are available, the most prominent being SQ3R[7] (survey, question, read, recite, review). The effect of this type of technique is the same as a DRA except that the student is to apply it to his studies without supervision. Independence in reading content material is the desired objective of this system.

Activities in which the child organizes and classifies ideas are useful in remediation. Children who cannot read in the content areas usually have difficulty with outlining skills. Beginning with completed outlines of material recently read, the teacher illustrates the method of following the author's train of thought. An outline format then is presented for the child to complete, followed by simple outlining of clearly organized material with little or no direction. The *Reading For Meaning*** workbooks, designed for the intermediate and secondary grades, have practice exercises to develop the child's ability to organize material through a gradual exposure to outlining techniques.

The *SRA Organizing and Reporting Skill Kit*** has individualized exercises which gradually introduce the concepts of note taking, reporting, and outlining.

The child's ability to follow directions has a direct relationship to his ability to perform in study situations. Composite in nature, this skill depends upon the child's ability to follow the sequence and organization of the author's thoughts, as well as his ability to obtain the main idea. The *Specific Skill Series*** includes sets of intensive exercises in following directions at the various grade levels. Once the ability to follow directions is mastered, remedial sessions should provide further experiences with this concept at regular intervals.

These examples of activities for following directions have been useful in helping children develop mastery of that skill. As has been suggested, the use of model cars, ships, and airplanes helps a child to realize the importance of following directions carefully. Reading the directions on the box and following them step by step to completion can be a highly useful reading and learning experience. If

---

[7]Francis P. Robinson, *Effective Study* (New York: Harper & Row, 1961), Chap. ii.

children cannot read all of the instructions, they should work in pairs, helping each other. Learning centers can be developed to help children follow directions. Using pages from telephone books or newspapers, children can be instructed to follow directions ranging from the simple to the complex (e.g., find a given phone number; find a given phone number and address; find the phone numbers of three dentists — give their names, get their addresses, and determine which lives closest to your home).

Another SRA study aid is the *Graph* and *Picture Study Skills Kit.*** Designed to be adapted to any subject area, these materials are useful in developing a type of useful reading often overlooked in remedial programs.

Clinical remediation: The reading specialist uses the techniques mentioned above and adds to them individualization of instruction through the use of certain materials designed for classroom use and having particular application to remedial cases with this skill deficiency. The *Be a Better Reader*** books provide specific suggestions for study in the major content areas, particularly for older students. The *Study Skills Library,*** which provides specialized instruction in developing the same type of concepts, is useful with younger children. Individualized for clinical use, these materials can serve a highly useful function with children who are deficient in this skill.

Adaptation of the language experience approach to content subjects has been very effective.[8] Reading specialists can work with classroom teachers to develop skill in presenting material and information to the children without using texts (i.e., lecture, discussion, tapes, films, pictures, demonstrations, experiments, and the like); drawing the children's verbal expressions of what they have learned; writing language experience stories based on the children's contributions; and developing reading and content skills from the written stories.

Reading specialists also can help content teachers rewrite materials which are too difficult. Basically, the rewriting involves cutting sentence length, eliminating complicated sentence structures, and reducing word difficulty through the use of synonyms.

---

[8]Robert M. Wilson and Nancy Parkey, "A Modified Reading Program in a Middle School," *Journal of Reading* (March 1970), 447-452.

Is there a total failure to respond to comprehension situations?

For the child who does not respond to any type of comprehension check, even at relatively easy levels of performance, remedial techniques are difficult to apply, for there is no place to begin. For these children, the level of material must be easy, the interest of the material must be high, the quantity of the material must be small, and the type of comprehension expected must be the simplest.

Classroom remediation: Again, the use of experience stories permits a start with relatively easy, interesting material of as small a quantity as desired. Again, the child is directed to demonstrate an understanding of the experience stories which, containing his own concepts, can usually be done without difficulty. Once a feeling for this type of directed activity is developed, the child is exposed through the DRA to easy, interesting printed material.

Placing the child in reading situations which call for action and reaction is often successful. Signs, posters, and flash cards which can be presented to him with directions for his reaction are developed from the opportunities which appear daily in and out of the classroom.

When comprehension is almost totally lacking, the continued use of materials similar to those used with the children previously is difficult to defend. One type of action material (i.e., material which involves a reaction from the child at each step) has been produced under the name of *Programmed Reading.*** As the child reads through the programmed books, he is expected to react to every sentence. His reaction is immediately reinforced by the correct response (see Chapter 8). These materials place children in situations which demand thought about what they are reading.

Clinical remediation: Intensified use of the language experience approach usually is justified in clinical remediation for children who are having difficulty with comprehension. Since the material contains the child's ideas, he *can* comprehend it. Working with material which has meaning for the child and then calling attention to those meanings should be the major focus of initial clinical remediation of severe comprehension problems. Instruction through the DRA also is recommended for a serious comprehension problem. Clinical procedures use the same materials discussed in the various comprehension sections but are highly individualized to prohibit the development from step to step without a thorough understanding of the meaning. Of specific value are *Non-oral Reading,*** basal materials, and *Programmed Reading.*** All material must be interesting and must include reading goals which are clearly understood by the child. By carefully leading the child to small quantities of interesting, meaningful material, it is possible to develop the basic skills needed in reading for comprehension.

Vocabulary exercises which involve the child in nonverbal responses to the printed symbol have considerable usefulness here. The *Nichols Slides,*** mentioned in Chapter 7, or their equivalent can be used by starting with very simple, direct commands and progressing as the child develops the skill (e.g., start with words such as *sit, stand,* and *jump,* and go to more complicated combinations of words such as *stand and sing now* or *jump three times.*)

With this type of child, drill activities without contextual emphasis certainly would be discontinued until the desired awareness of meaning was developed.

EXTENDED REMEDIATION

Again, the extension of diagnosis by the classroom teacher and the reading specialist established two additional areas of speed and distraction for remedial consideration. Normally, this remediation will be conducted by the reading specialist and occasionally by the classroom teacher upon the recommendations of the reading specialist.

Was the lack of response due basically to speed?

It is not unusual to find, after clinical diagnosis, that the responses of the child are, in fact, due to a slow speed. In these cases the child has been asked to read a selection (ample time must be alloted) and to give comprehension type responses. Not having completed the material, the child's comprehension responses appear to be unsatisfactory. Upon careful examination, it is often found that the child has responded properly to those questions related to the material which he has read and has missed those concerned with material he has not read. Remediation, then, should not be in terms of the child's responses but rather in terms of the reasons for the child's slowness. It is in this way that we become involved with the problem of reading speed in remediation, not by evaluating words per minute or by employing specific speed drills.

Using the first step in the DRA, the child reads for a specific purpose and is instructed to be flexible in his approach. Practice is accomplished on easy, interesting materials in order to be certain that the child's slowness is not due basically to poor sight vocabulary or to word attack problems. (Slow reading caused by these types of deficiencies is corrected by direct remedial efforts in the skill areas of sight vocabulary and word attack.) The child is then pressured by limiting the time permitted for reading small passages. This pressure can be gradually increased or reduced as the reading situation demands, and the child gains a sense of what is meant by "flexibility of reading rate." Graphs of progress can be developed to help the child realize his development and to motivate him to continue to try.

Most of the devices mentioned under orientation remediation are useful in developing efficiency in reading speed. The controlled exposure devices such as the *Controlled Reader*** and the *Rate-ometer*** are useful here; however, it must be noted that these devices should be used on easy, interesting materials and that the child should be directed through step one of the DRA to the type of comprehension expected.

Prepared materials are available for children to use for practice exercises in reading within certain time limits. The *SRA Laboratories*** have rate building exercises in which the child must read and answer the question in three minutes. The child should be started with rate building exercises at very easy levels. The emphasis here is on efficiency in relatively easy material of high interest. The *Standard Test Lessons in Reading*** also have the three minute time limitation.

Other available exercises are designed to motivate improved time performance by emphasizing such measures of reading rate as number of words read per minute. In remediation, none of this emphasis should be stressed without equal or greater emphasis on the quality of comprehension which accompanies the rate. The *Better Reading Books*** are an example of this type of material to be used with older children, providing charts for easy motivation to better speed and better comprehension.

Charts or graphs which illustrate the child's progress are always helpful. These should be constructed so that the child can note small gains in improved rate, so that the aspect of comprehension is charted as well as the reading rate, and so that the goals for which he is striving are realistically within his reach. If he reaches the graph's goal quickly, the teacher simply makes a new graph, again with easily reached goals.

Was the poor performance due to the fact that the child was easily distracted?

In many cases, the child's performance on any exercise or in any book may be due basically more to his distractability than to a lack of skills. When such a diagnosis is made, remedial procedures should be adjusted to reduce as many distractable elements as possible. Recommendations should also be made to the classroom teacher to facilitate learning situations in which the child can perform with a minimum of distractions. Specific suggestions include:

1. When working with older children, distractable children should be placed so that the actions of the other children are no more distracting than necessary. In the classroom, this would normally involve a front corner seat.
2. The person conducting the remediation should dress plainly, wearing clothes which do not call unnecessary attention to the teacher. We have found that elaborate dress such as fancy earrings appears to distract these children.
3. Remediation should not be conducted in physical surroundings in which pictures and other distracting objects are prominent. In clinical remediation, a plain room where a child's total efforts can be directed to the book before him should be used initially. In the classroom, distractable children should take their reading instruction in an area of the room which lacks extensive decoration.
4. When distractability is recognized as a serious limitation, it is often helpful to use books which contain a minimum of pictures, thus permitting the child to focus his entire attention upon the print and the skills necessary to read it.
5. Distractive children will need to have skill exercises in periods of shorter duration. They should understand that their entire attention will be expected for a short period of time, after which they may move to another activity and return to reading skill activities later. In the clinic, we have found

it helpful to vary the child's activity as much as possible. Unfortunately, such adjustments are difficult and at times impossible in the classroom, for they disrupt the activities of the other children. The classroom teacher, however, should provide a variety of activities and at least refrain from punishing the children for distractability over which they have no obvious control. In the more extreme cases, the children should run, jump, and play actively in other ways between their periods of skill activities in reading. Opportunities should be used to get them to be active in class as well as out. For example, the teacher could have them come to the board for some of their work and let them pass out materials to other children, thus providing them with opportunities to stand up. In this way, their tensions are released and they become more receptive to the required silent work at their seats.

6. Children who are easily distracted generally enjoy a program which has as much consistency as possible. When they can anticipate an interesting routine, they are more likely to be able to concentrate on it to its completion. In clinical and classroom remediation, efforts should be made to develop program constancy.

MOTIVATION

In each of the comprehension areas, motivation was discussed as an inherent part of the remedial program. In the general area of comprehension, motivation is the most appropriately intrinsic element, for the child readily senses his accomplishments. Comprehension, the goal in reading for both teachers and students, is a rewarding experience in itself, especially at the interpretation and problem-solving levels. Specifically, we note that motivation in comprehension includes:

1. Improved performance in the content area in school.
2. Charts and graphs of progress.
3. Free reading of enjoyable material.
4. Enjoyment of reading for interpretation and reading for problem solving.

5. Creating of successful comprehe.:sion situations.
6. Experience stories which permit the child to assume the role of the author.
7. Use of games requiring team work.
8. Active role required of a child in most reading.
9. Genuine appreciation of discovering the unknown.

Other Structured Remedial Programs

The reader's attention is directed to several carefully structured reading programs which involve a modified system for decoding. In each of these, the teacher, once committed, is expected to follow the program to a transfer stage where the child returns to reading traditional print. Of particular interest may be remedial programs being conducted with *ITA*** and *Words in Color.*** The reader is directed to the noted sources for further study.

REMEDIAL TECHNIQUES FOR THE RELUCTANT READER

The third type of problem reader, the child who has the reading skills but gives all indication of reluctance to use them, can be found in almost any classroom. Normally, this child will not be referred for clinical remediation on the basis of this deficiency alone. However, most children who come to the clinic are reluctant readers. The major responsibility for remediation in this area is with the classroom teacher, for the development of attitudes and habits can only *begin* in clinical remedial programs; their continuation and development must take place in the classroom.

Classroom remediation: First of all, it is important for this child to develop the attitude that free reading is an activity which the teacher feels is worthwhile. Therefore, free reading opportunities should occur periodically in all classrooms. Free reading in this case implies reading which is not followed by question and answer periods and reading in which the child is relatively free to choose the desired materials. As this child develops the understanding that free reading can be fun and is important enough to take school time, gradual changes of attitude are likely to be noted.

The development of an attitude of willingness to read obviously involves the availability of books. The problem reader must have books available to him for free reading at his seat, in the classroom library, in the school library, and at home. There is little chance to develop attitudes and habits towards reading when books are difficult or impossible to obtain. School administrators should note that attempts to be thrifty by cutting appropriations for classroom and school libraries place teachers in the position of being unable to encourage the reading habit.

Every opportunity should be utilized to promote free reading through the use of peer group recommendations. The child who has read an interesting book and wants to share it with a class can often create more interest than can the teacher. Sharing may be done through brief, voluntary, oral reports, through a classroom card file including the name of the book and the reasons that the child enjoyed it, or through a school book fair where interesting books are displayed.

The teacher can develop interest by reading to the children from books which would be too difficult for them to read themselves but which contain stories and ideas of interest. If he takes the time to read some of the children's books, he too will be able to provide book summaries to develop interest in new books as they appear in the library. He also subtly develops attitude by showing enthusiastic interest in his own personal reading.

The teacher may find it useful to consult book lists prepared by authorities to facilitate his guidance of children and the recommendations he will be expected to make. *Teacher's Guide to Children's Books*,[9] *Children and Books*,[10] *Your Children Want to Read*,[11] and *Good Reading for Poor Readers*,[12] are four examples. Through the use of such resources, the teacher also can recommend to parents books which would be appropriate gifts. Teachers should encourage parents to consider a book a valued, highly desired gift.

We often find that the reluctant child is reluctant to select a book which to him is a threat in terms of volume alone. Perhaps due to pressure from adults in his past, the child has developed an attitude that taking a book from the library commits him to read

---

[9]Nancy Larrick, *A Teacher's Guide to Children's Books* (Columbus, Ohio: Charles E. Merrill Publishing Co., 1960).

[10]May Hill Arbuthnot, *Children and Books* (Chicago: Scott, Foresman & Co., 1947).

[11]Ruth Tooze, *Your Children Want to Read* (Englewood Cliffs, N.J.: Prentice Hall, Inc., 1957).

[12]George D. Spache, *Good Reading for Poor Readers* (Champaign, Illinois: The Garrard Press, 1968).

the book from cover to cover. The teacher, of course, must discourage this attitude, for we all have been in situations where, after starting a book, we feel no desire to finish it. Nevertheless, too many false starts tend to discourage the child from sampling brief portions of books prior to selecting the books from the library. Two such materials which have been well received are the *Literature Sampler*** and the *Pilot Library*.** Both of these materials provide the teacher with a guide to the readability of the book and the interest factors involved, assisting him to direct the child to the books to which he will most likely respond favorably.

Learning centers which provide children with opportunities for selecting the materials they are going to use, for pacing themselves, and for correcting their own work have been used with considerable success. The *Learning Center Handbook*[13] provides instruction for those unfamiliar with learning center construction and use.

Clinical remediation: The type of activities mentioned above are required in clinical remediation as often as they can be applied. Extensive use is made of book series which, while maintaining high interest, have low vocabulary levels and facilitate interesting reading for problem readers. Without these books to reinforce the skills that are being developed in clinical remediation, the chance for transfer of these skills is seriously limited. The following high interest, low vocabulary books have been used effectively in programs of clinical remediation.

Series	Vocabulary level	Publisher
About Books	2-4	Children's Press
All About Books	3-6	Random House
American Adventure Series	2-6	Wheeler
Bucky Buttons	1-3	Benefic Press
Cowboy Sam	1-3	Benefic Press
Dan Frontier	1-3	Benefic Press
Deep Sea Adventure Stories	1-3	Harr Wagner
Dolch First Readers	1-2	Garrand
Interesting Reading Series	2-3	Follette
I Want to be Books	1-3	Children's Press
Sailor Jack	1-3	Benefic Press

---

[13]Waynant, Louise, ed., *Learning Center Handbook* (College Park: University of Maryland, 1969).

Books such as these are inexpensive and readily available for clinical remediation. For a more complete list, see Botel, *How to Teach Reading* (see Suggested Readings).

Free reading may be permitted in clinical remediation by using materials such as the *SRA Reading Laboratories*** and the *Reader's Digest Skill Builders.*** When used for free reading, these materials should be used without requiring the child to answer questions or to do the vocabulary exercises and, of course, should be selections at the recreational reading level.

Of particular value to the clinic are the *Literature Sampler*** and the *Pilot Library*** which, as in classroom remediation, save time in book selection.

REMEDIATION FOR THE NON-READER

Diagnosis occasionally uncovers a child who does not have a specific skill deficiency and might be termed a non-reader (see Chapter 5). Remediation for these children involves all of the best that has been discussed in the preceding pages. However, in these cases, instruction must be more precise and more thorough. The major characteristics of this instruction may well follow these recommended procedures:

1. Build upon the experiences of the child using the language experience approach (see page 186).
2. Develop basic sight vocabulary by using the Fernald or VAKT techniques. Reading specialists have found these techniques to be particularly valuable, although when used as a basic approach, they are reserved for the seriously handicapped. Since these children normally profit most from a consistent approach, it is important that the reading specialist follow these sight vocabulary approaches with careful consistency. Fernald[14] and Kolson[15] provide detailed descriptions.
   The following version is one which we have found to work effectively:

---

[14]Fernald, *Remedial Techniques in Basic School Subjects*, Chap. V.
[15]Clifford J. Kolson and George Kaluger, *Clinical Aspects of Remedial Reading* (Springfield, Illinois: Chas. C. Thomas, 1963), pp. 44-6.

a. A word is selected from the context in which the child is working. This word will be printed on a card, in sand, on the chalkboard, or on the paper from which the child will work.

b. The teacher then demonstrates how to trace the word while pronouncing it. Using the fore- and index fingers, he traces the word left to right and pronounces it.

c. The child then does the same. If he makes an error, he must be directed to start from the beginning of the word and try it again. The teacher should remember that he says the whole word as he traces it.

d. After several accurate tracings, the child is directed to reproduce the word while saying it. This reproduction is done with the copy in sight.

e. When he reproduces the word successfully, the child is then asked to reproduce the word without the copy in sight. Of course, he says it as he writes it.

f. When mastered, this word is placed on a card with a sentence contributed by the child.

g. The word can be reviewed as the teacher sees the need and it can be used in future works for reading. It is quite possible that the child will come to this same word in context and claim to not know it. He should be asked, "How does the word feel? Trace it."

At any step in this process, the child may fail. The procedure then is to go back to the preceding step, for it can be assumed that the preceding step has not been mastered.

Talmadge and others[16] have found a tracing approach to be the most successful technique to use when teaching children with cerebral dysfunction. The reader is cautioned that the technique is time consuming, must be accomplished precisely, and requires overlearning. As a result, there is no suggestion that these procedures be used over a long period of time in less serious cases. In fact, as soon as the child can learn words effectively by taking short cuts, we encourage him to do so. Once learned, tracing techniques can be ac-

---

[16]Max Talmadge; Anthony Davids; and Maurice W. Laufer, "A Study of Experimental Methods for Teaching Emotionally Disturbed, Brain Damaged, Retarded Readers," *Journal of Educational Research*, 56, no. 6 (February 1963), p. 312.

complished by the child without teacher supervision, except for the pronunciation of the unknown word.

As the child builds sight vocabulary through tracing, he should be placed in reading situations constantly. Initially, the reading will consist of the language experience approach using the concepts and vocabulary of the child. As the child progresses, easy, interesting material can be used from other sources. As a rule, it is desirable to have this child experience much success at each step in the program. It will be necessary, therefore, to limit word analysis exercises until the child starts to indicate confidence in a learning situation.

3. Many children who are classified as non-readers demonstrate difficulties in visual discrimination. Carefully working through the types of visual discrimination exercises found in most readiness programs is often helpful for such children (see Chapter 7). The Frostig** exercises may be required for children who are more seriously handicapped in this area. For the experienced reading specialist, the language experience stories will provide many opportunities to stress both auditory and visual discrimination.

4. Because this child needs as many stimuli as possible, the teacher may pursue oral reading further than usual. Note that the Fernald Approach makes optimum use of available stimuli.

Survival Program

Older children, ages 15–20, particularly in clinical situations, are often so seriously retarded in reading that there is little chance of their ever using reading for anything but the essentials of life. These young people often can profit most from sight vocabulary instruction which is directed towards their survival in our society. Although normally they would be dealt with in clinical situations, the pupils are often found in classrooms where clinical remediation is not available. What these people need is strong motivation and good teaching techniques to learn the sight words and concepts necessary for functioning in our society. The materials used for this type of instruction may consist of:

1. Driver's manuals
2. Road signs

3. Menus
4. The Essential Driver's List[17]
5. The Essential Vocabulary List[18]
6. Various sight words used in the occupation in which the young person has an interest
7. Rochester Occupational Series**
8. Ads in newspapers
9. Employment contracts
10. Income tax forms
11. Social Security forms
12. Newspaper headlines
13. Phone books
14. TV guides

The words and concepts involved may be taught in any manner that seems efficient.

The *Non-oral*** *technique, the Nichols Tachistoscope Slide*** concept, and the *Fernald*** technique have all been used effectively in these programs.

The young person involved in a survival program should understand the goals which we assume are self-motivating and should not normally be placed in other types of reading situations. He will not enjoy sitting down with a book, nor will he be attempting occupations which require extensive reading. It is through the learning of the essential sight vocabulary that he will receive the mose benefit. The survival program often encourages him to continue to strive for reading skills beyond "survival," in which case the remedial program may be continued toward some other short-term realistic goals.

When survival types of programs are desirable for the classroom, the young person should be placed in learning situations of minimum pressure. Specifically, he should not be expected to be responsible for reading assignments in his text and should not be required to fail on written tests. Rather, text assignments can be read to him or placed on tape for his use. Tests may be handled in much the same manner. However, we recommend that this child have a text and be permitted to use it as he desires if for no other

---

[17]Corlett T. Wilson, "An Essential Vocabulary," XVII, *The Reading Teacher*, (November 1963), 94-96.

[18]Wilson, pp. 94-96.

reason than giving him the status which is involved in using the regular text. With this child, the classroom philosophy is one of having him learn as much as possible via listening, pictures, and demonstrations, while reading instruction initially is limited to the above mentioned survival programs.

REMEDIATION FOR THE CULTURALLY DIFFERENT

From diagnosis, the reader will recall that certain groups of children, due to experiential backgrounds which are quite different from those of the average child, do not make normal progress in reading. Remediation for these children must be designed to permit development of experiential background, success in decoding activities, and personal success in the total reading act.

Both the classroom teacher and the reading specialist must take every opportunity to develop language experiences throughout all remedial sessions. When opportunities do present themselves, they should be structured. For example, if the child who is reading about the zoo has never been to the zoo, either a trip to the zoo, a film, or pictures must precede a reading lesson that has to do with those types of animals that one finds in a zoo. It can be assumed that in a normal school situation, the child has experienced considerable frustration by being placed in reading situations for which he has not had sufficient experiential background. There is no justification for this child being continually frustrated for these reasons. For those who desire a systematic program of language experiences, the *Peabody Language Development Kit*** and the *Ginn Language Kit A*** mentioned previously can serve as guides.

Decoding activities for these children should always be in terms of language involving concepts which they possess. This, then, assures motivation, for the child sees that the system actually does help him to decode words for which he understands concepts.

Although motivation is an important part in all remediation, for these children it is extremely important. Remedial sessions should have an aura of excitement about them, and the values of reading should be subtly stressed.

Selection of books for children from different cultures also should be of prime importance. Attempts to match books used in remediation with the culture of the children proves to be most worthwhile. Spache's book, *Good Reading for the Disadvantaged Reader* can serve as a useful reference.[19]

Beyond these suggestions there should be a program which is developed according to the precise needs of the individual child, as for all children.

PITFALLS OF REMEDIATION

In concluding the discussion of remedial techniques, the classroom teacher and the reading specialist should consider the following pitfalls which, when not avoided, disrupt the efficiency of many remedial programs.

Isolated Drill

Perhaps the major pitfall in remediation is the abundance, in a remedial session, of isolated drill activities in which the child obtains the impression that satisfactory performance in the drill itself is the reading act. To avoid this trap, all drill activities should be transferred to context in each lesson.

Failure to Establish a Program Which Complies with Established Goals

Another common pitfall in remedial programs is for instruction to become sidetracked into areas which do not meet the goals as they were established on the basis of the diagnosis. This occurs quite often when isolated drill appears to have become the goal of remediation. A conscious effort must be made to establish goals which are realistic and which can be understood by the person conducting the remediation, the child, the parents, and the child's classroom teacher. These goals then should serve as a guide to remedial approaches. Diagnostic teaching might well alter initial diagnostically established goals, however.

Failure to Illustrate Progress

As educators, we are quite often satisfied with the child's progress as he develops his reading skills. Progress, however, is not always clear to the child. It is common for the child to become discouraged and lose interest, even when working up to his full potential. It is im-

---

[19]Spache, George D., *Good Reading For the Disadvantaged Reader* (Champaign, Ill.: Garrard Publishing Co., 1970).

portant that the child have his progress illustrated through any techniques available.

Failure to Share Information about Remedial Progress

This pitfall is particularly directed at clinical remediation in which the child has gone through an extensive and successful remedial program. If the results of such programs are not readily available to the classroom teacher or to the parent, false assumptions may be gathered concerning the child's reading skills based upon previous performance. Therefore, effective communication lines must be maintained between the various people concerned with the remedial program. Most successful communication includes face-to-face explanations of the remedial program.

SUMMARY

Relying heavily upon the language experience approach, directed reading activities, and carefully constructed questioning, activities in the area of comprehension soon become the most enjoyable aspect of remediation. Children want to learn. They find that they can learn through reading when stress is placed on exciting, interesting activities and materials. When a child becomes bored in a comprehension activity, something is wrong with that activity for that child and it should be changed.

Attention paid to the comprehension strengths of the reader which permits him to be placed in successful, meaningful comprehension activities in every remedial session. Undo pressure results in frustration which, in turn, results in a disinterest in reading. Keeping interest high and keeping the child motivated to want to read more should be the aim of all comprehension activities. Instructional attention to comprehension strengths might well precede all other skill instructions.

SUGGESTED READINGS

Bloom, Benjamin S., *et. al.*, ed. *Taxonomy of Educational Objectives: Cognitive Domain*. New York: David McKay, 1956. Part II of this book deals with definitions of the cognitive domain. For those interested in more detailed information concerning the levels of thinking, this book is required reading.

Botel, Morton. *How to Teach Reading*, Chapter 2. Chicago: Follett Publishing Co., 1959. Botel's practical guide for teachers will again be useful to the educator who wants specific techniques for teaching comprehension as a thinking process.

Robinson, Francis P. *Effective Study*. New York: Harper and Brothers, 1961. The teacher of older students who desires to stress study skills in remedial sessions will find the SQ3R technique well-defined and explained in this book.

Sanders, Norris M. *Classroom Questions*. New York: Harper & Row, 1966. A brief paperback dealing solely with the various components of question construction and teacher planning. Filled with illustrated examples, Norris's work carefully covers many dimensions of question-asking.

Stauffer, Russell G. *Directing Reading Maturity as a Cognitive Process*. New York: Harper & Row, 1969. In the first two chapters, Stauffer presents vital information to all those who wish to become well informed about the cognitive processes.

Tinker, Miles A. and McCullough, Constance M. *Teaching Elementary Reading*, Chapters 8 and 9. New York: Appleton-Century-Crofts, Inc., 1962. Excellent suggestions are provided in this book for the teaching of comprehension skills to elementary school children. The reader will find these suggestions specific and practical.

Wilson, Robert M. and Hall, MaryAnne. *Reading and the Elementary School Child: Theories and Practices*, Chapter 8. New York: Van Nostrand Reinhold Co., 1972. Intensive attention is given to the developmental aspects of comprehension. This chapter is background reading for those who find difficulty with the terminology used in this chapter.

10

Evaluation in
Remedial Reading

Instruction which has been directed through effective diagnosis to meet the strengths and needs of the child stands a good chance of succeeding. Following remediation, be it classroom or clinical, the child is likely to show signs of being an improved reader. It is also likely that in most cases a post-remediation test will be the evaluation technique used by the educator to determine how much gain the child has made. While the assumption is logical, post-testing is plagued with problems and is not the entire answer to the problem of evaluation in remedial reading.

Has the pupil made *useful* progress? Post-test comparisons with performance prior to remediation measure how well the child has improved but only in those areas measured by the test. Has he improved so that his classroom performance will be better? Will he read more at home? Has his attitude toward reading changed? Are the gains which are indicated by the test of a permanent nature? Has the test measured the child's ability to perform in nontest reading situations? Are the gains a significant change in the child's reading skills? Other questions are concerned with the efficiency of the remedial program. Although the pupil has made real progress, were the gains made as a result of efficient diagnosis and remedial techniques? Could the child have accomplished more with less or more diagnosis, less or more remediation? Was this progress in terms of the educational goals which were established? Was the teacher able to direct the child toward useful goals and was his progress a result of that effort? Answers to these types of questions lead one to a truer evaluation of the effectiveness of a remedial program. The evaluation of teacher efficiency in the use of diagnostic and remedial techniques is essential, for through evaluation one can see more clearly the effectiveness of the reading program as contrasted with the educational gains normally expected over this period of time.

When evaluation is conducted following clinical remediation, additional complications not present in the evaluation of classroom remediation arise. First, the child may have been taken from the classroom, tested and tutored by someone other than the classroom teacher, and then sent back to the classroom to use his newly developed skills. This transfer from clinical to classroom situations is not always automatic, for many children in clinical situations perform for reasons that do not necessarily carry over to the classroom. We have experienced cases in which the child worked and improved during clinical remediation and was returned to the classroom with "adequate reading skills." However, upon returning to his classroom, the child was unable or unwilling to use these newly formed skills effectively. Upon investigation, we found that the child had enjoyed the individualized attention, responded to the motivation of the tutor, and though willing to work to please this particular educator, lost this desire upon returning to the classroom to be one of thirty-three children. To facilitate an effective transfer of skills learned in clinical situations to the classroom, we have made it a policy to conduct all clinical work in group instruction.

Another complication of evaluation in clinical remediation is determining how much of the child's improved skills performance has been due to work in the clinical situation and how much would have occurred if he had remained in the classroom. Although it is not always feasible to measure precisely, consideration must be made for improvement outside the remedial program. Classroom and clinical evaluation have much in common, however, and the reader will find a use for many of the following suggestions, be they applied to the classroom or to the clinic.

PRINCIPLES OF EVALUATION IN REMEDIAL READING

The following principles, common to all education, have particular application when evaluating the effectiveness of remedial reading programs:

Evaluation Must Be Broad in Base

Ample allowance must be made for factors such as improved medical attention, relaxation of home pressures, and reaction to both negative and positive diagnosis. If a child has been provided with glasses as a result of physical screening, a proper evaluation of his tutoring program must give consideration to the effect of the glasses as well as the instruction. In an examination of our clinic cases, for example, we found that children referred for inadequate visual screening performance made better progress (as a group) if the parents followed the referral advice than did children whose parents did not follow referral advice. Apparently, attention to the visual needs of these children had an effect upon the progress they made. The appropriate importance to be applied to each factor in evaluation is extremely difficult to determine; however, this principle insists only that they be considered in the evaluation of the child's progress.

Aspects of Evaluation: Broadly speaking, the aspects of evaluation in reading can be considered in terms of pupil growth and educator efficiency. In order to be seen as clearly separate aspects of evaluation, these aspects are discussed below individually. However, the reader is reminded that the two aspects of evaluation are closely related and that evaluation of one exclusive of the other is often not possible.

Evaluation Must Be Continuous

Actually, evaluation is the final act of continual diagnosis. It involves many of the same processes as diagnosis (i.e., an evaluation of the child's skill development and reading effectiveness). Evaluation of past performance should be considered diagnosis for future instruction; therefore, evaluation is continuous.

Evaluation Must Be Objective

Objective measures of performance should be used as an effort to control bias. One often reads evaluation reports which state that the teachers and pupils were enthusiastic about the progress which had been made. Although enthusiasm is a highly desirable factor, it cannot be the basis for evaluation of program effectiveness. Nonobjective evaluation techniques are certainly valuable and are not to be precluded by this principle. However, the principle that the basis of the evaluation must be as objective as possible still holds.

Evaluation Must Be in Terms of Established Goals

It is desirable and natural for considerable progress to be noticed in areas for which instruction had not been planned. Such progress, however desirable, must be considered secondary to the goals of the program. We cannot talk about attitude change, for example, unless the program pre-evaluated attitude and included attitude change in its objectives.

PUPIL GROWTH

The questions which arose at the beginning of this chapter indicate several aspects of evaluation in terms of pupil growth. An examination of several of these aspects will assist the reader to become more effective in pupil evaluation.

Changes in Classroom Performance

Of prime importance is the child's performance in the classroom. If there are not noticeable changes of behavior in classroom performance (skills and attitudes), there is cause to doubt the effectiveness of the remedial program. Classroom performance, although of basic importance, quite often is not considered in evaluation. Does the child make better grades in school following the remedial program? Does the child read more willingly and more often? Has the child gained independence in reading? Since improved school grades are usually a satisfactory indication of pupil growth, particularly for the child and his parents, grade improvement might be best noticed in the language-centered subjects. This author studied successful remedial reading cases and found considerable scholastic improvement in school grades.[1] Subsequent to this study, it was found valuable to conduct periodic follow-up studies of remedial students to determine effectiveness of remediation. Short questionnaires, preferably directed to the classroom teacher, can be used to obtain this information. If scholastic performance has not improved, most parents will consider the remedial program ineffective, regardless of other indications of improved skill performance.

---

[1]Robert M. Wilson, *The Scholastic Improvement of Successful Remedial Reading Students*. Unpublished Doctor's dissertation, University of Pittsburgh, 1960.

The classroom teacher can obtain information concerning change in classroom performance through school records available to him. He can follow a child's scholastic performance on a rather informal basis, while the reading specialist generally will be required to use interviews and questionnaires to obtain this information. In either case, the educator will be obtaining important information concerning the growth and development of the child after remedial efforts have been successfully terminated.

Changes of pupil attitude are of utmost importance to the teacher, to the parents, and, of course, to the child. In most cases, attitude changes are the most obvious indication to the classroom teacher that the program was effective. Similarly, parents often feel that attitude changes prove the worth of a given program. It goes without saying that, if the child can improve in his attitude toward reading and school in general, it will be obvious to him that the remedial program has made a difference.

Further evaluation must be made to determine whether changes in classroom performance are temporary or permanent. Temporary changes may indicate a lack of communication between one classroom teacher and the reading specialist. In such cases, many remedial programs have been disbanded or severely criticized because children were able to demonstrate only short-term gains. Implications for temporary gains include: no change of desire to read on the part of the child; skill improvement which has not been transferred to actual reading situations; or lack of communication between teachers who are working with the child. In the latter case, conflicting treatment of the child (e.g., one teacher's praising the child's efforts while another criticizes them) can undo much of the good accomplished in a remedial program.

A study of a child's grades over a period of several years can be conducted in the same manner as can a study of immediate scholastic performance (i.e., through the examination of school records or questionnaires). When the evaluation findings are positive, the educator will find this type of evaluation a rewarding experience. It is most assuring to know that the child has not only responded to the teacher's efforts but also has used his newly developed skills without the teacher's constant attention. For example, the following grades earned by John cover the two years prior to remediation and the two years after remediation.

TABLE 7

	Grade 2	Grade 3	Remediation in Grade 4	Grade 5	Grade 6
Reading	D	D	C	B	B
Language	C	C	C	B	B
Spelling	D	F	D	C	C

Without attempting to determine direct cause and effect relation-ships, Grade 4, the time of John's remediation, appears to have been a turning point in his grades. By noting that the changes appear to have been permanent, more reliance can be placed upon the evaluation. However, if John showed grade changes only in fifth grade and then regressed to his previous performances, the success of the program would need to be questioned.

Observant teachers might notice and record behavior changes which might not be reflected in grades earned during reading periods. For example, the teacher should notice whether the child now is able to contribute during word attack skill lessons or whether he does much better when attempting to answer questions following silent reading. Observed changes should be recorded and reported to parents as positive behavior change which can be praised and rewarded.

Changes in Reading Skills

In terms of grade level improvement: Evaluation of reading improvement usually is determined by test performance. Bleismer,[2] in sighting three basic post-remediation evaluation techniques, calls this a simple pre- and post-test comparison. If a child enters a remedial program reading at 4.5 grade level and concludes the reading program at 5.5 grade level, it can be concluded that he has gained 1.0 years in grade level. Obviously, the adequacy of the test instrument used to determine grade level performance limits this aspect of evaluation. It does not account for the child's chronological or mental age increase nor for changes which would have occurred without remediation.

---

[2]Emery P. Bleismer, "Evaluating Progress in Remedial Reading Programs," *The Reading Teacher* (March, 1962), pp. 344-50.

Reading skill performance as compared to grade level is of particular interest to both the classroom teacher and the principal, for it has much to do with the placement of the child in a particular room and within a class. Once it has been determined that a child can perform at a certain grade level, it is necessary to create situations that permit him to perform at that level.

In terms of reading potential: Evaluation in this area attempts to determine whether the child is working up to his potential. Bleismer[3] claims that potential will change with age and that estimates must be adjusted for effective evaluation. Regardless of the child's grade level performance and his ability to perform in an assigned classroom, growth up to potential is generally considered a desirable goal of remediation. If a child has an estimated potential of 5.0 and a reading level of 3.0, his working development is lagging behind his mental development by 2.0 years. If, after a semester of work, his reading level rises to 4.2, his potential will have to be reestimated before growth can be measured.

January			May		
Potential	Reading	Difference	Potential	Reading	Difference
5.0	3.0	2.0	5.8	4.2	1.6

Note that in this case, the child's reading potential increased as he grew older, thereby lessening the apparent effect of the difference in reading grade level changes. Remedial sessions accelerated his growth over his potential by .4 years (found by subtracting the differences). Reading potential techniques will be of more interest to the reading specialist than to the classroom teacher or the parent. One major problem with using potential as a standard occurs when remedial efforts are being made to improve potential. In those cases, potential is not a standard. For example, if a remedial program includes opportunities for language development, opportunities of potential improvement are also included. Such programs actually have resulted in considerable improvement on tests of intelligence.

In terms of past performance: Evaluation of skill improvement in terms of the child's previous performance rates is of some advan-

---

[3]Bleismer, "Evaluating Progress in Remedial Reading," pp. 344-50.

tage with older students. Again, Bleismer[4] is asking that the identifiable variables be controlled. Suppose that a boy has completed six years of school and has scored at grade level 4.6 before remediation was begun. This indicates an average growth of .6 years of reading skill for each year in school $(4.6 - 1.0 \div 6)$. Note that 1.0 must be subtracted as all children start with a reading level of 1.0 (the zero month of first grade). If this child obtained a reading level of 5.5 by the end of one year in remediation, he would have gained .9 years of skill in one year $(5.5 - 4.9 = .9)$. Yet he is not reading up to grade level and may not be reading up to expectancy. He has not progressed even one full year under intensive remediation. *But his improvement is greater than it has been in the past*, thus indicating that he is profiting from an effective remedial program.

Years in School	Average Yearly Gain Before Tutoring	Gain During Yr. of Tutoring	Growth Attributed to Tutoring
5	.6	.9	.3

Note that the gain of .9 years is greater by .3 years than could have been expected from the average of previous efforts. While of interest to the reading specialist and the classroom teacher, the rate of improvement during remediation is of little interest to the child or the parent, especially if the child remains limited in his ability to perform in the classroom.

Evaluation of past performance is limited by the unlikely assumption that past performance was evenly distributed. However, the older child who is seriously handicapped in reading is less likely to score effectively in the other aspects of evaluation even though he is making significant progress. This technique then provides an indication of his skill improvements, however slight.

All of the evaluation techniques suggested above are limited by the instruments being used to make comparisons. Standardized tests are inherently unreliable and cause notable gains to be suspect due to the error on the measuring instrument. Grade level scores on these tests are not equal units for measuring gains. If used at all, standard scores should be used. The test selected may not measure the skills which were the objectives of the remediation. The standard-

---

[4]Bleismer, "Evaluating Progress in Remedial Reading," pp. 344-50.

ization population may be mismatched with the remedial group.

It is recommended that standardized tests be used best to indicate gains with groups of children and that informal tests be used to measure the gains of individual children.

Two other problems occur when evaluating in terms of standardized tests. First, all standardized tests contain error in their measurement; the amount of error makes score changes possible by chance. Therefore, small gains over short periods of time cannot be measured by standardized tests. Second is the problem of the phenomenon referred to as regression. Stated simply, if a group of children were given a standardized test today and then the same test were readministered a week later, low scoring children would tend to improve their scores (scores would move toward the mean), while high scoring children would decrease their scores (scores would move toward the mean).

One solution to overcoming the limitations of standardized tests, is the use of informal measures, either teacher-made or commercially prepared. Informal tests constructed from the actual material which the child is ultimately expected to read are more reliable indications of reading ability than are standardized tests. Informal devices can be of three types:

1. Word lists taken from reading materials at various levels can be used to measure gains in word recognition.
2. Paragraphs followed by carefully constructed questions taken from materials of varying reading levels can assist in measuring gains in reading accuracy (when used orally) and in comprehension (when reading silently).
3. Skills quizzes constructed by teachers to assess a child's abilities to perform in the areas upon which instruction is given can be used to measure skill development.

In some cases it is worthwhile to administer two post-tests. One of these may be an informal measure as mentioned above; the other, a standardized measure. In any case, the educator will want to assure himself that the gains are due to skill improvement and not the design or the norms of the test. Since evaluation must be planned prior to remediation, the measuring instruments should be included in the pre-testing sessions (i.e., in the diagnosis) so that post-testing can be used for comparison.

Using diagnostic information as pre-testing data can be a useful technique. For example, the data from Table 11 in Chapter 4 can be reevaluated at the end of the tutoring period. The following table might serve as an example:

TABLE 8

Child	Word Recognition		Word Opposites		Phonics					
					Consonants		Blends		Vowels	
	pre	post	pre	post	pre	post	pre	post	pre	post
1	2-1	3-1	2-2	4	ok	ok	ok	ok	ok	ok
2	2-1	2-2	2-2	3-2	no	ok	no	ok	no	no
3	2-1	3-1	2-2	5	ok	ok	no	ok	no	ok

Changes in observed behaviors: When instruction is based on behavioral objectives, statements that can be observed in terms of behavioral changes, the child's ability to perform behaviors can be used for evaluation. For example, a behavioral objective might be *to be able to substitute initial consonants while reading unknown words orally.* Obviously, if a child can perform such a behavior, he has met the objective. His success may not be reflected in test performance but is observable in reading situations.

When behavioral objectives are to be used in evaluation, those objectives should be recorded, and specific examples of appropriate behaviors should be recorded when they are observed. Educators should not rely upon memory to recall what behaviors were used for instruction and instances of the child's ability to perform those behaviors.

Because they may be the most valid measure of short-term gains in reading skills, the use of behavioral objectives is encouraged. During a period of remediation, many behavioral objectives might be set. The values of evaluating the effectiveness of a remedial program using them are many. Teachers can interpret behaviors better than they can test scores. Parents can be asked to watch for behaviors and reward them. Improvement might not be measurable by test scores until the behaviors developed become overlearned and used in all reading situations. Short-term remedial sessions can be developed in terms of specific behavioral objectives and evaluated without the use of testing materials. Obviously evaluation via behavioral objectives emphasizes a child's strengths and successes (see Suggested Readings for further information).

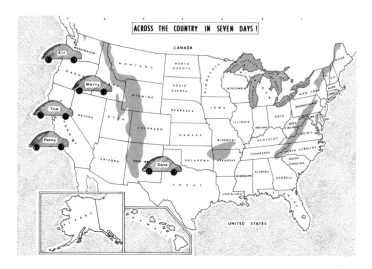

Contract Completion Can Be Reinforced Intrinsically
via the Use of Such Materials as an Auto Race across
the Country.

Changes in observed attitudes: Like behavioral changes, attitude
changes can be observed when care is taken to look for them and
when they are recorded in specific terms. Mager[5] suggests that attitude behaviors can be objectively observed. He classifies attitude
responses as either *approach* or *avoidance*. Approach responses
might include such behaviors as coming to remedial sessions on time
or early, being ready and eager to work, bringing books to class to
share, asking for help with certain skills, and so on. Avoidance responses might include such behaviors as skipping remedial sessions,
refusing to work unless directed, forgetting to bring books to class,
disrupting the learning of others, and the like. If teachers were to
record both types of responses at the beginning, during, and at the
conclusion of a remedial program, objectivity could be added to the
measurement and evaluation of attitude changes. Attitude changes
easily might be observed by parents and by teachers.

   We have often heard parents exclaim, "Now John enjoys reading!" or "He actually sits down and reads without our urging him
to do so!" As a desirable outcome of a remedial program, parental

---

[5]Robert F. Mager, *Developing Attitude Toward Learning* (Palo Alto:
Fearon Publishers, 1968), Chapter 4.

reports of attitude changes must be considered with evaluation of a remedial program. It is the child's fully developed desire and interest in reading that can mean significant changes in his performance in school. Without changes in attitude, gains made during remediation are usually temporary, for it is through improved attitude that the child will continue to strive to improve.

Questionnaires or interviews generally are used to aid evaluation of out-of-school attitude changes. Information can be obtained from the child as well as the parents to assure the reliability of the responses. The inherent danger of interviews and questionnaires is the tendency for respondents to maintain a "halo" effect; therefore, it is important that the interview or questionnaire be structured to avoid pointing to obviously expected responses. Although difficult, evaluation of attitudes will add to the total picture of the child's improvements as a result of remediation.

EDUCATOR EFFICIENCY

The efficiency of an educator is more difficult to evaluate and is therefore less likely to receive the evaluative efforts that pupil growth receives. Educator efficiency in programs should be evaluated in the following areas:

Adequacy of diagnosis: Due to emphasis placed upon the proper use of diagnosis and the time spent in accomplishing it, there is valid reason for its inclusion in evaluation. The educator must determine whether the diagnosis has uncovered the remedial needs of the child effectively and precisely. Further, he must decide that the diagnosis, while not overextended, is complete enough to cover the areas of the child's skill development. When there is a failure to evaluate in all areas, there is a likelihood that inefficiency will develop in remedial sessions. We have known teachers who used tests which, for them, appeared to supply essential information for a diagnosis; however, upon closer examination, these tests did not provide any information that could not have been determined more easily by other diagnostic techniques.

Adequacy of remedial approach: As educators become accustomed to working in remediation, specific approaches often develop into standard procedures with all children. The error resulting here, unless there are constant attempts at evaluation, is that diagnosis is relegated to a secondary position since a given remedial approach is used with all children. For example, if all children were to be tutored through the use of the experience story approach, then, although diagnosis has some importance, the diagnostic conclusions would be secondary to the remedial approach. It is through evaluation of remedial approaches that the educator is led to develop the variety of effective approaches prescribed by the diagnostic needs of the children.

Adequacy of remedial techniques: Similar to the difficulty described in remedial approaches, a prescribed technique used with all children regardless of the remedial approach is equally limiting and should be avoided through careful evaluation of remedial techniques. For example, a graph to illustrate progress will not motivate all children in all remedial techniques. The evaluation of techniques will save time in remediation and lead the educator to those techniques best suited to the needs of the child.

Adequacy of remedial materials: As educators become familiar with the manuals and contents of the wide variety of materials available in remediation, they are likely to select and use those that appeal most to them. This action is proper when these materials are selected after an evaluation of their effectiveness; however, if they are selected on the basis of familiarity alone, their adequacy should be evaluated. As the flood of materials continues, the educator should do more material evaluation.

A variety of techniques is available to assist the educator in the various aspects of evaluation discussed above. The teacher can and should consult with other teachers; ask for help from a reading resource person in his school or district; read evaluations of materials in the professional literature; talk with children about books they like and dislike; conduct experiments using certain materials with one group of children and other materials with another group; examine the activities required by the materials and compare them to objectives for the remedial program; and by giving children choices of materials to use, observe their consistent selection of one over another. In addition, more than one of these techniques should be used in the evaluation.

If requested, the reading specialist should be able to conduct an evaluation of the total school efforts in the area of diagnostic and remedial reading. Assuming that the reading specialist is acquainted with research design and controlled experimentation techniques and has the ability to interpret research data, there is little reason for not using such techniques. Austin, Bush, and Heubner[6] discuss the school survey in detail with specific suggestions for its implementation. If many teachers are unprepared for this type of evaluation, it will be necessary to call upon others, school or university personnel to assist. Such a course of action has an added advantage in many cases, because evaluation conducted by persons not directly involved in the program lessens the role of bias.

Pupil Self-evaluation

Pupil evaluation of remedial progress and of remedial programs should not be overlooked. Children often render insights toward remediation which elude educators. Teachers should seek pupil self-evaluation and program evaluation and they should use it in their evaluation of remedial programs.

Pupil-teacher conferences can be used for pupil evaluation. If they feel that they will not be penalized for their honesty, many children can provide accurate, useful statements concerning their feelings about how they have done, about their remedial sessions, or about their reactions to specific materials and techniques. Questionnaires also can be used in pupil evaluation. Questions concerning how they feel they have performed in terms of specific objectives, the portions of the program they enjoyed most and least, and the changes they would recommend might be included. Finally, contract evaluation can be used for self-evaluation. Such evaluation occurs immediately after the contract is completed when children can mark their own work honestly.

SUMMARY

Evaluation should be carefully planned for all remedial sessions. To make valid comparisons, pretesting and noting of behaviors prior to remediation are essential. To evaluate the successes of children during the program, teachers should be expected to use formal and informal tests, behavioral objectives in and away from school, mea-

---

[6]Mary Austin, Clifford L. Bush, and Mildred Huebner, *Reading Evaluation* (New York: The Ronald Press Co., 1961).

sures of attitude change, and information from parents. To assure this professional growth, teachers should continuously evaluate their own effectiveness in both diagnosis and remediation.

SUGGESTED READINGS

Ahmann, J. Stanley, and Glock, Marvin D. *Evaluating Pupil Growth.* Boston: Allyn-Bacon, Inc., 1959. In Chapter XIV, the authors discuss the aspects of evaluating personal-social adjustment. Chapter XVI is devoted to diagnosis and remediation. The entire book will provide the reader with an effective basis for evaluation.

Austin, Mary C.; Bush, Clifford L.; and Huebner, Mildred H. *Reading Evaluation.* New York: The Ronald Press Co., 1961. This entire book is devoted to the subject of evaluation in reading. Without restricting themselves to remedial evaluation, the authors have provided specific evaluation techniques and tests. The reading specialist will find this book to have particular value when he is considering an all-school survey.

Bleismer, Emery P. "Evaluating Progress in Remedial Reading Programs." *The Reading Teacher*, March 1962, pp. 344-50. A detailed explanation of three basic techniques for evaluating remedial programs is provided in this article. Reviewed in this chapter, these techniques can be studied more thoroughly by a quick review of this excellent article.

Farr, Roger. *Reading: What Can Be Measured?* Newark, Delaware: International Reading Association, 1969. Farr takes an objective but critical look at evaluation instruments used by reading personnel in the schools and clinics. He provides guidelines for the application of research to work in reading. Farr has made a significant contribution which should be considered required reading.

Mager, Robert F. *Developing Attitude Toward Learning.* Palo Alto: Fearon Publishers, 1968. This is a highly valuable book which stresses the need for teachers to observe objectively children's attitudinal responses to their instruction.

Mager, Robert F. *Preparing Instructional Objectives.* Palo Alto: Fearon Publishers, 1962. This is an extremely well-written short paperback designed to help teachers gain skills in developing behavioral objectives. For those unfamiliar with behavioral objectives, Mager's book is required reading.

Maginnis, George. "Evaluating Remedial Reading Gains." *Journal of Reading*, April 1970, pp. 523-28. Discussing several of the inherent problems involved in evaluation of remedial reading, Maginnis leaves the reader with several positive suggestions for avoiding those problems.

Strang, Ruth, and Linguist, Donald M. *The Administrator and the Improvement of Reading*. New York: Appleton-Century-Crofts, Inc., 1960. This booklet, designed for the administrator, has evaluation clues built into each chapter. Chapter 4 addresses itself to the evaluation of suitable reading programs. Appendix B is a guide for teacher self-appraisal. These two references will be of interest to the reader who desires more information on teacher effectiveness evaluation.

11

Parental Roles in Diagnosis, Remediation, and Prevention

"Let your child alone!" or "Don't worry, we'll handle it," are quite often the only suggestions that teachers have to offer parents who are seeking ways to help their child with reading difficulties. Today, such advice is inappropriate and will likely fall upon deaf ears for parents want to help their child, can help their child, and will help their child! As the educational level of our adult population rises, as the emphasis upon education for success in life continues, as education continues to be examined in the public press, and as commercial exploitations of parental concerns expand, it is no longer defensible to keep parents from assisting their child with reading, especially if he is experiencing difficulty. It is imperative that educators realize this fact and seek ways for parents to be most helpful in terms of the educational goals which have been established.

On the opposite side of the coin is the fact that left without guidance parents do things to "help" their child which may be inappropriate and often harmful. It is not uncommon for an uninformed parent, for example, to attempt to motivate his child through comparison with his brothers and sisters or playmates. More often than not, undirected parental activity merely compounds the child's aversion to reading and actually interferes with his progress in a remedial program. So, again, it behooves us to direct the parent to that role which will fulfill most effectively the educational goals which have been established.

Although not a hard and fast rule, it is our finding that parental anxiety is likely to mount as the child's progress in reading declines.[1] There comes a point where parental anxiety is felt by the child to such a degree that it complicates his reading problem. These parents, too, must have their concern and anxiety channeled into useful, helpful educational activities. It *does not* help to tell the parents not to worry; it is too late for this. The answer is to establish for them a role through which they can be most helpful.

Clinical and classroom diagnostic and remedial situations inherently demand that the parental role vary. The difference in roles is generally one of degree, for by the very nature of clinical situations, the parents are more actively engaged in what their child is doing. As the role of the parent is discussed in diagnosis, remediation, and prevention of reading problems, suggestions are termed in reference to the classroom teacher and the reading specialist so that they might direct the parent toward useful activities. It certainly is not to be assumed that all parents can perform all of the roles to be discussed. Final determination of the precise role of the parent is reserved for the educator who is working directly with the child.

PARENTS CAN HELP!

Parents teach their children to walk, to talk, and to do numerous other useful activities required in our society. Educators rely heavily upon the ability of the parents to do these jobs well. When they do not fulfill this responsibility, they leave the child ill-equipped for progress in school. As the child develops difficulties in his progress in reading, it is logical to call upon the child's *first teacher*, his parents, to assist the educator in any way that will be useful. The suggestions that follow, then, are based upon the following beliefs:

1. Parents can help.
2. Parents often know what makes their child react most effectively.

---

[1]Robert M. Wilson and Donald W. Pfau, "Parents Can Help!" *Reading Teacher*, XXI (May 1968), 758-61.

3. Children want parental support and assistance and strive to please their parents through school success.
4. Without parent-teacher teamwork, success with severely handicapped readers will be unnecessarily limited.
5. When directed toward useful roles, parents are usually willing to follow the advice of educators.

Parental Role In Diagnosis

Except for the classroom teacher, parents most likely will be the first to recognize that their child is not making satisfactory progress in the development of his reading skills. When the classroom teacher fails to observe the signs of frustration in a given child, one can be certain that such awareness will not escape the parents for long. The responsibility for the initial identification of the problem reader often in such cases falls to the parents. Parents properly may be directed to observe their child in reading and to call any of the following symptoms of frustrated reading to the attention of the classroom teacher or the reading specialist. These symptoms are:

1. Avoidance of reading.
2. Inability to complete classroom assignments or homework.
3. Inability to discuss with the parent material which he has just completed in reading.
4. Habitual difficulty in attacking unknown words, especially if the problem is noticed after two or three years of schooling.
5. Word-by-word, non-fluent oral reading, especially when the child has practiced this reading silently before reading it orally.
6. Complaints from the child of visual discomfort in reading periods of fifteen minutes or more.

By directing the educator's attention to specific symptoms such as these, parents may identify reading problems before they become serious enough to necessitate the more formal types of reading diagnosis and remediation. Upon receipt of observations such as these from parents, the educator should conduct as much diagnosis as is necessary to inform himself and the parents of the nature of the problem.

That many parents will become overly anxious while observing the child for these symptoms must also be considered. Nonetheless, it is just as important for the anxious parent to know that his child does *not* have a reading problem as it is for other parents to know the nature of their child's reading problem. In this way needless anxieties can be relaxed, thus creating better learning situations for the child.

Another important role of parents in diagnosis is the supplying of information in support of or in conflict with the tentative hypotheses which have been established in classroom diagnosis or initial screening techniques. The parents' role in clinical diagnosis, then, is to supply supporting observations concerning the child's work in school, his attitudes toward reading, his physical well being, and so on. Without this information, which is frequently obtainable through either questionnaires or interviews, the reading specialist is likely to err in making judgments based on relatively short exposure to the child. It is generally more effective to obtain information from parents after tentative hypotheses have been reached, lest the feelings of the parents tend to bias the examiner.

The parent has the complete responsibility for the follow-up in areas in which referral has been made. It is the right and the responsibility of parents to attend to the physical and emotional needs of their child; and it is the parents to whom we most often look for assistance in taking the child to the vision specialist, the neurologist, the psychiatrist, and other specialists.

As parents become involved in the diagnosis, it is important that they also be consulted concerning the findings. Perhaps nothing is more frustrating to parents than to know that their child has undergone extensive study, yet they have not been consulted about the findings. However, making diagnostic conclusions available to parents is far more than a courtesy, for quite often it is the parents to whom the suggestions for alleviating the problem most appropriately apply. A number of times we have consulted with parents concerning their child's problem, only to find that the child, from that point on, improved and no longer needed remedial help.

Although parents should be consulted concerning diagnostic conclusions, it is often wise to avoid a discussion of precise scores and specific findings. The tendency to overrate a score on a particular test without fully understanding the explanation of the test is a common difficulty of parents when they encounter test score results. It is usually preferable to provide parents with the general findings of the diagnosis, placing more emphasis upon the interpretation of these test scores than on the scores themselves. It may be better, for example, to indicate to the parents that the child reads well on about the second grade level and that he will need help in remediation in the area of word attack skills than to tell them that the child scored 2.6 on a given test and obtained a score of 75 percent on initial consonant sounds. However, adding to such comments specific statements about the types of skills a child possesses can help parents to understand the child's strengths. Such efforts should not be minimized, for while not attempting to cover-up the child's weaknesses, it is healthy to discuss the child's strengths. Therefore say, "he can read well on the second grade level," instead of "he cannot read at the third grade level."

It is important that the parents have confidence in the findings of the diagnosis, for they are then more likely to adhere to the ensuing recommendations. Of course, their confidence is going to depend a great deal upon the manner in which the diagnosis is explained. However, we have found that it often helps to explain or to demonstrate a test or two upon which the child was evaluated. The parents then develop a feeling for the performance of the child and feel that the educator really wants them to be informed. When used as the only form of reporting, written diagnostic findings are of limited value to the parents. Terms and implications often are not fully understood; questions arising from the reports are left unanswered. Parents can be better informed if diagnostic reports are explained at a consultation session in which questions can be answered and understandings assured. Summaries of these sessions may be written and sent to the parents, but not without consultation.

Parental Roles in Remediation

For the parent to have any role at all in remediation, there must be a general understanding of the educational goals set by the person conducting the remediation. It is not only ethically appropriate for the educator to inform the parents of such goals, but reaching the goal is far more feasible when the parents are effectively involved. The first task, therefore, is to inform the parent of realistic goals and of the general approaches to be used in attaining these goals. It is extremely helpful if these goals are short-range and easily attainable so that the child, the parent, and the educator all can see clearly that progress is being made. Of course, this will necessitate contacting the parent as the goals are readjusted and progress in the development of reading skills is made. Again, these contacts with parents are most effective when they receive the information in a consultation session.

The most appropriate role for the parent, after an understanding of the program has been made available, is to provide situations in the home whereby the skills learned in remediation can be *reinforced*. Although reinforcement activities may be time-consuming, the parent should recognize the necessity for providing reinforcement opportunities as his foremost responsibility. Specifically, this work involves the parent in:

1. Providing a quiet, comfortable, and relaxing place for reading in the home.
2. Providing a planned time during the day when the household becomes suitable for reading: the television is turned off; other members of the family pursue reading interests; and a pleasant attitude regarding this time is created.
3. Assisting the child with material that is difficult for him in either word pronunciation or sentences and paragraph meaning. This work, of course, involves the availability of one of the parents but should not be construed to imply that the parent must be "breathing down the child's neck." On the contrary, the parent (while reading something of interest to himself) simply may be in the same room and available to the child, if needed.
4. Assisting the child with follow-up exercises which are sent home after a remedial session. The parent must understand that the child is learning a skill and will probably not be letter-perfect in these attempts. The parent must not become angry with the child when he fails repeatedly in these types of exercises; rather, the parent should contact the educator conducting the remediation and inform him of this difficulty. Neither the classroom teacher nor the reading specialist will send material home for practice unless there is relative assurance that it can be completed with some satisfaction. However, there will be instances when, regardless of the care taken, the child will bring home materials which are too difficult for him to read without assistance.
5. Being available when an audience is needed or when discussion is desirable following either oral or silent reading. The parent should display interest in what the child has

read, thus permitting him to feel a sense of having done something which pleases the parent.

6. Providing the praise and reward for demonstrations of skill development that is a job well suited to parents. Since the materials sent home for practice should allow the child to demonstrate his strengths, positive reactions from parents can do much to help the child make concentrated efforts in forthcoming tasks.

These activities should be conducted in cooperation with the reading specialist or the classroom teacher; specific activities should be originated by these educators in terms of the goals which already have been explained to the parent. It is helpful to demonstrate these techniques to parents. Illustrating how effectively the recommended suggestions actually work with their child builds the parents' confidence in the recommendations.

On the negative side, the parent should understand what *not to do* as well as what *to do*. Depending upon the educational goals, the educator should anticipate the types of problems likely to arise and direct the parents away from them. For example, it is far better to have the parents in the role of reinforcing skills learned in remedial sessions than it is to have them attempt to teach these skills themselves. If the parents feel that there is a great deficiency in a sounding skill, for example, the educator should be informed and the parents provided with an explanation of when that skill will become a part of the program. Furthermore, it should be made clear that no matter how great the temptation to have the child "sound out the word," it is the parents' job to tell the child unknown words until the sounding skill is approached remedially. Note that these examples relate to phonics. We find that although it is in this area that most parents feel most anxious, it is the area in which they do the poorest job of assisting the educators. As a general rule, therefore, we direct their attention away from instruction in phonics while providing opportunities for the parents to notice the child's development in reading through carefully prepared home assignments. Once again, the child demonstrates his strengths to his parents through such activities as reading orally an experience story which he has mastered, drilling for five minutes on the word cards he has mastered, and discussing exciting problem-solving activities which he worked on in school.

Another parental role in remediation is the obtaining of books for the child to read. Normally, the educator will supply the first books from materials available in the remedial program; however, since the supply of books is often limited, parents can be encouraged to assume responsibility for obtaining books. The educator, in this case, will supply the parent with a list of appropriate books for the child to read at home, asking the parents to obtain these books from libraries, friends, book stores, and the like. Consideration for the level and the interest factors of available books should be evaluated in the recommendations made to parents. It is particularly worthwhile to recommend books to parents near the child's birthday or at Christmas so that books can be included on gift lists. More than simply supplying the child with a book, such activity develops the attitude that a book is something of considerable worth, for it is given as a special gift.

Parents commonly desire to supplement the efforts of the remedial program with commercially available materials. Unless these materials are in accordance with the educational goals which have been established and unless the educator knows of the materials and can recommend their appropriateness for this child, it is our feeling that *they should be avoided.* By placing the parent in the teacher's role, unsuitable commercial materials involve the parents to a degree which is unprofitable for them, the child, and the educational goals for which they are all striving.

Parental Roles in Prevention

It is well to discuss the role of parents once the child has developed a reading problem, but it is far more important to reach parents before children develop such problems. Next to the classroom teacher, parents can do more to prevent the development of difficulties than anyone else. But part of the problem here is to communicate effectively with parents who are *not* anxious about their child's lack of success in reading. When unconcerned, parents are less likely to seek assistance even if it becomes necessary, thus implying to the child that they do not care. Each school and each teacher should take every opportunity to present preventive information to parents. Programs during Education Week, PTA meetings, individual conferences with parents, and notes sent to the home may be used to help parents prevent the occurrence of reading problems.

The following suggestions are designed to inform parents of activities which diminish the possibility of reading problems developing. They should be recommended by educators with discretion and for application when appropriate. No attempt is made here to supply a formula which will work with equal effectiveness with all parents.

Physical care: Parents who desire to avoid the complications involved with failure in school (in reading, particularly) should reflect upon their child's physical needs. A visual examination prior to school entrance and at least every other year thereafter is excellent insurance. An annual physical examination with follow-ups which are recommended by the family doctor eliminates the necessity of waiting until symptoms of physical disability become so apparent that they interfere with success in school. Many physical difficulties go unnoticed until failure in school is so acute that remedial programs are grossly inadequate to handle the particular problem. For example, if the child has refused to read for years because of visual discomfort, there is a void of reading experiences in his background for which, at times, it is impossible to compensate.

From the number of children who come to school too tired to accomplish the expected assignments during a given day, it seems that parents might well require ample amounts of sleep for their children. Since most teachers consider the first period of the morning the most effective instructional time, it is imperative that children be awake and alert. Parents who need suggestions concerning the amount of sleep their children require should consult the family doctor.

Hand-in-hand with alertness is the need for a substantial breakfast to replace an inadequate breakfast or none at all. Children who go without breakfast, fighting hunger long before the noon hour, are incapable of efficient use of school time. Recommendations for minimum breakfast requirements are readily available; however, when in doubt, parents should consult the family doctor. If the parents send a child who is physically sound to school, the educational program has a greater chance for success.

Emotional climate: When the school receives a child who is secure, loved at home, and understood, intereferences with success in school are further reduced. Parents can implant an attitude that learning will be fun and, though difficult at times, always worthwhile. They can develop an attitude by incorporating: no threats for failures in school (e.g., withdrawing television privileges), no promises for success in school (e.g., paying for good grades), respect and confidence in the teachers, and interest and enthusiasm for what is being accomplished in school. Parents should avoid criticism of the school and the teachers in front of their children. As parents, they have a right to voice their objections, but they should do so to the school authorities and the teachers rather than to the children. When children have the attitude that the school is weak and the teachers are incompetent, learning difficulties are compounded. Furthermore, parents can be directed to avoid as much as possible the direct and/or subtle comparison of their child to his peers and siblings. The reaction of the child who is striving to do as well as his sister is seldom positive or desirable. More concern should be demonstrated over the child's ability to perform as well as he can; performance which matches his sister's should not be the goal needed to satisfy parents.

Setting an example: Probably all parents have heard that it is good for them to set an example for their children. In reading, parental example can be one of reading for enjoyment. The child who from his earliest years notices that both parents seem to enjoy spending portions of their leisure time reading can develop a favorable attitude toward reading before entering school. Some leisure reading may be done orally for the child or for the family. Note that all oral reading should be accomplished with as much skill as possible; therefore, parents should be directed to first read silently all materials which they plan to read orally. Parents are inclined to discontinue oral reading as soon as the child himself develops skills in reading; however, oral reading by parents should continue. Parents should take every opportunity to read to children the books which are of interest to the children but which are too difficult for their developed reading skills. Children who come to school with family leisure reading experiences have definite advantages in learning to read, for they realize the wonders that reading can unlock for them.

Providing language experiences: Parents are to be encouraged to use every opportunity to widen their child's language experience. Through such activities as reading to the child, taking him on trips, and discussing events with him, situations are created in which language can be developed through experiences. Parents should be encouraged to lead the child into discussions which will add listening and speaking vocabulary words to the experiences. It is, of course, the listening and speaking vocabularies upon which the reading vocabulary hinges. Parents miss opportunities to help their children by failing to discuss trips and experiences with them. Trips about which little is said are not necessarily useless, but all parents should be encouraged to reinforce trip experiences with language experiences relating to the trip. For example, during the trip, they can let children help read maps, menus, and road signs; they can take photographs during trips and discuss them later; they can help children write captions for photographs, to be placed on the backs of pictures. Alerted to the potential of structured language experiences, parents can learn to use them more effectively.

Regulation of child's out-of-school activities: Parents who permit the child to do as he wishes with all out-of-school time indicate their lack of concern about what he does. First, parents, must understand that a full school day takes a good bit of concentration and is mentally fatiguing. Therefore, the child should be exposed to opportunities after school for active, expressive free play. Outdoor play, which physically releases the child, is desirable when possible. Secondly, the school program relies upon the interest and excitement which can be developed by the teacher and the materials from which the child is learning. Therefore, unusually large amounts of television viewing may interfere with the school program. After five hours of murder, passionate love, dancing girls, and the funniest of comedies, it is difficult to imagine that the child is going to fully appreciate a program which features the elementary school band or a story in the first grade reader which must be limited to his reading vocabulary. Although no formula is prescribed, we have found that limiting children to an hour of television viewing an evening does not work undue hardships upon them. Of course, the parents cannot expect the child to sit in the living room and *not* watch the shows that the parents are watching. This suggestion, then, implies that television viewing for the family should be restricted, especially during school days. Consideration can also be given by parents to the need for children to accomplish home assignments and have some quiet time. Again, quiet time, of necessity, involves the entire family.

Following advice: Parents must be encouraged to follow the suggestions of school personnel in matters concerning the education of their children. The most difficulty in this respect is experienced concerning the age at which the child should enter first grade and the decision to pass or fail the child in a given year. Each school system has its own method for determining whether or not a child is ready to profit from first grade instruction. When, after careful consideration, the school advises the parent to withhold the child from first grade for one year, the parent must understand that it is foolhardy to insist upon entrance. A scene creates needless anxiety for the child, antagonizes everyone, and generally results in the entrance of the child into a program in which he will not be successful. Scores of children who have been referred to us are victims of early entrance against school advice; their parents all now realize their error and wish that they could share their mistake with others who might thus avoid it.

School advice in connection with the passing or failing of a child generally receives undue parental concern which is passed directly to the child. Educators not only want the parents to comply with this advice but to embrace it with enthusiasm so that the child feels that he has not let the parents down. Unfortunately, in our pass or fail system, other children pick up the connotation of *failure* which will, unwittingly, create some disturbance within the child. Failure need not be compounded in the home by parental anxiety. To start with, parents can refer to repeating a year instead of failing a year. Hopefully, the time is near when failures in school will not be marked by failure to be promoted at the end of the year. All children should be on a program of continuous progress making it realistically impossible for such failure to occur. In the final analysis, it is our present system, not the children, that creates the failures. Many schools have instituted continuous progress programs, much to the satisfaction of parents, children, and teachers.

Willingness to follow referrals: Assuming that the school will over-refer to some degree (if they follow the procedure given in Chapter 3), it is imperative that a maximum of parental support for the referrals be developed. Educators may develop a more thorough attitude and stimulate the parents through their own concern. It is not enough, therefore, to refer and then forget about it. Follow-ups on referrals should be requested and expected. It is the parents' responsibility to see that their child's progress continues unhampered by obstacles which are noneducational in origin.

Reinforcement of learned skills: As discussed under the parental roles in remediation, skills learned in school can be reinforced by understanding parents in the home. The suggestions made in the previous discussion apply equally well here but with special emphasis on the fact that home reading situations should *always* end pleasantly with the child having a feeling of satisfaction. Parents who cannot control their anxieties and tempers should be led away from these types of activities. When the child reads orally to anxious parents, difficulty frequently arises regardless of the care the teacher has taken to make sure that the child can read the book which has been sent home.

In practical terms, when the child comes to an unknown word, what should the parent do? In order to make the reading pleasant and meaningful, the parents should tell the child the word. If he misses it again, they should tell him again and again. Words missed with regularity should be noted and sent to the teacher for analysis of the type of error and the necessary instruction. We have found that parents are seldom satisfied with this limited role; thus, we suggest the following course of action. When a child misses a word again and again, it is helpful if the parent prints the word carefully on a card. When the reading is finished and the story has been discussed, a *few* minutes can be spent glancing over these cards. As each word is pronounced, the child should be asked to use it in a sentence which should be written on the back of the card with the unknown word underlined. Preceding the next reading session at home, a little game-like drill can take place in which the child reads the sentence and the unknown word. Casey[2] makes further suggestions concerning the parental role in these cases. Her booklet is available for distribution to parents and can be effective when her suggestions match the philosophy of the teacher.

Pitfalls in Parental Cooperation

Obviously, there are numerous opportunities for parental cooperation to go astray which create more harm than good. Educators must be alert to these pitfalls and, when signs of their appearance occur, use alternate approaches to parental participation.

Lack of contact: Perhaps the worst pitfall is to make no contact with the parent. As this entire chapter illustrates, since parental roles will be assumed, it is best that they be taken in terms of the school's program. Parental contacts should be continuous, calling

---

[2]Sally L. Casey, *Ways You Can Help Your Child With Reading* (Evanston, Illinois: Row Peterson & Co., 1950).

for follow-up sessions to reinforce parental behavior. All too often, one parental conference is seen as meeting the need for parental involvement. We have found, for example, that in a six-week summer program three formal parental conferences and numerous informal conferences are needed to help parents become effective.

Underestimating parental love: Parents — even those parents who appear to be unconcerned — love their children. However, parental love easily can be misdirected; for example, some parents criticize the school in attempts to make the child feel more comfortable with his failures. When parental love is ignored, the result can be a lack of cooperation between parent and educator. As has been suggested, sending the child home with activities which will permit him to demonstrate his strengths to the parents allows them to demonstrate their love for the child with positive reinforcement.

Needless anxiety: Many parents confront educators with demonstrations of considerable anxiety. They are afraid, frustrated, and upset. For such parents to become useful partners, educators need to work with them to overcome their feelings of anxiety, for overanxious parents find it extremely difficult to work with their own child in any activity. When conversing with parents, the educator should listen to what they have to say. Really listen. Postpone judgments. Extra care should be taken to make activities for such parents as positive in nature as possible. As parents start to relax and gain confidence in the school's program, they can become more helpful partners.

One parent: Educators often are forced to settle for the reactions and opinions of only one of the child's parents. One must avoid this pitfall, for the child acts to please *both* parents. Therefore, every opportunity should be made to involve both parents, even if a home visit is required to attain this end. Upon talking with the other parent, we have often reversed our opinion of the home and the learning climate.

Coaching: Parents often develop the attitude that they should coach the child for his remedial sessions. Coaching improperly involves the parent as a crutch and leads the educators to make false assumptions concerning the child's progress. The parent must be directed toward the roles mentioned in this chapter and away from coaching type roles.

Failure to follow-up: When a remedial program is finished, the parents deserve to be given a summary of the results. Without this follow-up, parental activities may continue as the educator has directed following diagnosis, thus creating feelings of discomfort and needless anxiety within the child. The summary, therefore, should include specific recommendations for future parental roles concerning the changing needs of the child.

Assuming the teacher's role: Sending workbooks home in which the parent is placed in a teacher's role is seldom useful and often harmful. Educators must clearly see the difference between the parent's role as reinforcer of learned skills as opposed to that of the teacher's of new skills — the educator's job. Workbook activities provide too many teaching situations for most parents to handle well. However, if the child has worked in a skill activity successfully in school, allowing him to demonstrate that success to his parents is exactly what is desired.

SUMMARY

Parents can help! The educator must evaluate the home situation and make specific recommendations to the parents of problem readers as to which roles are most appropriate to enable the parents and the educator to work as a team. All parental roles should be in keeping with the educational goals which the remedial program is attempting to accomplish. When the child's parent is not actively involved, needless limitations are placed upon the educator's effectiveness. Based on the premise that most parents are going to help the child with his reading, it behooves the educator to direct these efforts toward the most useful purposes.

SUGGESTED READINGS

Artley, A. Sterl. *Your Child Learns to Read.* Chicago: Scott Foresman and Co., 1953. This book is a guide for parents to use with the Scott Foresman Series. It is obvious, though, that it includes many practical suggestions for parents whose children do not happen to use this series in school. Of particular interest might be the graded booklist under the title "Guide for Building a Home Library."

Casey, Sally L. *Ways You Can Help Your Child With Reading.* Evanston, Illinois: Row Peterson and Co., 1950. This excellent little booklet provides specific, practical suggestions to aid parents in helping a child with his reading. Since it is inexpensive, educators may find this a valuable book to have available for parents.

Landau, Elliott D. *Creative Parent-Teacher Conferences.* Salt Lake City, Utah: E. D. Landau, 1968. This work presents guidelines for various types of conferences with which educators are confronted. It offers specific suggestions to make conferences effective.

Reading Teacher, May 1970. Through twelve articles featuring the role of parents in reading activities, the entire May 1970, issue of the *Reading Teacher* focuses on the topic of this chapter.

Smith, Nila B. *Reading Instruction for Today's Children.* Englewood Cliffs, N.J.: Prentice-Hall, Inc., 1963, Chapters 19 and 20. This book provides two thorough chapters with specific suggestions on how to advise and work with parents. Included are sections on materials, selections, and some critical *do's* and *don'ts.*

Wilson, Robert M., and Pfau, Donald W. "Parents Can Help!" *Reading Teacher* (May, 1968), pp. 758-61. This article summarizes a study in which parents of children were asked how they helped their children at home. Children were grouped as below average readers and above average readers. Those children receiving most parental assistance at home were the below average readers.

12

Professional Responsibilities
and Roles

Public concern over school reading programs continues to grow. Newspapers, magazines, radio, and television focus public attention on the strengths and weaknesses of reading programs. Professional concern about reading is reflected in the large number of reading journals being published and the extensive amount of reading research as well as the endless volumes of books announced each year. Public and professional concern combined have resulted in pressures on school systems to produce better readers and to supply more programs of reading support. Unfortunately, such pressures occasionally create more problems than they solve. Hastily developed programs may emerge; inappropriate materials may be incorporated; hiring of personnel with questionable qualifications may occur; too many duties may be placed on personnel already employed. Therefore, consideration of professional responsibilities and roles may help both the teachers and the administrators who are planning reading programs.

PROFESSIONAL RESPONSIBILITIES

"Am I qualified to help problem readers?" "How will I be able to start a program in my classroom, in my school?" "To whom should

I look for help?" These are questions educators ask when they realize that many children with reading problems could be helped by establishing special reading services. Preceding a discussion of programs, however, must be a clear understanding of the professional responsibilities of the educators attempting to establish programs for problem readers.

The Child

Regardless of the type of program or the competency of the person conducting it, consideration first must be given to the child who is to benefit from the program. Educators are professionally responsible for the direction of children toward those programs that seem to be best designed for their needs. Referral need not reflect negatively upon the educator if he decides that he cannot assist the child as well as another can; rather, his action is to his credit. Clearly, many educators feel threatened when they become aware that they cannot help certain children. To call for outside help seems to indicate a lack of competency. However, the diagnosis and correction of many of our reading problems cannot possibly be handled by any one person. Consequently, to call for assistance when it is needed is a sign of professional maturity.

Cooperation

As mentioned in previous chapters, diagnosis and remediation are programs that cannot be conducted without full cooperation from all persons involved with the child. Programs which are conducted in isolation are limited in their ability to offer the child the help that he needs. Therefore, programs should not be instituted without thorough communication with the parents and with the child's classroom teacher.

Referral

When possible, all referrals — medical, psychological, and psychiatric — should be made prior to remediation and the final formation of diagnostic conclusions. When the child demonstrates enough symptoms of difficulties in these areas, it is inefficient to start a remedial program without consultation. All conclusions should be considered tentative until final reports are available. The educator does not refrain from working with these children; however, the full efficiency of remedial programs normally will not be realized without referral reports.

Qualification

Since the terms reading specialist, reading consultant, reading supervisor, reading teacher, and reading tutor appear to be defined differently within various states and school districts, the educator clearly is obligated to represent himself as honestly as possible. The International Reading Association has established suggested requirements for reading specialists, and these requirements may serve as a guide to the educator concerning requirements of the IRA for reading specialists.[1]

School Rapport

When remediation is conducted outside the classroom, the educator is professionally responsible for the avoidance of casting unwarranted reflections of inadequacies upon the school program, particularly to parents. However, if the school program is suspect, the educator is professionally obligated to consult appropriate school personnel in an effort to remedy the deficiency.

Here, the reader's attention is called to the Code of Ethics approved by the International Reading Association as it appears in Appendix D of this book.

Guarantees

Seldom can an educator guarantee specific outcomes as a result of specialized reading services. Many variables may influence a given child's performance in reading. To offer guarantees to parents or school officials is clearly unethical. What can be offered, however, are the best services of the personnel who willingly will submit their efforts to carefully conducted evaluations.

Recently, groups of commercial contractors have offered guarantees for improved reading results. These guarantees generally offer a return of monies invested for children who have not improved up to a predetermined level. Educators should study such guarantees rather carefully prior to accepting them. Attention to articles

---

[1]*Roles, Responsibilities, and Qualifications of Reading Specialists* (Newark, Delaware: International Reading Association).

and reports under the title of performance contracting will be necessary.

THE READING SPECIALIST IN THE SCHOOL PROGRAM

The following suggestions are designed to assist the reading specialist in assuming the role which will best suit the needs of the schools for which he is responsible and the children within those schools. A reading specialist may assume responsibility for more than one of these program suggestions, for they are frequently related.

Diagnosis: As discussed in Chapters 2, 3, 4, and 5, clinical diagnosis is a major obligation of most reading specialists. When limited to diagnostic responsibilities, the reading specialist conducts the diagnosis and prepares the recommendations with directions for remediation. Many reading specialists feel that they can be most useful to the classroom teacher through diagnostic services; it may be difficult for the classroom teacher to find the time that clinical diagnosis requires.

Remediation: Following a diagnosis, the reading specialist can make a schedule and draw certain children from the classroom for the precise instruction which is needed. Naturally this calls for a suitable setting in which this remedial program can be housed, for the materials which will accomplish the goals most effectively, and for the cooperation of all school personnel concerned. Due to the very nature of clinical remediation, groups must be small, instruction individualized, and the schedule flexible. Instruction can also be provided within the classroom setting if the reading specialist is permitted to work with the teacher and with all types of children.

Clinic director: In larger school districts, the reading specialist may find himself directing a reading clinic in an attempt to serve severely handicapped children. Clinics usually are established in permanent buildings to which the children can be brought for help. As director of the clinic, the reading specialist may assume all of the above roles as well as the administrative functions of the clinic and the communication between clinic and classroom.

In-service education: Occasionally, the reading specialist will find it worthwhile to conduct in-service educational programs with teachers who have children in need of classroom diagnosis and remediation. Through demonstration, discussion, and consultation with authorities, the teachers will gain insights into effective methods of working with problem readers. The responsibility is linked closely to that of supervision when the supervisor finds a common lack of understanding among his teachers in certain areas.

Resource for classroom teachers: Many reading specialists find their training best utilized when they can serve as a resource person to the classroom teacher. Instead of working with children outside the classroom in diagnosis and remedial activities, the resource teacher can help classroom teachers by:

1. Helping the classroom teacher diagnose his children. Test administration, scoring, and interpretation can be conducted as a team, thus permitting the classroom teacher to learn diagnostic skills.
2. Helping teachers work in the classroom with children who are experiencing difficulty. Planning, and team-teaching special lessons as well as offering continued support to help the teacher better handle children with reading problems allows for teacher development as well as service to children.
3. Obtaining materials for the teacher. Instead of keeping reading materials in a reading room, the reading specialists can bring needed materials to the classroom teacher and help him use them effectively. The resource teacher may obtain materials which the teacher requests and may recommend new materials for certain situations. Resource teachers can also suggest professional materials such as books, pamphlets, and articles.
4. Planning with the teacher to develop effective instructional goals. The teacher, using the knowledge and skills of the reading specialist, can develop better plans for instruction.
5. Evaluating program effectiveness. By applying research and evaluation skills, the resource teacher can assist classroom teachers in looking objectively at their reading programs, modifying portions of the program which appear to be weak, and assisting them to emphasize portions of the program which appear to be strong.
6. Interpreting for teachers the reading research which might have application for the classroom. As a result of their own reading, attendance at conferences, formal course work, and discussions with their colleagues, resource teachers should be alert to the most recent trends, research, methods, and

materials. Working with teachers as an interpreter has several problems. For example, the resource teacher can come on too strong, making the teacher feel inadequate. Or he may inform the teacher concerning things about which he is already well informed. Or he may create the illusion of being an "expert" without offering specific application steps for a given classroom. However, the role of interpreter can be accomplished in a friendly, encouraging, supporting manner — a manner which teachers will accept.

Generally, reading resource personnel must be assigned duties which will allow them freedom to work effectively with teachers. They should not be assigned by administrative personnel to evaluate teachers. They should not *set* policies which teachers must follow, nor should they force themselves into situations where teachers do not want them. In effect, the resource person should be assigned duties in which he can practice the philosophy of acceptance and challenge to teachers.

Summer school: An increasingly large number of schools are establishing summer programs for children who have not made adequate progress during the school year. The reading specialist probably will be responsible for such a program, with particular emphasis being placed upon the screening and selection of the children who are to be assisted. In addition, he might be responsible for the selection of the teachers who will be involved. The financing of these programs, normally assumed by the school, may to a small extent be supplemented by a nominal fee paid by the parents. We have found that such a fee stimulates a more serious attitude toward the work required in the program. Through summer programs, it may be possible for children to remain in the classroom during the year, thereby providing them the fullest opportunity to benefit from the classroom program. Of course, children with serious reading problems cannot always profit from summer programs alone. To avoid the stigma of failure which is often attached to such programs, summer facilities can be developed for good readers as well. All types of readers, can then be involved, making it no disgrace to attend a summer reading program.

Public relations: Public relations duties, which include PTA meetings, conferences with parents, and home visits, might fall to the reading specialist. At such meetings, the school's reading program can be explained, questions answered, and misinterpretations corrected. The reading specialist can take full advantage of the suggestions mentioned in Chapter 10, *Parental Roles in Diagnosis, Remediation, and Prevention*, when provided with opportunities to meet the public. Public relations opportunities such as conferences with parents and home visits as well as public-speaking engagements may be available to the reading specialists.

Supervision of tutoring: Many schools ask qualified teachers to tutor problem readers after school hours and on weekends under the direction of the reading specialist. It is the reading specialist's responsibility to help select the children, make available appropriate diagnostic and remedial materials, and, again, keep communication open between the tutor, the classroom teacher, the parent, and others.

Training of paraprofessionals: As paraprofessionals become more available for reading assistance, the job of training those persons will fall upon reading specialists. The better the training, the more useful will be the paraprofessional. A model program for such training has been developed in Prince Georges County, Maryland. Hundreds of paraprofessionals are trained and supervised by reading specialists as they work with classroom teachers to reach individual children.

All schools are being encouraged to consider the maximum use of such personnel to assist over-burdened teachers. Reading specialists will need to consider the many duties which paraprofessionals can perform and develop training programs to make their work as effective as possible.

Pitfalls for the Reading Specialist

Complex as they are, the programs developed by the reading specialists are not without potential difficulties. Especially for those with little experience, there are certain pitfalls involved in establishing reading programs. Anticipation of several possible pitfalls before beginning such a program may relieve the reading specialist of frustrating situations which ultimately can cause considerable difficulty.

Overloading: It is common to find the reading specialist assuming responsibilities which overload him to a point of ineffectiveness.

First, he reasonably should not be expected to assume all the roles which have been suggested in this chapter; rather, he should start where he can be most effective and slowly expand as he sees opportunities. Secondly, in the diagnostic and remedial role, he cannot be expected to carry the student load that a classroom teacher does. The very nature of the clinical situation precludes large groups. When overloaded, the reading specialist's effectiveness will be limited unnecessarily.

Inadequate housing: Teachers' rooms, damp basements, and even worse locations have been relegated to the reading specialist to conduct diagnostic and remedial programs. Assuming that a program is worth having, the school district must make provisions for a well-lighted, comfortable, nondistracting environment for the children and the teacher. To be most effective, housing considerations should be built into the basic plans for the program's development.

Screening: Final responsibility for determining which children can be helped most effectively must be left to the reading specialist. Without diagnosis, a given classroom teacher is likely to select his dullest children for remedial attention, when dullness alone is not sufficient criteria for program enrollment. The reading specialist should provide for the screening of all referred children yet retain the right to reject any child that he feels cannot profit effectively from the established program. He will have to reject temporarily those children who add to the tutoring load, creating class sizes which cannot be taught effectively. Interschool relations may be strained unless clear-cut systems are established concerning the final responsibilities for the identification of children to be accepted in the reading specialist's programs.

The image: Specific efforts should be made to avoid the image that the reading specialist is the educator who works with failures. As previously suggested, the reading specialist should work in the classroom, participating in all types of programs for children. Such adjustment will help the children assigned to him by relaxing their anxiety about their failures. It will also prevent his getting a distorted opinion of the school's reading program. (This easily occurs when one works hour after hour, day after day with only the problems which a given system has produced.) Working with teachers in the classroom also aids reading specialists in maintaining perspective, especially concerning the difficulties teachers might have working with specific children in large groups.

Demonstrations: Normally, demonstrations are requested when teachers are uncertain of how to use a new technique or material. Traditionally, the demonstrator replaces the teacher and thereby falls into a trap of ineffectiveness. It is suggested that demonstrations be conducted in cooperation with the classroom teacher as a participant. Specifically, the classroom teacher plans the lesson with the reading specialist; the classroom teacher teaches that portion of the lesson which he understands; the classroom teacher remains in charge of the class; and the reading specialist assists with the planning and execution of the lesson. Immediately upon completion of such lessons, the classroom teacher and the reading specialist discuss what happened and how it can be applied in an everyday situation.

Using techniques such as those described above removes the teacher from the passive, observer role and places him in an active, participating role. Teacher behavior is more likely to be modified with such an approach.

THE CLASSROOM TEACHER IN THE SCHOOL PROGRAM

With various degrees of competency, classroom teachers participate in school programs with problem readers in several ways. An understanding of the possibilities may assist each teacher to serve most effectively.

Classroom diagnosis: As the teacher develops skill in the techniques of classroom diagnosis, he is likely to find himself assigned to children who are in need of this service. The best teachers will perform this type of function as an ongoing part of their teaching program. The administrator is cautioned that overloading excellent teachers is unwise, since excessive numbers of weak students obviously will hamper his efforts with all students assigned to him.

Classroom remediation: The teacher should use every opportunity, whether in a group or individually, to help the child in the skill areas which have been diagnosed as being deficient. When possible, flexible room assignments will place children with common problems with the same teacher, enabling him to use his time more effectively with the greatest possible number of children.

Tutoring: Having developed skills in diagnosis and remediation through either in-service or formal course work, many teachers serve as tutors in school-established programs. The teacher's activities in these programs are usually supervised by the reading specialist and are directed toward the instruction of individuals and/or small groups.

Demonstration: When a teacher is particularly skillful in either classroom diagnosis or remediation, other teachers should observe him. Observations may be made during after-school in-service programs or through released time. To create strong feelings about their teaching competencies, teachers should be permitted to evaluate their own strengths and to offer their rooms for observations. Reading specialists can assist teachers in the identification of strengths and urge them to offer their classrooms for the benefit of their colleagues.

Public relations: All teachers have the responsibility of interpreting the school's program to parents. Those who have studied the program more thoroughly may assist in programs such as the PTA in order to clearly illustrate its features. Parents may accept the classroom teacher in this role better than they do the reading specialist, for they know that the classroom teacher works with their children each day.

Pitfalls for the classroom teacher

The classroom teacher also must be alert to several pitfalls in his roles.

Overloading: Teachers who are skilled in diagnosis and remediation may become overloaded with poor readers. Ultimately, overloading is a detriment to his effectiveness with these children. Even when using free periods, short sessions before and after school, Saturdays, and summers, we have found many good teachers who need more time to do an efficient job. Even the healthiest teachers find that they must regulate their time so that relaxation and recreation are also part of their daily schedule. Their major responsibility continues to lie with the whole class and the education of all children assigned to them.

Short-cutting: Attempting to diagnose without using the suggestions in Chapters 2, 3, 4, and 5 leads to inadequate classroom diagnosis. However, after limited experience, the classroom teacher will start to modify and to refine these suggestions to his classroom and the needs of his children. After several diagnostic efforts, a teacher will realize that his children are all proficient in some area(s) and that study in those areas is not essential in his classroom diagnosis. This does not justify excluding major portions of classroom diagnosis.

Cooperation: Regardless of the certainty with which a teacher operates and of the feeling he has toward the total school reading program, he must remain aware of being a member of a team working toward the total education of the child. Gross distortions of the school program in an effort to satisfy his personal philosophy of reading must be avoided when they interfere with the overall school objectives. By cooperating and attempting to convince the school of the need for basic changes, the teacher will better serve his children and the school district. Needless to say, displeasures within the school should remain there and not be topics for community gossip.

Continued study: As changes occur in the field of reading, the teacher must have a system for continued study available to him. Some find that the study of educational periodicals serves this purpose. Specific reference is made to the journals of the International Reading Association,[2] the National Council of Teachers of English,[3] and the College Reading Association.[4] These organizations are striving to keep teachers informed of developments in the field of readin. Other teachers prefer in-service workshops and institutes; still others prefer formal course work in the colleges and universities. Of course, most teachers seek a suitable combination of methods. However, regardless of his method, the effective classroom teacher must remain alert to new ideas, lest he become stale and fixed in his ways.

Out-of-School Programs

Many educators take part in "out-of-school" programs designed to assist problem readers. Some find themselves teaching in these programs; others have parents asking them for their opinions of the programs; and still others find these programs to be interfering with

---

[2]*The Reading Teacher* and *Journal of Reading* (Newark, Delaware: International Reading Association).

[3]*Elementary English* and *The English Journal* (Champaign, Illinois: National Council of Teachers of English).

[4]*The Journal of the Reading Specialist* (Syracuse, New York: Syracuse University, College Reading Association).

the educational objectives of the school. A brief look at the nature of some of these programs may assist the educator to make decisions concerning them.

Teacher education clinics: Many teacher education institutions operate reading clinics to educate teachers. Children who are brought into these clinics for assistance are generally diagnosed and tutored by students doing advanced work in the field of reading. Normally the costs for services in teacher education clinics are small since the programs are not expected to pay for themselves. The effectiveness of these programs is generally related to the effectiveness of the supervision which the students receive and the prerequisites for entrance of college students into courses of a clinic nature.

Some teacher education clinics limit themselves to diagnosis, while others include remediation as well. Although the thoroughness of each program varies, they generally follow the lines of clinical diagnosis and remediation as presented in this book and are reliable.

Privately operated clinics: A variety of privately operated clinics are usually available in large population centers. Designed for financial profit, these clinics generally charge fees much higher than do teacher education clinics. The effectiveness of these clinics is clearly limited by the personnel and materials available for diagnosis and remediation. Referrals to this type of clinic should be made only after acquaintance with the personnel and the attitude of the clinic. Private clinics can accept this as a challenge: Work with the schools! Unless cooperation is achieved, the effects of privately operated clinics are limited indeed. The College Reading Association is constantly attempting to focus professional attention on the need for understanding and evaluating private clinics.

Private tutoring: Ranging from excellent to horrible, programs designed by private tutors are generally restricted by the proficiency of the tutor and by the materials available for precise diagnosis and remediation. These private tutoring programs are most effective with mildly retarded readers. Children with severe problems seldom benefit; however, it should be noted that there are many excellent, well-qualified private tutors performing highly satisfactory services. Unfortunately, there are others who cause more harm than good. Private tutors are obligated to work closely with the school which has the child in an instructional program every day. There is no justification for programs which do less. Referral should be based only on a personal evaluation of effectiveness.

Commercial programs for parents: Often advertised as panaceas, programs which place parents in teachers' roles assume that all children have a common deficiency and that instruction with a given technique can be done without diagnosis. Unless the educator is familiar with the contents of the program and unless a diagnosis has been conducted to pinpoint the remedial area, these programs are not recommended. Further discussion of these programs was mentioned in Chapter 11. Not all such programs are inherently bad; on the contrary, some of them are well designed and have been used with considerable success. The educator simply is advised to study them closely. An assessment must also be made in each case of the parent's suitability as a teacher of his own children.

Temporary programs: Several private companies have organized crash programs designed to send materials and instructors into schools and industry to improve general reading skills. As crash programs, many of these are well designed and taught excellently; others are not. The long-term gains of such programs properly may be questioned, and these companies should be willing to answer questions and submit to research concerning these claims. The educator will have to evaluate the relative worth of any such program.

Out-patient, parental instruction: Several clinics have been established to diagnose children and then train parents to conduct remediation. Amazing results have been reported with this technique; however, the long-term gains are again in need of evaluation. Out-patient clinics usually handle large numbers of children and usually request periodic return for reevaluation and retraining for the parents. Since the programs are out-patient in nature, their overall costs are not great, although the per hour cost may be high. Note that these programs are generally designed for children with specific disabilities and usually should follow referral from medical personnel, psychologists, psychiatrists, or reading specialists.

Pitfalls of Out-of-School Programs

The basic limitations of each of these have already been mentioned. Specifically, however, the pitfalls of such programs are:

Goals: Do these programs assist us toward the most desirable educational goals or do they, in reality, interfere? Once this question is answered, referral may be made more specifically. When it is established that the programs are not in agreement with the school's goals, attempts should be made to reconcile the differences. When reconciliation is not possible, educators should strongly recommend nonparticipation by the parents of the children assigned to them.

Personnel: The effectiveness of all of these programs is dependent upon the supervisory as well as the instructional personnel. Weakness in personnel means weakness in the program. No compromise can be made by educators in demanding that out-of-school programs meet certain standards of quality. Again, efforts should be made to reconcile differences.

Intention: Since each of these programs has other aims beyond simply assisting children, it must be determined if assisting children is even included in their aims. Naturally, they will claim to help problem readers, but do dollar signs or teacher education become so important that the child does not matter? When alternate aims prevail, the worth of the program is suspect.

Accountability

That educators and commercial companies should be held accountable for their efforts with children is an issue of great interest, for this is, of course, the whole purpose of diagnostic teaching. Teachers should be accountable for providing efficient instruction based upon diagnostic technique. Lock stepping children through one commercial program and indifference to individual learning styles are not to be tolerated. The teacher who knows the strengths and weaknesses of his children and who provides the best instruction he can based on that knowledge is truly teaching with accountability.

Accountability has nothing to do with obtaining the same results with all children. It has nothing to do with helping each child to read on some type of mythical grade level. It refers to helping each child to successful learning — a task which can only be done with a diagnostic teaching approach.

SUMMARY

Once the professional roles of the classroom teacher and the reading specialist are understood, programs can be developed to incorporate them appropriately. An awareness of the types of programs available within the realms of the school permits educators to strive in developing those which the needs of their community demand. All facilities, county, state, college, and university, should be incorporated when it is felt that they can be helpful.

Out-of-school programs for children must be evaluated and cooperation should be encouraged, when possible. In areas where out-of-school programs proliferate, more concentrated efforts will be needed to assure educational programs of the most effectiveness for children.

Accepting and Challenging by Teaching to Strengths Can Make Learning to Read Enjoyable and Successful

SUGGESTED READINGS

Cohn, Stella M. and Cohn, Jack. *Teaching the Retarded Reader*. New York: Odyssey Press, 1967. The Cohns discuss in detail the roles and responsibilities of reading personnel in establishing and administering reading programs. Based on experience in the city schools of New York, it offers many practical suggestions.

Gans, Roma. *Common Sense in Teaching Reading*, Chapter 20. Indianapolis: The Bobbs-Merrill Company, Inc., 1963. The reader will find this chapter a stimulating adjunct to the material covered in this book. Dr. Gans had added many practical considerations which will be helpful to those who are attempting to develop programs.

Kolson, Clifford J., and Kaluger, George. *Clinical Aspects of Remedial Reading*, Part III. Springfield, Illinois: Charles C. Thomas, 1963. In this section of their book, Kolson and Kaluger provide excellent supplementary information to that presented in this chapter. On pp. 101-103, they have included what they consider to be the hallmarks of a good clinic. The reader will find these suggestions very beneficial.

Robinson, H. Alan, and Rauch, Sidney J. *Guiding the Reading Program.* Chicago: SRA, 1965. The reader will find this entire book an excellent source of information. Subtitled *A Reading Consultant's Handbook*, the emphasis is on developing reader insights into all aspects of the reading program from the specialist's point of view. This, it would seem, is required reading for the reading specialist.

Spicknall, Stella and Fischer, Drema, eds. *A Handbook for the Reading Resource Program in Prince George's County.* Upper Marlboro, Maryland: Board of Education, 1969. This handbook describes the various duties of reading personnel in resource roles. The work, done in Prince George's County, Maryland, is one of leadership in seeing the reading specialist as a resource person.

APPENDIX A

Appendix A, provided for the reader's reference, is based upon the tests which have been cited in this book. No effort has been made to include all known reading tests, nor have evaluations of the tests' merits been included. For that type of information the reader is referred to Buros' *Mental Measurements Yearbooks*.

The age range of each test is approximated. We realize, of course, that in diagnosis the use of a test will depend upon the instructional level, not the age, of the child. The educator must determine this instructional level and then select the appropriate test.

Administration time for tests often varies with the age of the child. The reader should accept these times as approximate—a factor which may determine the use of a test in a particular situation.

Publishers are coded. The key to the code is in Appendix C. The reader is referred to the publisher for the cost of the tests, the specific directions, and other desired information.

Designed to Assist in Evaluation of:

Name of Test	No. of Forms	Type	Age Range	Approximate Administration Time, Reading Section	Speed	Comprehension	Vocabulary	Word Attack	Spelling	Auding	Other	Publisher's Code
ACHIEVEMENT												
Botel Reading Inventory	2	Individual and Group	6-18									FOL
Phonics Mastery				15-25 min.				X				
Word Recognition				4-12 min.			X					
Word Opposite (Reading)				20-30 min.		X	X					
California Achievement Test	4	Group	L. Prim. 6-7 / U. Prim. 7-9 / Elem. 8-12 / Jr. Hi. 12-14 / Adv. 15-20	1 hr.		X	X		X		Arithmetic, Language	CAL
Dolch Basic Sight Words	1	Individual	6-8	15 min.			X					GP
Durrell Listening-Reading Series	1 / 1	Group	Prim. 6-8 / Inter. 9-12	80 min.		X	X			X	Compares Listening Ability with Reading Achievement	HBJ

Test		Admin.	Grades	Time					Subject areas	Publisher
Gates MacGinitie ReadingTest-Survey	3	Group	8-15	1 hr.		X	X	X		TC
Gates MacGinitie Reading Test	3	Group	Prim. 6-7 Adv. 7-8 Basic 9-12	40-60 min.			X	X		TC
Iowa Test of Basic Skills	2	Group	8-14	70 min.			X	X	Language Work-Study Arithmetic	HMC
Metropolitan Achievement Tests	4	Group	6-8 9-12 12-18	50 min.	X		X	X	Science Language Arithmetic Social Studies	HBJ
Stanford Achievement Tests	4	Group	6-8 8-9 10-12 12-15	45 min.			X	X	Arithmetic Study Science Social Studies	HBJ
Wide Range Achievement Tests	1	Individual	6-18	40 min.		X				CAL
DIAGNOSTIC California Phonics Survey	2	Group	13-20	40 min.		X				CAL
Diagnostic Reading Scales (Spache)	1	Individual	6-14	1 hr.	X	X	X	X		CAL

Designed to Assist in Evaluation of:

Name of Test	No. of Forms	Type	Age Range	Approximate Administration Time, Reading Section	Speed	Comprehension	Vocabulary	Word Attack	Spelling	Auding	Other	Publisher's Code
Diagnostic Reading Tests	2-4	Group and Individual	5-13	Varies	X	X	X	X				CDRT
Diagnostic Reading Test (Bond-Balow-Hoyt)	1	Group	8-14	90 min.				X		X		L&C
Doren Diagnostic Reading Test	1	Group	8-12	3 hrs.			X	X				ETB
Durrell Analysis of Reading Difficulties	1	Individual	6-12	40-60 min.	X	X	X	X	X			HBJ
Gates-McKillop Reading Diagnostic Test	2	Individual	6-12	1 hr.	X	X	X	X	X	X		TC
Gilmore Oral Reading Test	2	Individual	6-14	15 min.	X	X	X	X				HBJ
Gray Oral Reading Test	4	Individual	6-18	15 min.	X	X	X	X				B&M

Test	No.	Format	Age	Time	Skills	Arithmetic	Pub.
Monroe-Sherman Group Diagnostic Reading Aptitude and Achievement Tests	1	Group	8-14	90 min.	X X X X		NEV
Reading Versatility Test	2	Group	11-15 16-Adult	25 min.	X X		EDL
The Roswell-Chall Diagnostic Reading Test of Word Analysis Skills	2	Group	7-12	5-10 min.	X		EP
Standard Reading Inventory	1	Individual	6-14	40-50 min.	X X X		PP
INTELLIGENCE							
Arthur Point Scale-Knox Cube Sub Test	1	Individual	5-13	10 min.		Memory of Sequence	STO
California Test of Mental Maturity	1	Group	5-6 6-8 9-13 12-14 14-19 15-21	50 min.		Language and Non-Language	CAL
Durrell Listening Series	1	Group	5-7 8-11 12-14	25 min.		X Part of Durrell Listening-Reading Series	HBJ
Full-Range Picture Vocabulary	2	Individual	2-Adult	10-15 min.		X	PTS

Designed to Assist in Evaluation of:

Name of Test	No. of Forms	Type	Age Range	Approximate Administration Time, Reading Section	Speed	Comprehension	Vocabulary	Word Attack	Spelling	Auding	Other	Publisher's Code
Illinois Test of Psycholinguistic Abilities	1	Individual	2-10	1 hr.							Language Development	VIP
Peabody Picture Vocabulary Test	2	Individual	2½-18	15 min.						X		AGS
Slosson Intelligence Test	1	Individual	2-Adult	10-30 min.							General Mental Maturity	SEP
Stanford-Binet Intelligence Scale	1	Individual	2-Adult	1 hr.							General Mental Maturity	HMC
Wechsler Intelligence Scale for Children	1	Individual	5-15	1 hr.							Verbal Performance, Mental Maturity	PSY
SCREENING TESTS Vision: Keystone Visual Survey Telibinocular	1	Individual	5-Adult	15 min.							Far and Near Point, Visual Skills	KEY

Test	No.	Individual/Group	Age	Time	Description	Source
Reading Eye Camera	1	Individual	6-20	10 min.	Photograph Eye Motion	EDL
Spache-Binocular Reading Tests	1	Individual	5-Adult	5 min.	Binocular Reading Efficiency	KEY
Auditory: Audiometer	1	Individual or Group	3-Adult	15 min.	Auditory Acuity	MAI
Wepman Auditory Discrimination Test	2	Individual	5-10	10 min.	Auditory Discrimination	JMW
Personality: California Test of Personality	2	Group	5-8 9-13 13-15 14-21	50 min.	Personal and Social Adjustment	CAL
Incomplete Sentences	1	Group and Individual			Personal and Social Adjustment	MCH
Dominance: Harris Test of Lateral Dominance	1	Individual	5-Adult	5 min.	Hand, Eye and Foot Dominance	PSY
STUDY SKILLS California Study Method Survey	1	Group	12-18	40 min.	Study Habits	CALIF.
Survey of Study Habits and Attitudes-Brown Holtzman	1	Group	14-21	20 min.	Study Habits	PSY

Designed to Assist in Evaluation of:

Name of Test	No. of Forms	Type	Age Range	Approximate Administration Time, Reading Section	Speed	Comprehension	Vocabulary	Word Attack	Spelling	Auding	Other	Publisher's Code
PERCEPTION												
Frostig Developmental Test of Visual Perception	1	Group and Individual	3-8	30-45 min. (Ind.) 40-60 min. (Gr.)							5 Aspects of Visual Perception	CPC
Purdue Perceptual Motor Survey	1	Individual		1 hr.							Perceptual Motor Abilities	CEM

APPENDIX B

Appendix B provides a reference for reading aids based upon the materials which have been cited in this book. Specific information concerning these materials may be found in publishers catalogues and brochures. The publishers' key may be used by checking with Appendix C.

Many of the cited materials may be used in a variety of ways to help problem readers. The cited use is based upon our experience, but in no way is intended to suggest that a material be limited to these functions.

The suggested age level must be considered flexible and regarded as the difficult level. The educator will find many of these materials to be used with children of older age and interest levels.

Teacher-made materials are often more suitable to the need of children experiencing severe difficulty with reading.

| | | | | Designed to Assist in Instruction of: | | | | | |
Name of Material	Approximate Age Level	Interest Level	Reading* Readiness	Sight Vocabulary	Word Attack	Comprehension	Speed	Other	Publisher's Code
MACHINE TYPE AIDS Controlled Reader	6-Adult	6-Adult	3-4		X	X	X		EDL
Delacato Stereo-Reader Service	6-10	6-10	3-4	X			X		KEY
Dolch Sight Words and Phrase Slides	6-8	6-8		X			X	Use with or Without Tachistoscope	KEY
Flash-X	Use with child's personal vocabulary		3	X			X		EDL
Iowa Reading Films	14-18	14-Adult	4			X	X		IOWA
Language Master	6-16	6-16	1-2-3	X		X			BHC
Leavell Language Development Service	6-9	6-9		X				Stereoscope Exposure to Print	KEY
Nichols Slides	7-15	7-18		X		X		Designed for use with Tachistoscope	KEY
Rateometer	Use with child's instructional material		4				X	Reading Rate Controller	AVR
Reading Accelerator	Use with child's instructional material		4				X	Reading Rate Controller	SRA
Tachistoscope	6-Adult	6-Adult	3-4	X			X		KEY

BOOKS AND WORKBOOKS			1	2	3	4		
Basic Reading Skills	9-11 / 12-14	12-14 / 15-18	X / X	X / X				SF
Be a Better Reader	12-18	12-18	X	X	X			PH
Better Reading Books	10-15	10-18	X	X		X	Study Skills	SRA
Cordts Phonics	6-10	6-12	X					HRJ
Developing Your Vocabulary	9-12	9-12	X	X				SRA
Diagnostic Reading Workbook	6-12	6-12	X	X	X			CEM
Elementary Crossword Puzzles	10-12	10-12	X				Crossword Puzzle Designs	EPC
Frostig Visual Perception Materials	6-8	6-8	3					CPP
Herr Phonics	5-11	5-11	X					ERA
ITA	6-8	6-8	X	X	X		Initial Teaching Alphabet	ITA
Let's Read	6-7	6-7	2	X	X	X	Linguistic Basal	CLB
The Macmillan Reading Spectrum	6-12	6-15	X	X	X			MAC

*1=Language   2=Auditory   3=Visual   4=Orientation

Designed to Assist in Instruction of:

Name of Material	Approximate Age Level	Interest Level	Reading* Readiness	Sight Vocabulary	Word Attack	Comprehension	Speed	Other	Publisher's Code
Merrill Linguistic Readers	5-7	5-7		X	X	X		Linguistic Basal	CEM
Michigan Tracking	6-Adult		3-4				X		AAP
Palo Alto Sequential Steps in Reading	6-8	6-8	1-2-3-4	X	X	X			HBJ
Phonetic Keys to Reading	5-12	5-12	2	X	X	X		Basil Phonics Approach	EC
Phonics Skilltexts	6-10	6-12			X				CEM
Phonics We Use	6-10	6-12			X				LC
Phonovisual	5-7	5-7	2		X			Basic Phonic Approach	PVP
Reading for Meaning	10-18	10-18				X		Study Skills	JBL
The Reading Skill Builders	6-14	6-Adult		X	X	X	X		RDS
Reading Skilltexts	6-14	6-14		X		X			CEM
Rochester Occupational Reading Series	13-18	13-Adult		X		X		Job Type Reading Material	SRA

*1=Language   2=Auditory   3=Visual   4=Orientation

Specific Skill Series								
Using the Context	6-11	6-11		X	X			BL
Getting the Facts	6-11	6-11			X			
Following Directions	6-11	6-11			X			
Locating the Answer	6-11	6-11			X			
Working with Sounds	6-11	6-11	2		X			
SRA Reading Series	5-12	5-12	2	X	X	X		Linguistic Basal — SRA
Standard Test Lessons in Reading	7-18	7-18			X	X		TC
Storybooks	6-7	6-7		X				Contextual Practice for Programmed Material — WMcH
Words in Color	6-8	6-8	3	X	X	X		Colored Letters in Beginning Reading — LM
KITS AND PACKAGED MATERIALS								
Dolch Teaching Aids								Gamelike Procedures to Develop Vocabulary — GP
Consonant Lotto	6-7	6-9		X				
Vowel Lotto	7-8	7-10		X				
The Syllable Game	8-9	8-11		X				
Picture Readiness Game	5-6	5-6	1-3					
Match	5-6	5-8	3	X				

Name of Material	Approximate Age Level	Interest Level	Reading* Readiness	Sight Vocabulary	Word Attack	Comprehension	Speed	Other	Publisher's Code
								Designed to Assist in Instruction of:	
Basic Sight Cards	6-8	6-9		X					
Sight Phrase Cards	7-8	7-10		X					
Picture Word Cards	6-7	6-8		X					
What the Letters Say	5-6	5-7			X				
Group Word Teaching Game	7-9	7-11		X					
Durrell-Murphy Phonics Practice Program	5-7	5-7	2		X				HBJ
EDL Study Skills Science Social Studies Reference	9-14	9-14						Study Skills	EDL
Gillingham	1-3	1-3		X	X			Spelling	ES
Building Pre-Reading Skills Kit-A-Language	6-7	6-7	1-2						Ginn
Graph and Picture Study Skills Kit	9-12	9-15						Teaching the Use of Study Aids	SRA

*1=Language 2=Auditory 3=Visual 4=Orientation

Material	Interest Level	Reading Level	Level	Chk 1	Chk 2	Chk 3	Chk 4	Description	Source
The Literature Sampler	12-18	12-18			X			Provides Samples of Books	LM
Linguistic Block Series	6-7	6-7			X	X			SF
Map and Globe Skills Kit	9-14	9-16						Use of maps and globes	SRA
Non-Oral Reading Series	6-8	6-8	1		X		X		PES
Organizing and Reporting Skills Kit	9-12	9-12						Study Skill	SRA
Peabody Language Development Kits	5-7	5-10	1-2						AGS
Phonics We Use Learning Games Kit	6-12	6-12	2			X		Games	LC
Pilot Library	9 / 11 / 13-14	7-12 / 9-14 / 10-18						Provide Samples of Books	SRA
Reading Attainment System	11-16	11-16		X	X	X	X	High Interest Low Vocabulary Books	AAP
Reading for Understanding	8-13 / 13-18 / 10-21	6-13 / 6-18 / 6-21			X / X / X				SRA
Reading Lab I-Word Games	6-9	6-9	2			X			SRA

Name of Material	Approximate Age Level	Interest Level	Reading* Readiness	Sight Vocabulary	Word Attack	Comprehension	Speed	Other	Publisher's Code
Reading Pace-makers	8-15	8-15		X		X		High Interest Book Set	RH
Speech To Print Phonics	5-7	5-9			X				HBJ
Spelling Learning Games Kits SRA Kits	6-12	6-12	2		X			Games	LC
Reading Lab									
IA	6	6-8		X	X	X	X		SRA
IB	7	6-9		X	X	X	X		SRA
IC	8	6-10		X	X	X	X		SRA
IIA	9	7-12		X	X	X	X		SRA
IIB	10	8-13		X	X	X	X		SRA
IIC	11	9-14		X	X	X	X		SRA
IIIA	12-13	13-16		X	X	X	X		SRA
IIIB	13-14	10-17		X	X	X	X		SRA
IVA	14-17	13-19		X	X	X	X		SRA
Tactics in Reading	12-18	12-18		X	X	X			SF
Teaching Reading Through Creative Movements	7-8	7-8	1-2						KIMBO

Designed to Assist in Instruction of:

*1=Language   2=Auditory   3=Visual   4=Orientation

Visual-Lingual Reading Program	6-7	6-7	1		X	X		TT
Webster Classroom Reading Clinic	7-13	7-18		X	X	X	High Interest Low Vocabulary Books	WMCH
PROGRAMMED MATERIALS David Discovers the Dictionary	9-11	9-15					Dictionary Skills	COR
Goals in Spelling	7-10	7-12			X			PSP
Lessons for Self Instruction	9-11	9-15					Dictionary Skills	CAL
Programmed Reading	5-9	5-14		X	X	X		WMcH
PACKAGED TRADE BOOKS Invitations to Story Time	5-6	5-6	1				Interest	SF
Invitations to Personal Reading	6-12	6-12				X	Book Preview	SF
Scholastic Literature Kits	12-15	12-15				X	Interest	SBS
Scholastic Pleasure Reading Library	5-14	5-14				X	High Interest Low Reading Levels Critical Thinking	SBS
The Owl Books	5-7	5-7				X	Interest	HRW

APPENDIX C

AAP   Ann Arbor Publishers
611 Church Street
Ann Arbor, Michigan
   48104

AGS   American Guidance
   Service, Inc.
720 Washington Avenue
   S.E.
Minneapolis, Minnesota
   55414

AVR   Audio-Visual Research
1509 Eighth Street, S.E.
Waseca, Minnesota
   56093

BL   Barnell Loft Ltd.
111 S. Centre Avenue
Rockville Centre,
   New York 11571

BHC   Bell & Howell Company
7100 McCormick Road
Chicago, Illinois

B&M   Bobbs Merrill Company,
   Inc.
4300 West 62nd Street
Indianapolis. Indiana
   46206

CAL   California Test Bureau
5916 Hollywood
   Boulevard
Los Angeles, California
   90029

CPP   Consulting Psychologists
   Press
Palo Alto, California
   94306

CDRT   The Committee on
   Diagnostic Reading
   Tests, Inc.
Mountain Home, North
   Carolina 28758

CEM   Charles E. Merrill
        Publishing Company
    1300 Alum Creek Drive
    Columbus, Ohio 43216

CLB   Clarence L. Barnhart
    Reference Books
    Box 359
    Bronxville, New York

Cor   Coronet Learning
        Programs
    Coronet Building
    Chicago, Illinois 60601

EC   The Economy Company
    529 N. Capital Avenue
    Indianapolis, Indiana
    46204

EDL   Educational Develop-
        mental Laboratories
    Huntington, New York
    11746

EnC   Encyclopedia Brittanica
        Press
    425 N. Michigan Avenue
    Chicago, Illinois 60611

EP   Essay Press
    P.O. Box 5
    New York, New York
    10024

EPC   Educational Publishing
        Company
    Darien, Connecticut

ERA   Educational Research
        Association
    2223 S. Olive
    Los Angeles, California

ES   Educational Service Inc.
    P.O. Box 112
    Benton Harbor, Michigan

ETB   Educational Test Bureau
    720 Washington Avenue,
        S.E.
    Minneapolis, Minnesota
    55414

FOL   Follett Publishing
        Company
    1010 W. Washington
        Boulevard
    Chicago, Illinois 60607

GP   The Garrard Press
    Champaign, Illinois
    61820

Ginn   Ginn & Company
    72 Fifth Avenue
    New York, New York
    10011

HBJ   Harcourt, Brace &
        Jovanovich, Inc.
    Tarrytown, New York
    10591

HMC   Houghton Mifflin
        Company
    53 West 43rd Street
    New York, New York
    10036

HRW   Holt, Rinehart and
        Winston, Inc.
    383 Madison Ave.
    New York, New York
    10017

IOWA   The State University of
        Iowa
    Bureau of Audio-Visual
        Instruction
    Iowa City, Iowa 52240

ITA   ITA Publications Inc.
    20 E. 46th Street
    New York, New York
    10017

JBL   J. B. Lippincott Company
East Washington Square
Philadelphia,
     Pennsylvania 19103

JMW   Joseph M. Wepman, PhD
950 E. 59th Street
Chicago, Illinois

KEY   Keystone View Company
Meadville, Pennsylvania
     16335

KIMBO   Kimbo Educational
     Records
Box 55
Deal, New Jersey 07723

LC   Lyons E. Carnahan
Educational Publishers
Affiliate of Meredith
     Publishing Co.
407 E. 25th Street
Chicago, Illinois 60616

LM   Learning Materials, Inc.
100 East Ohio Street
Chicago, Illinois

MAC   The Macmillan Company
Front and Brown Streets
Riverside, New Jersey
     08075

MAI   MAICO Electronics Inc.
21 N. 3rd Street
Minneapolis, Minnesota

McH   McGraw-Hill Book
     Company
New York, New York
*The Improvement of
    Reading*
Ruth Strang, Constance
    McCullough, and
    Arthur E. Troxler.
    1967. pp. 172-173

NEV   Nevins Publishing
     Company
Pittsburgh, Pennsylvania

PAR   Programs for Achieve-
     ment in Reading, Inc.
Abbott Park Place
Providence, Rhode Island
     02903

PES   Primary Educational
     Service
1243 W. 79th Street
Chicago, Illinois

PH   Prentice-Hall, Inc.
Englewood Cliffs, New
     Jersey 07632

PP   Pioneer Printing Co.
Bellingham, Washington
     98225

PSP   Popular Science
     Publishing Co., Inc.
McGraw Hill Text Film
     Dept.
330 W. 32nd Street
New York, New York
     10036

PTS   Psychological Test
     Specialist
Box 1441
Missoula, Montana 59801

PSY   Psychological Corporation
304 East 45th Street
New York, New York
     10017

PVP   Phonovisual Products,
     Inc.
Box 5625
Washington, D.C. 20007

RDS	Reader's Digest Services, Inc. Pleasantville, New York 10570	STO	C. H. Stoetling Company 424 N. Homan Avenue Chicago, Illinois 60624
RH	Random House 457 Madison Avenue New York, New York 10022	TC	Bureau of Publications Teachers College Columbia University New York, New York 10027
SBS	Scholastic Book Service Sylvan Avenue Englewood Cliffs, New Jersey 07018	TT	Tweedy Transparencies 207 Hollywood Avenue East Orange, New Jersey 17018
SEP	Slosson Educational Publications Press 140 Pine Street East Aurora, New York, New York, New York 14052	UIP	University of Illinois Press Urbana, Illinois 61601
SF	Scott Foresman & Company 433 E. Erie Street Chicago, Illinois 60611	WMcH	Webster Division McGraw Hill Book Company 1154 Roco Avenue St. Louis, Missouri 63126
SRA	Science Research Associates, Inc. 259 E. Erie Street Chicago, Illinois 60611	WWS	Weston Woods Studios Weston, Connecticut 06880

IRA Code of Ethics*

Introduction

The members of the International Reading Association who are concerned with the teaching of reading form a group of professional persons, obligated to society and devoted to the service and welfare of individuals through teaching, clinical services, research, and publication. The members of this group are committed to values which are the foundation of a democratic society—freedom to teach, write, and study in an atmosphere conducive to the best interests of the profession. The welfare of the public, the profession, and the individuals concerned should be of primary consideration in recommending candidates for degrees, positions, advancements, the recognition of professional activity, and for certification in those areas where certification exists.

Ethical Standards in Professional Relationships

1. It is the obligation of all members of the International Reading Association to observe the Code of Ethics of the organization and to act accordingly so as to advance the status and prestige of the association and of the profession as a whole.

---

* *Code of Ethics,* International Reading Association, Newark, Delaware.

Members should assist in establishing the highest professional standards for reading programs and services, and should enlist support for these through dissemination of pertinent information to the public.

2. It is the obligation of all members to maintain relationships with other professional persons, striving for harmony, avoiding personal controversy, encouraging cooperative effort, and making known the obligations and services rendered by the reading specialist.

3. It is the obligation of members to report results of research and other developments in reading.

4. Members should not claim nor advertise affiliation with the *International Reading Association* as evidence of their competence in reading.

Ethical Standards in Reading Services

1. Reading specialists must possess suitable qualifications *(See Minimum Standards for Professional Training of Reading Specialists)* for engaging in consulting, clinical, or remedial work. Unqualified persons should not engage in such activities except under the direct supervision of one who is properly qualified. Professional intent and the welfare of the person seeking the services of the reading specialist should govern counseling, all consulting or clinical activities such as administering diagnostic tests, or providing remediation. It is the duty of the reading specialist to keep relationships with clients and interested persons on a professional level.

2. Information derived from consulting and/or clinical services should be regarded as confidential. Expressed consent of persons involved should be secured before releasing information to outside agencies.

3. Reading specialists should recognize the boundaries of their competence and should not offer services which fail to meet professional standards established by other disciplines. They should be free, however, to give assistance in other areas in which they are qualified.

4. Referral should be made to specialists in allied fields as needed. When such referral is made, pertinent information should be made available to consulting specialists.

5 Reading clinics and/or reading specialists offering professional services should refrain from guaranteeing easy solutions or favorable outcomes as a result of their work, and
their advertising should be consistent with that of allied
professions. They should not accept for remediation any
persons who are unlikely to benefit from their instruction,
and they should work to accomplish the greatest possible
improvement in the shortest time. Fees, if charged, should
be agreed on in advance and should be charged in accordance with an established set of rates commensurate with
that of other professions.

Index